Deficit Politics in the United States

From the clashes between Federalists and Republicans in the 1790s until today, partisan battles over taxing, spending, and public debt have shaped American political development. These battles were formerly constrained by fiscal norms that mandated balanced budgets and low debt. In his Farewell Address, President George Washington counseled the nation to "cherish public credit" by using "it as sparingly as possible."

In the 1980s, however, tax cuts and spending increases created large structural deficits and much higher debt levels. With only a brief interruption in the late 1990s, deficit politics has been a mainstay ever since.

Over this period, the Republican Party has passed large tax cuts but has failed to retrench the large entitlement programs that continue to raise spending. Likewise, the Democratic Party has expanded the domestic role of government but has abandoned the broad-based taxation it supported in the 1990s. Funding their domestic agenda with matching revenues is now as unappealing for Democrats as entitlement cutbacks are for Republicans, contributing to the current stalemate of Republican tax policy, Democratic spending policy, and soaring deficits and debt. The economic risks this entails are serious, yet an end to the era of deficit politics is nowhere in sight.

Dennis S. Ippolito is the Eugene McElvaney Professor of Political Science at Southern Methodist University. His most recent book on budget policy was a revised edition of *Why Budgets Matter: Budget Policy and American Politics* (Pennsylvania State University Press, 2015), the first edition of which was published in 2003. His other books on budget policy include *Deficits, Debt, and the New Politics of Tax Policy* (Cambridge University Press, 2012); *Budget Policy and the Future of Defense* (National Defense University Press/Institute for National Strategic Studies, 1994); *Uncertain Legacies: Federal Budget Policy from Roosevelt through Reagan* (University Press of Virginia, 1990); *Hidden Spending: The Politics of Federal Credit Programs* (University of North Carolina Press, 1984); *Congressional Spending* (Cornell University Press, 1981); and *The Budget and National Politics* (W.H. Freeman, 1978). In 2010, he received the Aaron B. Wildavsky Award for Lifetime Scholarly Achievement in Public Budgeting and Finance from the Association for Budgeting and Financial Management of the American Society for Public Administration.

Europa Economic Perspectives

Providing in-depth analysis with a global reach, this series from Europa examines a wide range of contemporary economic issues from areas around the world. Intended to complement the *Europa Regional Surveys of the World* series, *Europa Economic Perspectives* will be a valuable resource for academics, students, researchers, policymakers, business people and anyone with an interest in current world economic affairs.

While the *Europa World Year Book* and its associated *Regional Surveys* inform on and analyse contemporary economic, political and social developments, the Editors considered the need for more in-depth volumes written and/or edited by specialists in their field, in order to delve into a country's or a region's particular economic situation, or to examine economic theories in the context of current global economic affairs. Volumes in the series are not constrained by any particular template, but may explore any aspect of a country's recent economic issues in order to increase knowledge.

International Monetary Reform
A Specific Set of Proposals
John Williamson

Small States and the European Union
Economic Perspectives
Edited by Lino Briguglio

Advances in Geoeconomics
Edited by J. Mark Munoz

The Economic Crisis and its Aftermath in the Nordic and Baltic Countries
Do As We Say and Not As We Do
Hilmar Þór Hilmarsson

Deficit Politics in the United States
Taxes, Spending, and Fiscal Disconnect
Dennis S. Ippolito

Deficit Politics in the United States

Taxes, Spending, and Fiscal Disconnect

Dennis S. Ippolito

Routledge
Taylor & Francis Group
LONDON AND NEW YORK

First published 2022
by Routledge
4 Park Square, Milton Park, Abingdon, Oxon OX14 4RN

and by Routledge
605 Third Avenue, New York, NY 10158

Routledge is an imprint of the Taylor & Francis Group, an informa business

British Library Cataloguing in Publication Data
A catalogue record for this book is available from the British Library

Library of Congress Cataloging-in-Publication Data
A catalog record has been requested for this book

ISBN: 978-0-367-76506-4 (hbk)
ISBN: 978-1-032-20124-5 (pbk)
ISBN: 978-1-003-16726-6 (ebk)

DOI: 10.4324/9781003167266

Typeset in Times New Roman
by Taylor & Francis Books

To Melanie Kay

Contents

	List of figures	viii
	List of tables	ix
	Preface	xi
1	From Balanced Budgets to Deficit Politics	1
2	From Deficit to Surplus: The Reagan-Clinton Transition	39
3	From Surplus to Deficit: The George W. Bush Presidency	88
4	Stabilizing the Deficit: The Obama Presidency	117
5	Raising the Deficit: The Trump Presidency	149
6	The Future of Deficit Politics—And Why It Matters	185
	Bibliography	211
	Index	217

Figures

2.1 Inflation-Adjusted Defense Spending, Fiscal Years 1940–1990 54

6.1 Spending and Revenues in the Deficit Politics Era, 1980–2031 (as a percentage of GDP) 186

Tables

1.1 Spending, Revenues, Public Debt, Surpluses/Deficits, and Extraordinary Expenses of the Federal Government, 1789–1860 6
1.2 Spending, Revenues, Surpluses, and Debt, 1920–1930 (as a percentage of GDP) 12
1.3 Spending, Revenues, Deficits, and Debt, 1940–1946 (as a percentage of GDP) 17
1.4 Revenues, Outlays, and Surplus/Deficit, 1969–1980 (as a percentage of GDP) 33
2.1 Economic Recovery Tax Act of 1981 (P.L. 97–34): Major Provisions 43
2.2 Comparison of Tax Rates, Existing Law and Tax Reform Act of 1986 51
2.3 Revenue Effects of Major Legislation Enacted During the Reagan Presidency, 1987–1991 (in billions of dollars) 52
2.4 Discretionary Spending, 1981–1989 (as a percentage of GDP) 57
2.5 Components of Deficit Reduction, 1981–1989 (as a percentage of GDP) 62
2.6 The 1987 Gramm-Rudman-Hollings (GRH II) Deficit Ceilings and Congressional Budget Office Deficit Projections (in billions of dollars) 63
2.7 Omnibus Budget Reconciliation Act of 1990: Major Provisions and Deficit Savings (in billions of dollars) 67
2.8 Omnibus Budget Reconciliation Act of 1993: Major Provisions and Deficit Savings (in billions of dollars) 72
2.9 Taxpayer Relief Act of 1997: Major Provisions and Revenue Effects (in billions of dollars) 80
2.10 Components of Deficit Reduction, 1990–2000 (as a percentage of GDP) 84
3.1 The Bush Administration's 2001 Budget Program "Highlights" 89
3.2 Economic Growth and Tax Relief Reconciliation Act of 2001: Estimated Revenue Effects of Major Individual Income Tax Provisions by Income Group (in billions of dollars) 95

3.3 Jobs and Growth Tax Relief Reconciliation Act of 2003: Major Provisions and Estimated Revenue Effects, Fiscal Years 2003–2013 (in billions of dollars) 99
3.4 The Surplus to Deficit Reversal, 2000–2007 (as a percentage of GDP) 112
4.1 Spending, Revenue, and Deficit Impact of the American Recovery and Reinvestment Act of 2009 (in billions of dollars) 120
4.2 Spending, Revenue, and Deficit Effects of the Patient Protection and Affordable Care Act of 2010 (in billions of dollars) 127
4.3 The Simpson-Bowles Comprehensive Deficit Reduction Plan (in billions of dollars) 133
4.4 The Long-Term Path of Federal Spending Under the Ryan Budget Plan (as a percentage of GDP) 136
5.1 Budget Deficit Effects of the Better Care Reconciliation Act (BCRA) and American Health Care Act (AHCA) (in billions of dollars) 153
5.2 Major Provisions of the Tax Cuts and Jobs Act of 2017 (TCJA 2017) 163
5.3 Baseline Revenue Projections and Actual Revenue Levels, 2017–2021 (as a percentage of GDP) 166
5.4 The Obama Budget Baseline and Trump Administration Budget Policy (as a percentage of GDP) 174
5.5 The Budgetary Effects of Laws Enacted in Response to the 2020 Coronavirus Pandemic, March and April 2020 (in billions of dollars) 175
6.1 The Composition of Federal Spending in the Deficit Politics Era (as a percentage of GDP) 187
6.2 Baseline Spending Projections, 2020–2031 (as a percentage of GDP) 189
6.3 The Growth of Social Security and Federal Health Programs, 1990–2050 (as a percentage of GDP) 190
6.4 Baseline Revenue Projections, 2020–2031 (as a percentage of GDP) 192
6.5 Revenues, by Category, 1980–2030 (as a percentage of GDP) 193
6.6 Deficits and Debt: Baseline Estimates and Biden Administration Budget Estimates, 2022–2031 (as a percentage of GDP) 203

Preface

One of the more intractable problems facing the United States today is the escalating growth in federal deficits and debt. The federal budget has been in deficit for most of the past several decades, and the only uncertainty about the years ahead is just how large future deficits will turn out to be. Since the 1980s, long-standing differences between the Democratic and Republican parties over the size and role of the federal government, amplified by intense electoral competition, have destabilized the budget. The result is an era of deficit politics without precedent in U.S. history.

Of course, deficits are sometimes necessary, as in times of war or economic crisis. The large deficits incurred during the Great Recession of the late 2000s and the recent COVID-19 pandemic, for example, allowed the federal government to provide assistance to citizens and businesses and to protect the economy. The concern lies instead with structural deficits—an excess of spending over revenues caused by budget policy decisions for which the president and Congress are responsible. When structural deficits continue to grow, there are heightened levels of risk—adverse economic consequences, fiscal vulnerabilities, or other disruptions.

While there is uncertainty about the immediacy of these risks, the obvious question is why policymakers have failed to lessen them. The United States is, after all, an extremely wealthy nation, with lower tax burdens and spending levels (measured against the size of its economy) than other major democracies. Keeping budgets at or reasonably close to balance should not be all that difficult, since Democrats and Republicans routinely extol the virtues of balanced budgets and fiscal responsibility. Indeed, the Republican party, whose deficit record in recent decades has been especially dismal, has long championed a constitutional balanced-budget amendment.

The purpose of this book is to examine why and how this era of deficit politics has unfolded. Its starting point is an historical overview of the balanced-budget rule that remained a distinctive feature of American politics for nearly two centuries. Chapter 2 covers the 1980s and 1990s transition, when the balanced-budget rule was redefined to accommodate competing Republican and Democratic policy goals. Since presidents play such a key role in budget policy leadership, this chapter and those that follow are organized by presidential administration—from Ronald Reagan's through Joseph Biden's. The chapters analyze as well the role of Congress in facilitating or countering presidential policy agendas. The growing imbalance between mandatory and discretionary spending over this period is also taken into account, as it creates additional difficulties for policymakers in controlling budget outcomes.

The basic assumption of this book is that prudent management of deficits and debt is an essential quality of democratic governance. As George Washington counseled in his Farewell Address, it is the responsibility of political leaders to present to the public "a candid construction of the conduct of the government" in order to obtain "a spirit of acquiescence in the measures for obtaining revenue." Taxes are, in effect, a political check on government. In assessing programs that government seeks to undertake, cost is an inevitable consideration, and an honest presentation of these costs includes the taxes that will be required. The routine use of debt financing to obscure these costs may have undesirable economic consequences at some point; it almost certainly corrodes transparency and accountability between government and the taxpaying public.

With deficit politics, political leaders can offer tax cuts or spending programs that have immediate electoral benefits, while ignoring basic fiscal principles and disregarding whatever long-term damage might result. I hope that a better understanding of the deficit politics problem will lead to a more informed and honest debate about the difficult budget policy choices that lie ahead. At stake, after all, is the fiscal competence of the federal government.

During the writing of this book, as in my previous work, I have benefited greatly from the insights and perspectives of many scholars and would like to acknowledge that intellectual debt. I also want to thank Dominic Heaney at Routledge for his invaluable encouragement and counsel at every stage of the project. Christine Carberry helped to research and prepare the manuscript from its beginning to its completion. As always, she has added an entirely new dimension to the word meticulous, and, as always, I am sincerely grateful for her assistance. Finally, Southern Methodist University, my academic home for several decades, generously provided a research leave and support for my work.

1 From Balanced Budgets to Deficit Politics

The First Federal Congress met in New York City on March 4, 1789, and the challenges it faced were enormous. Foreign threats—that Alexander Hamilton had characterized as "the dangers … from the arms and arts of foreign nations"—had been mounting, and Hamilton was even more concerned with the "dissensions between the States themselves and from domestic factions and convulsions."[1] The new Constitution called for "a more perfect Union," but Congress first had to translate its design and principles into a functioning and effective government.[2]

Congress also inherited the seemingly mundane but critically important task of restoring the nation's credit. When the Revolutionary War ended in 1783, the United States had accumulated an enormous debt—an estimated $43 million held by foreign and domestic creditors.[3] Lacking the power to tax, the Articles of Confederation government could not meet its debt obligations. Interest payments were delayed or missed entirely, the size of the debt continued to grow, and the public credit rapidly deteriorated. Hamilton, the nation's first secretary of the treasury, was directed by Congress to prepare a "proper plan for the support of the Public Credit."[4] His plan was reported to Congress on January 14, 1790, and its key recommendations were adopted later that year. But debates over the plan were bitter and protracted, and Hamilton's subsequent *Report on a National Bank* further galvanized critics of his broad interpretation of federal fiscal powers.[5]

The Federalist "High Finance" program that Hamilton implemented achieved its immediate goal. By the mid-1790s, the public credit of the United States was firmly established in both domestic and European credit markets.[6] Nevertheless, Hamilton's belief that the federal government should manage and secure, rather than retire, its debt prompted Thomas Jefferson (and James Madison) to organize an opposition party that rejected deficit finance. For Jefferson, whose antipathy to federal debt was visceral, balanced budgets were a vital safeguard against corruption and economic inequality.[7] Balanced budgets with limited taxation and spending would further insure that the federal government upheld what Jefferson believed were the "genuine principles" of the Constitution.[8] When the Jefferson administration took office in 1801, it pledged to eliminate federal deficits and debt. Jeffersonian Republicans, reorganized and rechristened as Democrats in the late 1820s,

DOI: 10.4324/9781003167266-1

would go on to dominate national elections for more than half a century. Although intraparty factions fought over many issues, Jefferson's beliefs about balanced budgets and a limited federal government defined this first fiscal era in American political development.

The Civil War gave rise to a political majority with a more positive view of federal power. While the new Republican party believed in balanced budgets and low debt, it also embraced federal support for economic and industrial development. A protective tariff system was created to subsidize American manufacturers and industries, and tariff revenues (and excise taxes) were used to fund public works projects and other spending programs. Instead of limiting what the federal government could do, post-Civil War balanced budgets supported federal efforts to meet domestic needs. Then, when income taxes became the main source of federal revenues during World War I, the Republican party's approach to balancing the budget changed. Lower taxes and lower spending were now Republican priorities. The federal budgets of the 1920s were larger than Jefferson's small government ideal, but balanced-budget conservatism was a limiting vision nonetheless.

With onset of the Great Depression and World War II, federal budgets reached entirely new levels of spending, taxation, and debt. This transition to modern government was the work of a Democratic party majority whose electoral dominance would continue until the 1980s. Over this period, the balanced-budget rule became more flexible, as policymakers adopted countercyclical fiscal policies to stabilize and strengthen the economy. Nevertheless, presidents and Congresses were still expected to balance budgets when possible and otherwise to limit deficits and debt burdens.

For roughly two decades after World War II, for example, a political consensus on Cold War defense budgets provided the necessary support for tax policies and revenue levels that kept budgets at or close to balance. With the social welfare expansions of the late 1960s and 1970s, that consensus eroded, and balanced-budget discipline was more difficult to maintain. Finally, in the 1980s, electoral realignment and partisan divisions over spending and taxation ushered in the era of deficit politics—a willful disregard of deficits and debt without precedent in the nation's history.

The balanced-budget rule that Jefferson advocated so forcefully in the early 1800s was more than an accounting device. It incorporated ideas about the role of the federal government in American life and the spending and tax policies that defined that role. While ideas about the size and role of government later changed, the rule itself proved markedly resilient for nearly two centuries. A closer look at this history provides a helpful perspective for understanding the deficit politics phenomenon that ultimately subverted it.

Jeffersonian Balanced Budgets, 1789–1860

The framers of the Constitution were intent on remedying the fiscal defects that had plagued the Confederation government, and the Article I powers to tax, spend, and borrow they approved were deliberately broad. The borrowing authority was, as a prominent nineteenth-century historian noted, "well-nigh complete; there is no limitation as to time, manner, place, amount, security, payment, or interest."[9] During the constitutional ratification process, this unchecked federal borrowing authority raised serious concerns, and some states called for a constitutional amendment requiring congressional supermajorities to authorize any federal borrowing.[10] Similar reservations were raised about the taxing and spending provisions, which contained elastic language as well. Ratification was secured despite these concerns, but debates over federal fiscal powers continued during the 1790s and beyond.

There was greater acceptance, by comparison, of constitutional provisions that assigned to Congress the power of the purse—which Madison hailed as "the most complete and effectual weapon with which any constitution can arm the immediate representatives of the people."[11] Congressional control of taxing, spending, and borrowing was, for Madison, a necessary check on the executive. Almost immediately, however, the First Congress found itself trying to defend that authority against executive encroachments.

Rejecting the Hamilton Model

In establishing the Department of the Treasury in 1789, Congress debated whether the secretary of the treasury should be authorized to *report* "plans for the improvement and management of the revenue."[12] While the departments of Foreign Affairs (State) and War created earlier that year were directly accountable to the president, the Treasury's unique role raised concerns about executive interference with congressional prerogatives. This possibility was sufficiently troubling that Congress debated whether a multimember Treasury board might be a safer alternative for managing the federal government's financial affairs.[13]

In the end, Congress decided that a single executive should head the new department, but the word "report" was rejected. The final text of the Treasury Department statute approved on September 2, 1789 provided instead that the secretary could "prepare" revenue plans, along with plans "for the support of public credit."[14] Despite this precaution, Alexander Hamilton, who was then unanimously confirmed as treasury secretary, seized the initiative on fiscal matters and championed executive policy leadership. Congress eventually rebelled against executive direction, but Hamilton's spending, tax, and debt program encountered strong opposition almost from the beginning.

Hamilton's tenure began with a highly controversial plan for managing the nation's debt. Article VI of the Constitution mandated that "All Debts contracted and Engagements entered into, before the Adoption of this Constitution, shall be as valid against the United States under this Constitution, as under the Confederation." Hamilton's plan included honoring the nearly $55 million in domestic debt and foreign debt at its original, or par, value and assuming the approximately $25 million in outstanding debt incurred by the states.[15] Congressional approval for these measures was secured only after Hamilton agreed to support relocating the nation's permanent capital to a federal district on the Potomac.

In 1791, Hamilton again marshalled congressional support for legislation chartering the First Bank of the United States. He then persuaded President Washington to sign the measure, despite Secretary of State Thomas Jefferson's strong objections to its constitutionality.[16] At Hamilton's urging, and again in the face of opposition from Jefferson and his followers in Congress, the first federal excise tax was enacted in 1791. Other internal taxes soon followed, including federal taxes on carriages and land. The far-reaching tax program implemented by Hamilton and his successor, Oliver Wolcott, included sinking funds (or pledged revenues) for servicing the debt, and within a remarkably brief time the public credit had been restored and strengthened.[17] Hamilton's focus, however, was on managing the debt rather than eliminating it. A secure public credit, in his view, would allow the nation to borrow easily and cheaply during wartime or other emergencies. It would also help to buttress an expansive federal spending and tax program and "promote the development of the central state."[18]

The political aims of Hamilton's debt program and national bank proposal were complementary. The assumption of state debts, for example, was intended to build support for the new federal government among the prosperous and influential individuals who held those debts. Tying their self-interest to the federal government would, Hamilton believed, counter interstate tensions and rivalries that had proved so troublesome. The national bank's objectives were equally ambitious. In addition to facilitating federal financial transactions, such as borrowing and transferring funds, the national bank's holding of government debt would allow it to issue currency, in the form of bank notes, that would circulate nationally and increase the capital available for commercial transactions and investment. Hamilton's national bank, in other words, was designed to promote economic and commercial development.

Hamilton's entire approach to fiscal matters was executive-centered. He favored broad discretion for executive officials in the expenditure of funds, which meant general or lump-sum appropriations from Congress. In addition, unexpended appropriations were routinely transferred between department accounts, and borrowing "in anticipation of the revenue" was utilized.[19] By the mid-1790s, Congress was rebelling against these practices. Lump-sum appropriations were replaced by increasingly detailed spending specifications, and general appropriations bills were divided into separate measures for general government and for the military.[20] Further divisions of annual appropriations bills would take place over the next several decades. In 1795, the House Ways and Means Committee was made a standing, or permanent, committee, expressly to counter "the existing bias in favor of … the power of the Executive branch."[21]

The Jeffersonian Reaction

More importantly, the 1790s ushered in a political realignment, as Jeffersonian Republicans wrested power from the Federalists and vowed to balance budgets, cut spending and taxes, and reduce debt. When the Jefferson administration took office in 1801, immediate steps were taken to implement this "small government" program. By the end of Jefferson's presidency in 1809, and despite additional borrowing for the Louisiana Purchase, the total public debt had dropped from more than $80 million to just over $50 million.[22]

The War of 1812 required substantial borrowing, in part because Congress delayed action on the Treasury Department's plans for wartime taxation, but the postwar drive for debt reduction was relentless. At war's end, the public debt stood at $127 million; a nearly uninterrupted string of surpluses over the next two decades eliminated virtually all of it. An extended economic recession that began in the late 1830s followed by the Mexican–American War from 1846–1848 brought to an end what President Andrew Jackson had celebrated as "the rare example of a great nation … altogether free from debt," but the public debt in the 1850s was still less than it had been in the 1790s.[23]

In sum, while the pre-Civil War period found Congress bitterly divided over any number of national issues—especially slavery—the power of the purse was governed by relatively stable fiscal norms (see Table 1.1). Budgets were, under normal conditions, balanced—nearly two-thirds of the annual budgets from 1789–1860 were in surplus. Domestic spending was extremely limited—nearly 70 percent of federal expenditures during this period were for the military or military-related purposes (Army, Navy, and veterans' pensions) and for interest on the public debt. Congress also controlled federal taxation. After the War of 1812, excises and other internal taxes virtually disappeared, and Congress relied instead on tariffs and revenues from the sale of public lands. Nevertheless, the public debt in 1860 was some $15 million less than the consolidated debt of 1789, despite the nearly $220 million incurred in "extraordinary expenses" over the period.

Finally, pre-Civil War presidents usually deferred to Congress when it came to fiscal matters. This deference reflected a shared understanding of the separation of powers and constitutional order. In his multivolume treatise on the Constitution published in 1833, Supreme Court Justice Joseph Story summarized the prevailing view about the congressional power of the purse: "[The legislature] has, and must have, a controlling influence over the executive power, since it holds at its own command all the resources, by which a chief magistrate could make himself formidable."[24] Presidential deference was also policy-based—most chief executives after Jefferson shared Congress's commitment to the balanced-budget, small government model.[25]

Notably, that model did not extend to the states, many of which did not share the federal government's aversion to internal improvements. For the first two decades of the nineteenth century, state borrowing and debt had

Table 1.1 Spending, Revenues, Public Debt, Surpluses/Deficits, and Extraordinary Expenses of the Federal Government, 1789–1860

			Extraordinary Expenses	
Total Spending	*Total Revenues*	*Public Debt*	*Wars*	*Territorial Acquisitions*
$1.731 billion	$1.806 billion	$64.8 million	$171 million	$48.3 million
Total number of surpluses		46		
Total number of deficits		24		

Sources: "Total number of surpluses" and "Total number of deficits" are calculations. John Joseph Wallis, "Federal government finances – revenue, expenditure, and debt: 1789–1939," Table Ea584–587, and Scott Sigmund Gartner, "Estimated costs of U.S. wars: 1775–1992," Table Ed168–179, in *Historical Statistics of the United States, Earliest Times to the Present: Millennial Edition*, edited by Susan B. Carter, Scott Sigmund Gartner, Michael R. Haines, Alan L. Olmstead, Richard Sutch, and Gavin Wright (New York: Cambridge University Press, 2006), https://hsus.cambridge.org; U.S. Department of State, Office of the Historian, "Milestones in the History of U.S. Foreign Relations," https://history.state.gov/milestones.

Note: *Public Debt* is as of the end of 1860. *Wars* includes "incremental direct costs … incurred over the duration of the war only" for the War of 1812 and the Mexican–American War (see Gartner source). *Territorial Acquisitions* includes the Louisiana Purchase, the cessions of Florida and California, and the Gadsden Purchase. 1789–1791 is reported as one fiscal year period (see Wallis source).

been relatively low. Starting in the 1820s, a growing number of states began to borrow heavily and debt levels skyrocketed. Collective state debts exceeded $190 million in the early 1840s and reached nearly $260 million in 1860.[26] Much of this debt supported public works and commercial enterprises that the federal government had refused to fund, and state finances often suffered as a result. But reliance on state governments had been one of the principles that animated Jefferson's opposition to Hamilton in the first place, so they were subject to different fiscal rules.

Republican Balanced Budgets, 1860–1932

In 1860, Abraham Lincoln was elected president, and Republicans gained control of both the House and the Senate. The Republican party's electoral supremacy would continue, with occasional interruptions, for the next 70 years. For well over half of this period, Republicans held the presidency and both houses of Congress; unified Democratic control totaled only six years. The Republican version of the balanced-budget rule served a different governmental purpose. As Civil War debt was reduced in the 1870s and 1880s, Republicans kept protective tariffs and excise taxes in place, and the excess revenue they generated was then used to fund internal improvements (public works) and veterans' pensions that helped to bolster the party's electoral support.

This unorthodox program eventually strained Congress's capacity to coordinate revenues and spending. Nearly three decades of consecutive balanced budgets came to an end in the early 1890s, and deficit problems continued until World War I. The substantial debt incurred during that war then led to major budget process reforms designed to manage federal finances more effectively. World War I also led to a significant change in federal tax policy as individual and corporate income taxes replaced tariffs as the principal source of federal revenues. Once the war was over, Republicans were determined to reduce these taxes. Over the next decade, they proceeded to retire wartime debt, while cutting taxes and limiting domestic spending.

Civil War Debt Retirement

The Civil War was a long and extremely bloody conflict, and the Treasury Department had difficulty in funding wartime operations from the outset.[27] The uncertain future of the federal government made it impossible to borrow easily and cheaply, and Congress was repeatedly forced to issue unsecured paper currency to cover revenue shortfalls. Tariff rates and alcohol and tobacco excises were increased, and the nation's first individual income tax was enacted, but tax collections lagged, and revenues remained flat until 1863. By 1865, revenues had increased substantially, and federal borrowing had been stabilized, but postwar inflation and debt management problems persisted for quite some time because of this haphazard war finance system.[28]

When the Civil War ended, federal debt was more than $2.7 billion. In 1866, interest on that debt was $133 million—more than double the total federal spending in the years prior to the war.[29] In order to fund and retire this debt, Congress tightened its controls over noninterest spending. New House and Senate Appropriations Committees were charged with enforcing strict economic restrictions on annual spending bills, and these committees had considerable success in doing so for over two decades. In 1890, the public debt had been reduced to $1.1 billion, and total spending was lower than it had been in the late 1860s.

The commitment to economy, however, began to wane as interest costs declined, and "excess" revenues became available. The centerpiece of Republican fiscal policy was economic protectionism to promote industrial and commercial development. The Civil War income tax was repealed in the early 1870s, but tariff rates remained high, and alcohol and tobacco excises continued to generate substantial revenues as well. This enhanced revenue capacity allowed Republicans to pursue an ambitious spending agenda, namely extensive internal improvements (public works and infrastructure), generous veterans' pensions, and a costly naval rebuilding program.

The growing appetite for new spending gradually undermined the Appropriations Committees, whose independence and "excessive economy-mindedness" had long frustrated other committees.[30] In 1877, the House transferred its politically lucrative rivers and harbors appropriations bill to the Commerce Committee, which already controlled its program authorizations. By 1885, similar transfers of jurisdiction had removed almost one-half of the annual budget from Appropriations Committee control.[31] The impact on spending was predictable. Rivers and harbors expenditures, for example, had totaled $53.8 million from 1869–1879; over the next decade, this spending increased to more than $100 million.[32] Additional spending for other federal public works projects received equally strong congressional backing, with especially generous support directed to construction of the transcontinental railroad.[33] Federal funding of internal improvements, once considered constitutionally suspect, was now a major part of the national agenda.

The pension program for Union veterans of the Civil War started out fairly modestly, with pension costs during the 1870s averaging less than $30 million annually. In 1879, however, Congress passed the Pension Arrears Act, which increased benefits and raised spending for veterans' pensions to almost $90 million a decade later. The 1890 Dependent Pensions Act, described by a leading veterans' organization as "the most liberal pension measure ever passed by any legislative body in the world," then greatly expanded the number of eligible beneficiaries. By 1893, spending for veterans' pensions had risen to nearly $160 million.[34]

Civil War debt retirement ultimately stalled, as the appropriations process fragmented, and politically popular spending programs proliferated. Presidential efforts to restrain spending were sporadic and generally ineffective. Even Grover Cleveland's record-breaking 241 vetoes of general and private pension bills during his first term had little long-term impact.[35] Congress's power of the purse in the pre-Civil War period had certainly not been immune to the spending needs of districts and states, but limited taxation and balanced-budget principles had kept these pressures in check. Post-Civil War Congresses, however, found that they could fund popular domestic spending programs and still manage to balance budgets with reliably abundant revenues.

The Return of Deficits

In the early 1890s, however, tariff revenues began to fall. As spending continued to grow, surpluses narrowed, and, in 1894, the budget was in deficit for the first time since 1865.[36] Over the next two decades, there were 14 additional deficits, and the public debt increased from $960 million in 1893 to $1.2 billion in 1915. Many of these deficits were unavoidable, caused by economic disruptions (the financial "panics" of 1893 and 1907), war (the Spanish–American War in 1898), and borrowing to help to fund construction of the Panama Canal.[37] Others, however, suggested that Congress was finding it increasingly difficult to control spending and coordinate spending with revenues.

Congress acknowledged some of these shortcomings, passing legislation in 1905 and 1906 that required agencies to manage their appropriated funds more efficiently. This legislation was aimed at "coercive deficiencies," whereby agencies deliberately overspent appropriations during a fiscal year and forced Congress to provide additional funding. Congress refused, however, to adopt the comprehensive presidential budgeting reforms that a number of study commissions had recommended and early twentieth-century presidents had endorsed.[38]

Nevertheless, presidents were becoming much more involved in the legislative process. Theodore Roosevelt, for example, argued that "wise legislation and honest and intelligent administration" required executive direction.[39] His administration's domestic policy initiatives and efforts to expand U.S. international involvement marked a major advance in presidential activism. William Howard Taft, Roosevelt's successor, held a more restrained view of presidential power but agreed that "the scope of modern government in what it can and ought to accomplish for its people has widened far beyond the principles laid down by the old 'laissez faire' school of political writers."[40] The "Progressive Era" modernization of the federal government advanced still further with Woodrow Wilson's presidency, as his administration worked closely with Congress to enact federal labor laws, broaden business regulation, and establish the Federal Reserve system.

Wilson also set in motion the transition to a modern tax system. In 1910, Congress had levied a corporate income tax (designated as an excise to avoid constitutional challenges) and proposed a constitutional amendment allowing the federal government to tax individual income. When ratification of the Sixteenth Amendment was secured in 1913, the Wilson administration and Congress enacted a modest income tax, while cutting tariff rates to their lowest levels in decades. During World War I, corporate and individual income tax rates were substantially raised, and income taxation became the main source of federal revenues.

The deficit problem that emerged between 1890 and 1915 was relatively small in terms of scale but did contrast with the balanced-budget record of the previous century. The lack of an executive budget and a fragmented appropriations procedure no doubt contributed to the problem, but Congress was also responding to demands for a greater federal role in meeting national needs. Extensive public works and a growing bureaucracy—the number of federal civilian employees increased from 162,000 in 1890 to more than 395,000 in 1915—were an important part of this new role. In the early 1900s, state and local governments still accounted for two-thirds of overall government spending.[41] Much of what government did at that time (education, law enforcement, health and welfare services, highway construction) remained the responsibility of state and, especially, local governments, but the federal government had moved well beyond the strict fiscal limits of the Jeffersonian era.

Balanced-Budget Conservatism

The United States entered World War I on April 6, 1917. In the years leading up to the war, federal spending had averaged about $725 million annually. When the war ended, the budget was nearly $18.5 billion, the public debt was $25.5 billion, and the debt-GDP ratio was above 30 percent. Despite these high costs, the financing program for World War I was quite successful.

Coordinated borrowing and taxation, together with extensive economic regulation, minimized borrowing costs and kept inflation in check.[42] The first war-related tax bill, the Emergency Revenue Act of 1914, was passed before the United States entered the war, and much larger revenue measures were then enacted in 1916, 1917, and 1918. These bills substantially increased taxes for individuals and corporations, and excise taxes were raised as well. Between 1915 and 1920, individual and corporate income tax revenues increased from $80 million to nearly $4 billion. In 1920, income and excise taxes generated approximately 80 percent of total revenue; the revenue share for tariffs, by comparison, was less than 5 percent.[43]

In the 1918 midterm elections, the Republican party regained control of the House and the Senate. Two years later, Warren Harding won the presidential race with ease, and Republicans expanded their House and Senate majorities. Unified Republican control continued for the next decade, and the balanced-budget rule was used to advance a new partisan agenda. The goal, in this case, was a fiscal model that combined debt reduction, reduced revenue levels, and limited domestic spending.

Budget Reform

In 1921, Congress finally acknowledged that the federal budget process needed presidential direction. The Budget and Accounting Act of 1921, which President Harding praised as the "greatest" budget reform in U.S. history, mandated a comprehensive, annual executive budget.[44] This included the "expenditures and appropriations necessary in his judgment" for all executive departments and agencies, estimates of current revenues and proposals for raising or lowering revenues, and recommendations for how surpluses were to be used or deficits addressed. A new staff agency, the Bureau of the Budget, was set up in the Treasury Department to assist the president in putting together his budget, which would then serve as the starting point for the congressional budget process.

Congress also centralized its own spending controls, restoring exclusive jurisdiction over appropriations bills to the House and Senate Appropriations Committees. House Rule XXI, adopted in 1921, barred legislative committees from reporting bills or amendments that included appropriations.[45] The Senate passed a similar rule the following year. A new congressional staff agency, the General Accounting Office, was authorized to audit the expenditure of appropriated funds by the executive branch to insure compliance with congressional directives.

Budget Policy

With these procedural and organizational changes in place, the executive branch and Congress proceeded to reshape budget policy. On the tax side, Secretary of the Treasury Andrew G. Mellon, who served from 1921–1931, argued that economic efficiency—the proposition that low tax rates promote economic growth—should guide his party's approach to tax policy. Mellon's commitment to balanced budgets, however, insured that revenue-raising requirements were taken into account as well.

Corporate income taxation during the war, for example, had included both a "normal" rate on net income and an excess profits surcharge on income above certain levels. The excess profits tax was reduced in 1919 and repealed entirely two years later. The normal tax rate, however, was then raised, and only minor adjustments were made thereafter.[46] Equally as important, the taxable exemption level remained low over this period, and, with the exception of oil and gas depletion allowances in 1926, Congress did not adopt major corporate tax preferences. As a result, the percentage of net income paid in corporate taxes remained fairly stable throughout the 1920s.[47]

Mellon's concern that high tax rates would impair economic growth led to much lower marginal tax rates for individuals. The top marginal rate on individual income had risen to 77 percent during the war but was reduced to 25 percent in the mid-1920s. Rates for other income brackets were cut as well, and increased exemptions and dependent allowances entirely eliminated tax liabilities for many individuals and families. Congress also approved a number of tax preferences, such as preferential rates on capital gains, that lowered average tax rates and revenues. Compensating changes, particularly adjustments in the income brackets at which marginal tax rates applied, insured that the progressivity of the income tax was retained and revenue losses were minimized.[48] Estate and gift tax rates were cut during the 1920s but remained well above prewar levels, and these taxes continued to supply substantial revenues until the very end of the decade. In addition, Congress revived the protective tariff system that had been a mainstay of federal finances after the Civil War. The Fordney-McCumber Tariff Act of 1922 raised tariff rates and nearly doubled tariff revenues over the next several years. These revenues helped fill the gap in excise tax collections, since Prohibition virtually eliminated alcohol excise revenues and other wartime excises had been cut or eliminated.

Overall, however, the revenue system of the 1920s depended heavily on income taxes. Despite the many postwar changes, individual and corporate income taxes continued to provide approximately 60 percent of total revenues. While revenue levels dropped by more than $2.5 billion from 1920–1922, they remained fairly stable thereafter. Whatever their reservations about income taxation, Republicans did not ignore the revenue requirements of their balanced-budget program.

Domestic spending commitments during the 1920s were limited, and the newly formed Bureau of the Budget played an important role in accomplishing this. From the outset, the Bureau's leadership centralized policy controls over executive departments and agencies to insure that presidential budget decisions were enforced. With presidential budgets typically highlighting spending discipline and efficiency, Congress rarely approved nonpriority spending. Republicans continued to fund internal improvements and federal administrative services, but domestic policy innovations were almost nonexistent. As a result, spending remained concentrated in three areas: military spending, veterans' pensions and benefits, and interest on the public debt. In 1930, for example, these spending categories accounted for 70 percent of the budget. Military spending was much higher than prewar levels, since active duty forces were larger. In addition to the basic pension and compensation benefits for veterans, Congress established a readjustment program in 1918 that funded vocational training, rehabilitation, and limited medical services, and death and disability insurance were made available as well. Finally, interest costs on wartime debt were substantial, averaging approximately 30 percent of total spending for much of the decade. The margin for other programs was therefore narrow. From 1922–1930, total spending remained at or below $3.3 billion annually, and domestic spending was usually less than $700 million. Federal grants to the states were increased, but most of the additional funding was for highway construction, and Congress also provided more generous support for agricultural credit and loan programs.[49] But spending-GDP ratios remained relatively low, budgets were balanced each year, and debt-GDP ratios dropped by nearly one-half (see Table 1.2).

Table 1.2 Spending, Revenues, Surpluses, and Debt, 1920–1930 (as a percentage of GDP)

Fiscal Year	*Total Spending*	*Total Revenues*	*Surplus*	*Total Public Debt*
1920	7.3	7.6	0.3	27.9
1921	6.8	7.5	0.7	32.4
1922	4.5	5.5	1.0	31.5
1923	3.7	4.5	0.8	26.3
1924	3.3	4.4	1.1	24.4
1925	3.2	4.0	0.8	22.5
1926	3.0	3.9	0.9	20.2
1927	3.0	4.1	1.2	19.1
1928	3.1	4.0	1.0	18.2
1929	3.0	3.7	0.7	16.3
1930	3.6	4.4	0.8	17.7

Source: Calculated by the author from John Joseph Wallis, "Federal government finances – revenue, expenditure, and debt: 1789–1939," Table Ea584–587, and Richard Sutch, "Gross domestic product: 1790–2002 [Continuous annual series]," Table Ca9–19, in *Historical Statistics of the United States, Earliest Times to the Present: Millennial Edition*, edited by Susan B. Carter, Scott Sigmund Gartner, Michael R. Haines, Alan L. Olmstead, Richard Sutch, and Gavin Wright (New York: Cambridge University Press, 2006), http://hsus.cambridge.org.

Budgets and the Economy

A steep economic contraction in 1920–1921 was followed by less severe recessions in 1924 and 1927. The economy recovered in each instance without federal intervention, reinforcing the conventional view that spending discipline and balanced budgets were all that was needed to stabilize the economy. When the 1929 economic downturn began, the Hoover administration and Congress approved a limited tax cut for individuals and corporations but nevertheless expected the budget to remain in surplus. One year later, with the surplus disappearing, the administration reversed course and called for increased taxes to keep the budget in balance. Congress also passed the Smoot-Hawley bill that raised tariffs on manufactured goods and agricultural products. As the economy continued to deteriorate, income tax revenues fell sharply, and Smoot-Hawley triggered a decline in international trade that depressed tariff revenues as well. From 1930–1932, total revenues plummeted from $4.1 billion to $1.9 billion.

New spending in response to the economic contraction was limited. Funding for public works and federal credit for banks and businesses were made available, but emergency relief to individuals and families was left to state and local governments. As the budget declined from a surplus of $738 million in 1930 to a deficit of $2.7 billion two years later, Hoover warned that "a large excess of expenditures … can not be continued without disaster to the federal finances."[50] Hoover's commitment to balanced-budget principles, even under such exceptional circumstances, was shared by members of Congress in both parties. The Reconstruction Finance Corporation (RFC) Act of 1932 authorized several billion dollars' worth of loans to businesses and state governments, but the Hoover administration and Congress continued their efforts to cut spending as the depression deepened. Moreover, even the RFC was expected to be self-financing, with loan repayments offsetting the agency's Treasury debt, and was not viewed as new or additional spending. Tax policy was likewise restrictive. The 1929 tax cut was repealed one year later, and the 1932 Revenue Act then raised individual and corporate tax rates. The top marginal rate for individuals, for example, more than doubled, and the normal corporate tax rate of 13.75 percent was higher than its wartime level. The problem, of course, was that revenues continued to fall as the sharp decline in individual and corporate income negated the changes in tax rates.

Given the severity of the Great Depression, the spending cuts and tax increases needed to balance the budget were simply not feasible. Even more importantly, the futile attempts to balance the budget made it impossible for the federal government to fund needed relief and recovery efforts. As President Franklin D. Roosevelt recounted years later, the Great Depression had taught federal policymakers an important lesson about modern budget policy:

> In the early thirties—prior to 1933—fiscal policy was exceedingly simple in theory and extraordinarily disastrous in practice. It consisted in trying

> to keep expenditures as low as possible in the face of shrinking national income ... [and] came near to bankrupting both our people and our Government.
>
> Following 1933 the fiscal policy of the Government was more realistically adapted to the needs of the people ... The deliberate use of Government funds and of Government credit to energize private enterprise ... had a profound effect both on Government and on private incomes.[51]

Democrats and Balanced Budgets, 1932–1980

In 1932, Franklin Roosevelt received nearly 90 percent of the Electoral College votes for president, while Democrats increased their House majority to 313 seats and took control of the Senate by a 59–37 margin.[52] Four years later, Roosevelt's landslide reelection was part of an even larger Democratic wave. When the 75th Congress convened in 1937, there were only 89 Republicans in the House and a mere 17 in the Senate. Over the next half century, the New Deal coalition Roosevelt built never matched this level of electoral dominance, but its majority party status was never seriously threatened.

Between 1932 and 1980, Democrats controlled both the House and the Senate for all but four years (1947–1948 and 1953–1954 being the exceptions). Presidential elections were more competitive, but Democrats still managed to win eight of 12 contests over this period. In addition, Harry Truman was the only Democratic president who had to deal with a Congress controlled by the opposition party, and his ordeal lasted only two years. By comparison, the Republican party achieved unified control only once and that ended after two years. Democratic majorities in both the House and the Senate were sometimes narrow, and liberal-conservative splits among congressional Democrats frequently hampered the party's legislative agenda. But the major changes in budget policy over this extended period—from the Great Depression through the World War II and Cold War decades and the Great Society "welfare shift" of the late 1960s and 1970s—were Democratic party initiatives. Balancing "modern government" budgets, however, often proved difficult, and conflicts over spending and tax policy became especially divisive during the 1970s.

In 1980, the Republican party offered voters a fiscal program that promised tax cuts and balanced budgets. Republican victories in the presidential and U.S. Senate elections that year helped to set in motion a partisan realignment that brought the Democratic majority era to an end. It also created a disconnect between tax policy and spending policy that has persisted, with only a brief interruption in the late 1990s, to this day.

The Great Depression

The 1932 Democratic party platform called for an "immediate and drastic reduction" of at least 25 percent in federal spending and "a federal budget annually balanced" between spending and revenues.[53] Once in office, however, Roosevelt and congressional Democrats increased spending for emergency relief and for numerous domestic programs. By the end of the decade, federal spending had risen to 10 percent of GDP, roughly triple what it had been under Hoover, and the 1940 deficit stood at nearly $3 billion. From 1933–1940, cumulative deficits exceeded $21 billion. In addition to deficit stimulus, long-term changes in spending and tax policy were set in motion during these years.

Spending Policy

The New Deal's peacetime budgets were heavily weighted toward depression-related relief programs, public works projects, aid to agriculture, and public assistance grants to the states.[54] Defense spending and veterans' pensions accounted for nearly one-half of federal outlays in 1930. Their combined share of the New Deal's budgets was less than 25 percent. The scale of New Deal public works projects marked a major advance in the long-running debate over "internal improvements." Massive water and power projects were developed to spur regional economic development, and rural electrification loans and subsidies served the same purpose. Funding for urban highway construction was authorized for the first time, and the federal government launched new programs to subsidize and regulate a national air transportation network. Federal financial assistance was provided as well for other components of a diversified transportation system, notably shipping and railroads.[55]

Federal support for the agricultural sector was also much more comprehensive than in the past. Beginning with the Agricultural Adjustment Act of 1933 and moving forward with additional legislation over the next several years, the federal government provided credit and price supports for various commodities and set production limits to balance supply and demand. This agricultural policy structure has been modified over time but remains an important component of federal domestic policy.

The most important domestic policy expansion of the New Deal, however, was the Social Security Act of 1935. This landmark legislation established permanent financial assistance programs for the elderly and the poor. The latter included several grant-in-aid programs for the states, and federal funding for these and other income security programs totaled $1.5 billion in 1940.[56] The Social Security program, a wholly federal initiative, distributed only $28 million in benefits in 1940 but has since become the largest spending program in the federal budget. The welfare state that the United States has built over the course of many decades rests upon the programmatic base created by the New Deal.

Tax Policy

In 1935, President Roosevelt called upon Congress to pass a "wealth tax" on high-income individuals and to expand corporate taxation to include corporate dividends. Progressive tax rates for individuals had, in the past, been based on the ability to pay. Roosevelt argued that progressivity should have a redistributive purpose, with the aim of reducing "an unjust concentration of wealth and economic power."[57] Congress agreed to raise individual tax rates—including a 79 percent marginal rate for incomes over $5 million—but the overall changes in income taxation were considerably more modest than Roosevelt had proposed. Corporate tax revisions included higher rates and dividend taxation, but were also less far-reaching than the administration had hoped to institute.

While Roosevelt continued to push his tax agenda, congressional support for tax reform was short-lived. In 1938 and 1939, Congress eased or repealed corporate tax changes it had previously enacted and approved new tax preferences for individuals and corporations. The New Deal-inspired debates over progressivity and equity therefore had a limited impact on revenue levels and tax policy during the 1930s. The individual income tax, for example, generated less than 15 percent of federal revenues in 1940. As a percentage of personal income, it stood at 1.3 percent, essentially unchanged from its level in 1930.[58] Taxes on corporate profits did increase with higher rates, but corporate income taxes provided less than 20 percent of federal revenues in 1940.

The single largest source of federal revenues during the 1930s continued to be excise taxes. The end of Prohibition in 1933 reintroduced the tax on alcohol. By the end of the decade, alcohol, tobacco, and various other excises accounted for nearly $2 billion in revenues, nearly as much as the individual and corporate income taxes combined. The payroll taxes included in the 1935 Social Security Act, however, quickly generated substantial revenues. In 1940, social insurance taxes totaled $1.8 billion, more than one-fourth of total federal revenues.

Taken together, the spending, tax, and fiscal policy initiatives of the New Deal transformed the domestic role of the federal government. It now included a permanent social welfare responsibility for broad segments of the population. Domestic policy activism, including financial assistance and regulation, had been integrated into major sectors of the economy, such as agriculture, housing, and transportation. The tax side of the budget included an important new revenue source—the social insurance tax—and the debate over income taxation reflected a heightened emphasis on progressivity and equity. Finally, spending stimulus was legitimized as an effective fiscal policy tool, regardless of deficits.

The growth of the federal government during the 1930s also marked an important change in fiscal federalism. When the New Deal began, state and local government spending exceeded federal spending by a ratio of approximately 2:1.[59] With the exception of World War I, that ratio had been in place for several decades. By 1940, federal spending had risen to 45 percent of total government expenditures, and it reached 60 percent ten years later. The balanced-budget conservatism of the 1920s envisioned a very different federal government than that which emerged from the Great Depression.

Wartime Budget Policy

The budgetary impact of World War II was enormous. Federal spending increased from less than $10 billion in 1940 to over $90 billion in 1945. For the fiscal years 1943–1945, outlays averaged well over 40 percent of GDP (see Table 1.3). Taxation increased rapidly as well, with revenue-GDP in 1944 and 1945 averaging more than 20 percent—the highest levels ever recorded. Nevertheless, unprecedented government borrowing was also necessary. When the war ended in 1945, the public debt was more than $235 billion—an astonishing 104 percent of GDP. While the Roosevelt administration failed to achieve its goal of funding two-thirds of wartime spending with tax and other revenues, its tax and borrowing program, together with the Federal Reserve's cooperation in controlling interest rates, helped the United States to avoid serious wartime finance problems.

Tax Policy

The largest World War II tax increases applied to individuals and corporations. In 1944 and 1945, individual and corporate income taxes provided over 75 percent of total federal revenues, with wartime excises supplying a good portion of the remainder. As was the case during World War I, the corporate tax increases included higher normal rates and additional taxes on excess profits. Both were repeatedly raised, as wartime spending and revenue demands escalated. There were even more far-reaching changes in individual income taxation. What had been a limited income tax for several decades, even during World War I, became a mass tax between 1940 and 1945. Personal exemptions were reduced, filing requirements were strengthened, and tax rates on all income brackets were substantially raised. The administrative mechanism for a mass tax system, such as tax withholding, monitoring, and

Table 1.3 Spending, Revenues, Deficits, and Debt, 1940–1946 (as a percentage of GDP)

Fiscal Year	*Total Spending*	*Total Revenues*	*Deficit*	*Total Public Debt*
1940	9.6	6.7	3.0	43.6
1941	11.7	7.5	4.3	41.5
1942	23.8	9.9	13.9	45.9
1943	42.6	13.0	29.6	69.2
1944	42.7	20.5	22.2	86.4
1945	41.0	19.9	21.0	103.9
1946	24.2	17.2	7.0	106.1

Source: *Historical Tables, Budget of the United States Government, Fiscal Year 2021* (Washington, D.C.: Government Printing Office, 2020), Tables 1.2, 7.1.

auditing, was put in place as well. By the end of the war, approximately 75 percent of the labor force was filing taxable returns, roughly five times the percentage during World War I.[60]

In addition, World War II tax rates were extremely high for all of the two dozen taxable income brackets, ranging from 23 percent for taxable income below $2,000 to 94 percent for taxable income above $200,000.[61] The revenue productivity of the wartime individual income tax resulted from this combination of steep progressivity and a compressed taxable income bracket structure. By the end of the war, the individual income tax generated considerably more revenue than the corporate tax, and the disparity between the two has become even greater over time. It was World War II, then, that established the individual income tax as the cornerstone of federal finances and set the stage for the "tax wars" of recent decades.

Defense Spending

The Roosevelt administration's singular focus on wartime defense budget requirements was an impressive demonstration of "guns vs. butter" discipline. In 1945, national defense outlays accounted for 90 percent of total federal spending, compared to less than 20 percent at the beginning of the war. With few exceptions, spending for domestic programs dropped steadily during the wartime emergency. In 1940, domestic program spending totaled $7.2 billion, which represented nearly 75 percent of total spending. Five years later, current dollar domestic spending was $6.1 billion, or 6.5 percent, of the 1945 budget.

The limited funding for domestic programs during World War II—and the obvious preoccupation of Democrats and Republicans with matters related to the war—defused what had been increasingly heated partisan debates over domestic policy in the 1930s. The long-term fate of the New Deal agenda, however, was far from settled. President Harry Truman, who became president when Franklin Roosevelt died on April 12, 1945, directed the last stage of the war through its official end on September 2. Two months later, he presented Congress with a lengthy domestic postwar agenda. Truman was determined to expand and extend the New Deal, but he soon found himself simply trying to defend it.

From Retrenchment to Cold War

Given the high level of wartime taxation, there was widespread support in Congress for a postwar tax cut. The Revenue Act of 1945, passed in early November, had repealed the corporate excess profits tax, but only modest reductions in individual and corporate tax rates were approved. Even so, Truman chided Congress for exceeding the Treasury Department's tax cut plan and announced his opposition to any future cuts until "the budgetary situation and the economic situation" had improved.[62] Truman was, with good reason, concerned that "ill-advised tax reductions" would add to postwar inflationary pressures, but he was also intent on preserving sufficient revenue capacity to fund domestic spending.

Later that month, Truman called upon Congress to broaden the Social Security program's coverage and benefits, increase grants to the states for public assistance programs, and create a new national health insurance system that would cover all Americans. When Congress failed to act, Truman included these requests in his budget message to Congress the following January. While Democrats had substantial House and Senate majorities in the 79th Congress, conservative opposition to Truman's proposals within the party was strong, and Republican opposition was unyielding. As a result, Truman's legislative program quickly stalled.

Then, in November 1946, Republicans gained control of both the House and the Senate and announced a very different policy agenda. Republican leaders were intent on "shrinking the government"—passing large tax cuts, retrenching domestic programs, and restoring Congress's power of the purse with a new legislative budget process. On June 3, 1947, Congress approved sharp reductions in income tax rates. Echoing the economic efficiency argument that Andrew Mellon had made during the 1920s, Republican leaders argued that lower tax rates would promote economic growth. Harold Knutson, chairman of the House Ways and Means Committee, also made it clear that Republicans planned to curb "much of the government's income by reducing taxes and compelling the government to retrench."[63] Truman promptly vetoed the Republican bill, and an override failed in the House.

Republicans then passed an essentially identical measure that Truman again vetoed. The House overrode Truman's veto, and the Senate barely sustained it. In 1948, an election-year tax cut was approved by Congress. This bill included the low-income tax relief that congressional Democrats favored, and Truman's veto was overridden. Nevertheless, Truman had managed to keep much of the World War II individual income tax system intact for more than three years.

On the spending side, Republicans failed to retrench domestic spending. Their procedural vehicle for doing so, a congressional legislative budget that set an advance limit on all appropriations bills, never worked as intended. In 1948, for example, Congress adopted a legislative budget that mandated less spending than Truman had requested, but the House and Senate then approved appropriations bills that provided higher spending. Shortly thereafter, the legislative budget experiment was abandoned.

With Truman's reelection in 1948 and Democratic control of both the House and the Senate restored, domestic retrenchment lost whatever momentum it might have had. As Truman had cautioned in his January 1946 budget message, abandoning the domestic responsibilities that the federal government had taken on during the New Deal would exact "an excessive price in terms of our national welfare."[64] Truman's attempt to expand these responsibilities made little headway, but he succeeded in protecting the basic social welfare and domestic public goods programs that the New Deal had established. Continued high revenue levels following the war allowed Truman to fund these programs and, at the same time, move the budget toward balance. Then, with the onset of the Cold War, a bipartisan compromise was eventually forged that supported much larger defense budgets, consolidated the New Deal domestic agenda, and restored balanced-budget discipline.

The Truman Defense Buildup

Post-World War II demobilization was rapid, with defense-GDP outlays falling from 37 percent in 1945 to less than 4 percent three years later. With the Truman doctrine in 1947 and the Marshall Plan in 1948 signaling the beginning of the Cold War, U.S. military and economic aid expenditures increased, but neither the Truman administration nor Congress envisioned massive defense budget increases. Strategic national security reassessments and the onset of the Korean War in June 1950, however, catalyzed a comprehensive and costly buildup of U.S. military capabilities. From 1950–1953, the defense budget quadrupled, and defense-GDP expenditures rose from 5 percent to nearly 14 percent. Truman nevertheless continued to press for balanced budgets. Two tax increases were approved in 1950 and a third in 1951. The "guns vs. butter" discipline of World War II was revived, as domestic spending was tightly controlled. The budget did fall into deficit during the Korean War years, but the deficits were relatively small, and debt-GDP levels actually declined.

The costly Cold War defense program that Truman ultimately embraced was troubling even for Pentagon supporters in Congress. In 1949, the chairman of the House Appropriations Subcommittee on Defense, George H. Mahon, noted being "shocked and disturbed" by the "vast sums we are spending and preparing to spend for national defense."[65] When the Soviet Union successfully tested an atomic weapon later that year, administration planning for even larger defense budgets began in earnest. The landmark NSC-68 report, submitted in the spring of 1950, made the case for a comprehensive buildup of U.S. conventional and strategic forces to counter the mounting Soviet threat. The estimated costs of that buildup were subsequently calculated at $40 billion annually, roughly triple the defense budget then before Congress.[66] With additional spending for Korean War operations, fiscal year 1953 defense outlays reached $53 billion (compared to $9 billion in 1948), accounting for nearly 70 percent of total federal spending. The wartime deficit, which peaked that year, was only 1.7 percent of GDP.

Truman's Cold War defense program required unusually high revenue levels, particularly for individual income taxes. The highest revenue levels during World War II were recorded in 1944 and 1945, when revenue-GDP averaged 20.2 percent. The corresponding revenue-GDP for Korean War operations was 18.4 percent in 1952 and 1953. Truman had, in fact, called for even higher revenue levels, but Congress would not go along. Nevertheless, the Truman presidency demonstrated the importance of presidential leadership in building congressional and public support for the costly national security commitments of the Cold War and, at the same time, insuring the revenue capacity that balanced budgets required.

The Eisenhower "Consensus"

The 1952 election gave the Republican party unified control of the White House and Congress for the first time since 1928. The party's House and Senate majorities, however, were narrow, and President Dwight Eisenhower did not pursue the tax cut and domestic retrenchment agenda that conservative Republicans were promoting. Instead, his balanced-budget program comprised Cold War defense budgets, selective increases in domestic programs, and stable tax levels.

The first sign that revenue raising was an administration priority became clear when congressional Republicans attempted to speed up the scheduled repeal of wartime tax increases in 1953. Eisenhower's Treasury Department blocked this effort and also persuaded Congress to extend the corporate excess profits tax for an additional six months. The administration then sponsored a comprehensive rewriting of the Internal Revenue Code in 1954 that included numerous technical revisions. The overall reduction in estimated revenues, however, was quite small, and much of it was offset by extending a number of expiring wartime taxes.

Eisenhower's opposition to major tax cuts was especially noteworthy, given his personal beliefs about fairness and economic efficiency. His January 1955 budget message, for example, conceded that high taxes were "a serious obstacle to the long-term dynamic growth of the economy" and imposed excessive burdens on individuals.[67] Still, he criticized congressional demands for immediate tax cuts and insisted that none would even be considered until the budget was in surplus.[68] Then, when the budget returned to surplus in 1956 and 1957, Eisenhower suggested using excess revenues for debt reduction rather than tax cuts, and he continued to do so through the final years of his presidency.

The spending program of the Eisenhower administration reflected a similar commitment to fiscal moderation. The Truman administration's final defense budget called for accelerated defense spending increases to meet the immediate Soviet military threat. Eisenhower rejected that planning scenario on economic and social grounds. His "new concept for ... financing our national security program" was unveiled in 1954, and it emphasized budgetary commitments that could "be maintained over the extended period of uneasy peace."[69] A paramount concern was insuring that "the external threat of Soviet power" be countered without "weakening our economy and changing our way of life."[70]

Eisenhower's solution was a budget ceiling or "directed verdict" that would serve as a de facto limit on defense budgets. To simplify matters, 10 percent of gross national product (the size of the economy measure used at that time) was used by the administration for defense planning purposes, and the "New Look" strategy military leaders were instructed to follow deemphasized costly conventional force deterrence in favor of increased reliance on nuclear forces. There were congressional reservations about Eisenhower's defense strategy and budget targets. Some Democrats, for example, were concerned that Eisenhower was ignoring important military capabilities, a critique that ultimately coalesced into the missile gap, conventional forces gap, and other alleged military shortcomings in the 1960 Democratic presidential campaign. Republican complaints that defense costs were too high, on the other hand, occasionally surfaced as well. In any case, Eisenhower's defense budget requests were ultimately approved by Congress with few major changes. The administration's peacetime defense budgets for 1955–1961 totaled $289.6 billion; congressional appropriations for the entire period were $287.6 billion.[71] In addition, Eisenhower's priority on Air Force funding was accepted, with the Air Force share of the budget eventually equaling combined funding for both the Army and the Navy.

The final component of Eisenhower's fiscal program involved stable budget shares for domestic programs. Here again, Eisenhower made it clear from the outset that Social Security and other New Deal social programs would remain in place. The administration remained opposed, however, to expanded social welfare commitments, in particular the national health insurance program that liberal Democrats continued to promote. Spending for capital investment projects, such as the interstate highway system, increased significantly under Eisenhower, but the pattern for other discretionary domestic programs was mixed. Outlay-GDP levels for social welfare and other domestic programs had declined during the Korean War but were close to prewar levels by the end of the decade.

The fiscal record of the peacetime Eisenhower presidency was shaped by balanced-budget considerations that required compromises on budget policy. The priority assigned to defense, for example, was supported by majorities in both parties who embraced Cold War strategic imperatives, but the consolidation of New Deal domestic programs was a bipartisan compromise that satisfied neither liberal Democrats nor conservative Republicans. The high revenue levels of the late 1950s were likewise troubling to Republican opponents of heavy taxation and to Democratic proponents of tax fairness. These compromises, and Eisenhower's budget policy leadership, produced three balanced budgets (1957, 1958, and 1960). The three peacetime deficits were relatively small, and debt-GDP levels continued their long-term decline, falling below 45 percent at the end of the decade.

The Welfare Shift

Between 1960 and 1980, the spending priorities of the federal government changed radically. The defense budget share was cut by more than one-half—

from 52 percent in 1960 to less than 23 percent in 1980. This defense transfer supported a massive increase in domestic spending, particularly for social welfare programs. But growth in domestic spending was so steep that the level of total spending rose as well—from just over 17 percent of GDP in 1960 to more than 21 percent two decades later. As this spending trajectory accelerated, additional revenues were not provided. The only major income tax increase during the 1960s was a temporary wartime measure in 1968. The record for the 1970s was even more one-sided, with five tax cuts from 1971–1978.[72]

Over this two-decade period, the balanced-budget rule continued to play a role in budget policy debates, but balanced-budget constraints became noticeably weaker. Growing partisanship over spending policy lessened bipartisan support for revenue raising. The congressional budget reforms of 1974 reduced the importance of presidential budgets, particularly with respect to fiscal policy and spending priorities. A more assertive Congress could, and did, decide that deficit finance was a politically cost-free means of expanding the welfare state. As a result, the deficit levels of the late 1970s were considerably larger than those over the previous three decades.[73]

The Kennedy-Johnson Transition

The Kennedy administration's original budget program mirrored Eisenhower's fiscal priorities. John F. Kennedy's presidential campaign had highlighted the need for enhanced military capabilities, and a series of requests for increased defense spending was submitted to Congress in 1961. In order to meet "present revenue requirements," Kennedy also asked Congress to suspend the scheduled expiration of the higher corporate income and excise tax rates initially approved in the 1950s.[74]

Two years later, however, the administration proposed a major tax cut. Despite nearly $20 billion in projected deficits for 1963 and 1964, Kennedy argued that tax cut stimulus was needed to spur economic growth. The choice, Kennedy explained, was "not between a tax cut and a balanced budget … [but] between chronic deficits arising out of a slow rate of economic growth, and temporary deficits stemming from a tax program designed to promote … more rapid economic growth."[75] The Revenue Act of 1964, which was signed into law by Lyndon Johnson, contained across-the-board cuts in individual tax rates and was by far the largest tax cut since World War II. Positive economic growth after its enactment provided an immediate political boost for Democrats, but it also set a precedent for pro-growth tax cuts regardless of deficit effects.

President Johnson's budget program then signaled a shift in spending priorities. The pace of defense budget increases had already slowed under Kennedy, but the budget Johnson sent to Congress in January 1964 called for an actual cut in military spending and a reallocation to domestic programs. The Great Society's expansion goals were announced later that year, and

Johnson's legislative agenda went well beyond the modest domestic policy reforms that Kennedy had proposed. In terms of its ambition and scope, Johnson's vision was modeled on the New Deal.

With Johnson's landslide reelection in 1964 and overwhelming Democratic majorities in the 89th Congress, Great Society legislation moved through Congress quickly and in great volume. The cumulative changes in social welfare policy and domestic public goods commitments were enormous and expensive. Johnson promised to finance them without tax increases or higher deficits, which left defense budget cuts as the preferred option.

In fiscal year 1965, defense spending was $4 billion less than in the previous year, domestic spending increased by roughly $3 billion, and the $1.4 billion deficit was the smallest in five years. Johnson's fiscal year 1966 budget forecast a similar result—despite domestic spending increases, "the ratio of federal spending to our total output will continue to decline."[76] The rapid escalation of the U.S. military commitment in Vietnam, however, quickly brought defense transfers to a halt.

In March 1965, the first Marine and Army combat units were sent to Vietnam. By the end of the year, troop levels had increased from 23,000 to almost 185,000. Three years later, the total was 550,000. This was several times larger than the U.S. force in Korea, but the costs and financing of the Vietnam War were managed very differently.

Johnson refused to let the war delay or downscale his domestic agenda, insisting instead that Congress "grasp the opportunities of the Great Society."[77] And, as noted earlier, the 89th Congress complied. In July 1965, for example, Congress approved new healthcare entitlements for the elderly (Medicare) and the poor (Medicaid). It then expanded the welfare state with new public assistance and income security benefits. Johnson's "guns and butter" fiscal program was sharply criticized by congressional Republicans and even some fellow Democrats, but they could do little to slow its advance.

From 1965–1969, the peak years of Vietnam War funding, defense outlays increased by approximately $30 billion, but social welfare and domestic spending rose by almost the same amount. During the Korean War, the defense budget share had more than doubled—from 32 percent in 1950 to 69 percent in 1953. Under Johnson, the defense budget share was essentially unchanged.

Johnson also wanted to avoid wartime taxation. In 1965, he called upon Congress to cut excise taxes. With the 1964 income tax cuts about to take full effect, Johnson wanted to insure that the "tax system … makes a maximum contribution to our economic growth."[78] Congress agreed, passing an even larger reduction than Johnson had proposed.

In 1966, with spending and deficits beginning to climb, Johnson adjusted course only slightly. He asked Congress to strengthen revenue collection enforcement and to suspend some excise tax reductions it had approved the previous year. Congress complied, as it did with a request to suspend corporate tax preferences that were about to be implemented. Entirely absent from the administration's tax program were any of the individual and corporate tax increases that had been imposed at the outset of World War I, World War II, and the Korean War.

Republicans picked up 47 House seats and four Senate seats in the 1966 midterm elections, and the 90th Congress that convened in January 1967 was more receptive to calls for fiscal restraint. The immediate concern was that rising deficits would make it difficult to keep inflation at an acceptable level, and the Johnson administration responded with an income tax surcharge proposal. In January, Johnson recommended a temporary 6 percent surcharge but warned Congress that anything larger could "depress economic activity … and thereby fail to secure the revenues it was designed to achieve."[79]

In the fall, the administration reported that its initial deficit projections had been much too low. With the deficit estimate having tripled to $24 billion, the administration conceded that a much larger tax increase was needed to halt "a spiral of ruinous inflation."[80] The new surcharge target was 10 percent, and additional revenue-raising measures were recommended as well.

At this point, however, conservative Democrats joined congressional Republicans in demanding that domestic spending cuts be part of the deficit-reduction agenda. This effort was led by Wilbur Mills, the influential chairman of the House Ways and Means Committee. In October, his committee voted overwhelmingly to postpone any consideration of a tax increase until the administration submitted a formal request for domestic appropriations cuts. Johnson's initial offer of a $4 billion reduction was summarily rejected by Mills, who insisted that $6 billion would be needed before moving ahead on a tax bill. Johnson was forced to comply, and the Revenue and Expenditure Control Act of 1968 was finally signed into law on June 28, 1968. The income tax surcharge, its most important revenue-raising provision, was initially limited to 12 months but was extended for an additional six months the following year.

The impact on revenues was dramatic, with revenue-GDP in 1969 reaching 19 percent, its highest level since 1945. Spending growth was minimal, given the cuts in domestic appropriations, and the budget surplus of $3.2 billion was the largest in over a decade. It would also turn out to be the last surplus for nearly three decades.

The Johnson administration's rationale for a temporary rather than a permanent tax increase was unclear. Johnson was hesitant to embrace the idea of a "war tax," and the economic policy arguments the administration offered instead were inconsistent and confusing. But deficit critics, like Mills, also favored a temporary increase. Mills was convinced that permanently higher revenues would eventually be used to fund domestic programs once the war ended.[81] As he explained, "Today tax policy … is being controlled almost completely by expenditure policy. This is one of the basic concerns to me, to try to find some effective way to bring about a change in the rate of increase in expenditures."[82]

Traditional fiscal norms, however, were changing in ways that Mills and other balanced-budget proponents could not foresee. Johnson had already set a precedent "for relegating war taxes to the back burner. Whether or not one believes that 'shared sacrifice' through higher taxes was ever an important value … that principle had plainly suffered a setback."[83] Three decades later, George W. Bush would eviscerate what was left of that principle. More immediately, the Congresses of the 1970s found that they could also avoid politically difficult tax increases and finance domestic programs with deficits.

Nixon-Ford and Divided Government

Richard M. Nixon's narrow victory in the 1968 presidential election left Democrats in firm control of Congress. His landslide reelection in 1972 also failed to have much of an impact on Congress. The 93rd Congress began with a 243–192 Democratic majority in the House and a 57–43 advantage in the Senate. Nixon resigned in August 1974 and was succeeded by Vice President Gerald Ford. The November midterms that followed produced even larger Democratic majorities, and the 1976 and 1978 election cycles had similar results. The 94th–96th Congresses had Democratic margins of roughly 2:1 in the House, and the party's Senate majorities averaged more than 60 seats. By 1980, these Democratic Congresses had raised domestic spending to historic levels. They also resorted to deficit financing for this spending, since defense budget cuts were insufficient.

President Nixon's first term featured repeated confrontations with Congress over spending policy. Congress continued to cut the administration's defense budgets, even though the United States was still fighting the Vietnam War. From 1969–1973, when the war officially ended, current dollar defense spending fell by 7 percent. The decline in inflation-adjusted spending was nearly 30 percent. Over the same period, the domestic program appropriations bills that Congress passed were well above Nixon's spending requests. Numerous presidential vetoes followed, some of which were sustained.[84] In other cases, Nixon simply refused to spend funds that Congress had appropriated. The number and scale of Nixon's executive impoundments was unprecedented, and Congress was predictably outraged.

For congressional Democrats, this battle over spending policy was framed as a "peace dividend." The term was disingenuous, given that both domestic spending and defense spending had increased by similar amounts under Johnson. More importantly, defense experts in Congress generally agreed that the non-Vietnam, or base, defense budget had been underfunded. This critique had been highlighted by Nixon in his 1968 campaign, echoing the Republican platform warning that the United States had "frittered away any superior military capabilities, enabling the Soviets to narrow their defense gap, in some areas to outstrip us, and to move to cancel our lead entirely by the early Seventies."[85]

Once in office, however, Nixon was unable to build public or congressional support for increased defense spending as the increasingly unpopular Vietnam War dragged on. What Nixon tried to do instead was to limit the transfer of defense "savings" to domestic programs and to adjust defense strategy and programs accordingly.[86] Nevertheless, real defense spending fell sharply during Nixon's first term.

With social welfare programs, the Nixon administration and Congress found areas of agreement that, in terms of total spending, were more consequential than the appropriations clashes. Social Security benefits were increased by 15 percent in 1969, 10 percent in 1971, and 20 percent in 1972. The administration and Congress then indexed future benefits, with cost-of-living adjustments scheduled annually. Both the Social Security wage base and tax rate were raised to fund these benefit expansions, which proved to be much more costly than expected when inflation rates soared in the late 1970s. The first-term increases under Nixon, however, were still quite substantial. From 1969–1973, Social Security spending rose by nearly $22 billion, considerably higher than the $13 billion total increase in discretionary spending over this period. Spending for healthcare entitlements also grew steadily and without serious policy disputes. In 1972, for example, Medicare coverage and benefits were expanded.

There were, by comparison, numerous conflicts over public assistance entitlements. In August 1969, Nixon proposed a guaranteed family income plan, with income support based on family need and size, to replace existing welfare programs. Nixon's Family Assistance Plan was a more ambitious welfare reform than the Johnson administration had believed feasible, but it was nonetheless rejected by congressional Democrats as inadequate. Democrats then blocked the administration's efforts to combine education and health categorical grants into block grants that would allow the states greater discretion, and proposed reforms in higher education student assistance were also rebuffed by Congress.

There were some important agreements on other public assistance entitlements. In 1972, several federal state assistance programs for the disabled and aged poor were combined into a new supplemental security income program, with higher benefit levels and exclusively federal funding. Eligibility and benefit levels for the food stamp program were liberalized, and Medicaid eligibility was expanded. Spending growth in public assistance entitlements lagged well behind the Social Security and Medicare increases, but the Nixon administration never mounted a wholesale assault on "welfare." In fact, mandatory programmatic spending-GDP rose from 5.5 percent in 1969 to 7.2 percent in 1973, a much larger increase than had taken place under Johnson.

On the revenue side, Nixon abandoned his attempts to increase taxes—and to balance the budget—as economic problems mounted. Inflation was a continuing challenge, but in 1970 the unemployment rate began to climb. Nixon then unveiled his economic recovery program, the stimulus component of which included a large tax cut. Four months later, Congress cleared the Revenue Act of 1971, which reduced individual and corporate taxes by an estimated $26 billion over a three-year period. In an attempt to assuage concerns that deficit stimulus would add to inflation pressures, the administration promoted an alternative budget concept—the "full employment budget," which measured what the government would spend and collect in taxes if the economy was operating at optimal capacity. According to the administration, its budget would be at or near balance under these conditions. In addition, there were wage and price controls to provide more immediate inflation relief, and complementary changes were made in international exchange rates and trade policy.

In 1972, Nixon stepped up his challenge to Congress over domestic spending. Citing the need to control the deficit, Nixon called upon Congress to adopt a $250 billion spending ceiling and allow him to cancel any spending above the ceiling. In the end, Congress refused to cede its "power of the purse," but the outcome was in doubt for some time. This episode convinced Democrats that budget reform was needed to strengthen Congress's hand. When Nixon then decided to bypass Congress by impounding funds, the reform effort became even more pressing.

Following Nixon's reelection, the spending ceiling and domestic appropriations conflicts resumed in 1973. As the Watergate scandal unfolded, however, Nixon's demands for "a rigid ceiling on spending" and an end to Congress's "momentum of extravagance" became less and less compelling.[87] By 1974, the administration was in full-scale retreat, but Congress moved ahead with legislation to curb presidential impoundments and enhance its control over budget policy. Less than a month before he was forced to resign, Nixon signed into law the Congressional Budget and Impoundment Control Act of 1974. What he applauded as "the most significant reform of budget procedures since the Congress and this country began" was a complicated measure that created Budget Committees, budget resolutions, and impoundment controls.[88] In the hands of the post-Watergate Democratic Congress, the new budget process soon accelerated the spending policy transfers Nixon had fought against so strenuously.

In the fall of 1974, Gerald Ford proposed a tax increase to reduce the deficit and check inflation, but Congress took no action. Over the next several months, as unemployment became a more urgent concern, Ford recommended a limited, temporary tax cut stimulus. Congress then passed a larger tax cut that included new tax preferences and an additional $2 billion in stimulus spending. When another tax cut was being considered in 1976, Ford attempted to attach spending offsets, but none were accepted. Spending-GDP in 1976 rose to 20.8 percent, its highest level since 1946. The 1976 deficit was more than $73 billion, nearly triple the largest Vietnam War deficit.

The defense budget, however, did not benefit from this spending largesse. At the end of his presidency, Ford was able to halt the protracted decline in real defense spending, but the defense budget share had dropped below 25 percent at that point. Whatever the merits of the Democratic party's "peace dividend" rationale, Congress had managed to transfer a massive amount of spending to domestic programs. A portion of that transfer supported the expansion of discretionary domestic programs. The remainder was redistributed to social welfare programs, particularly retirement and healthcare entitlements.

From 1969–1977, Congress also legitimized the routine use of deficit finance. Cyclical deficits during recessions—a mild slowdown in 1970 and a much more serious contraction that began in November 1973 and lasted through early 1975—were to be expected. Deficits at other times, however, were structural, as congressional support for tax increases vanished. Thus, by the mid-1970s, the policy imbalance between spending and revenues was much greater than it had been prior to the Nixon and Ford presidencies. The balanced-budget rule that congressional Democrats managed to ignore when dealing with Republican presidents would be taken more seriously by Jimmy Carter, but the results were much the same. Carter's presidency began with pledges of party unity, but the usual budget policy conflicts quickly surfaced.

The Carter Presidency

The Democratic party's goals in 1977 included national health insurance and welfare reform, as well as a substantial reduction in defense spending. Jimmy Carter added a fourth—balancing the budget by 1981. None were achieved.

The Carter administration's retreat on the defense budget occurred quickly. The administration's first defense budget proposal, a revision of Gerald Ford's fiscal year 1978 plan, was the first of what congressional Democrats expected to be a multiyear reduction program. In the following year, however, the president reversed course and called upon Congress to approve "prudent real growth" in future defense budgets.[89]

The problem facing Carter was the growing recognition that post-Vietnam defense cutbacks had compromised critical defense needs. An influential Congressional Research Service report in 1976 had pointed to growing disparities between U.S. and Soviet military capabilities.[90] That same year, the Central Intelligence Agency's analysis of comparative defense spending concluded that Soviet investments in strategic forces were much greater than those of the United States and that Soviet advantages in other defense programs were significant as well.[91] Carter's Defense Department came to a similar conclusion, estimating a 25–45 percent Soviet spending edge and conceding that "relative defense spending, annual or cumulative, is the best single crude measure of relative military capabilities."[92]

Carter's dilemma was that many congressional Democrats opposed any rebalancing of discretionary spending priorities. His "prudent real growth" defense program was thus too modest to remedy acknowledged shortfalls in funding, but too costly to accommodate the increases in discretionary domestic programs that liberals demanded. His attempts to compromise these differences were ineffective, and they compounded the difficulties he had in managing social welfare policy reform.

National health insurance proved to be an especially divisive issue for Democrats. When Carter took office, congressional Democrats assumed that a comprehensive plan could be enacted reasonably quickly. In April 1977, however, Carter insisted that Congress first enact healthcare cost controls. Healthcare cost inflation had been outpacing general inflation for years, with hospital costs an especially serious concern. From 1967–1976, for example, the consumer price index had risen by 174 percent.[93] Hospital operating room charges, however, had gone up by 290 percent and hospital patient rooms by 282 percent. Apart from the potential costs of a national health insurance program, the federal budget was facing much higher spending for Medicare and Medicaid, so Carter saw his cost control initiative as an important first step in making healthcare more affordable for the federal government and also for the states.

Despite Carter's insistence that Congress take immediate action, none of Congress's health policy committees reported out a cost control bill in 1977. The Senate passed a watered-down version the following year, but the House failed to act on the Senate-passed measure. In 1979, the House effectively ended the debate, voting down Carter's "top-priority anti-inflation measure" in favor of a national study commission on hospital costs.[94]

As the healthcare cost control debacle unfolded, the Carter administration decided to move ahead with a less costly, phased-in national health insurance program. The first phase included catastrophic coverage, and its limited benefits were sharply criticized by congressional liberals. Senator Edward M. Kennedy, who would challenge Carter for the 1980 presidential nomination, was the leading proponent of comprehensive national health insurance, and he introduced his Health Care for All Americans Act in 1979. For Kennedy, Carter's approach would do nothing to reform a "separate and unequal" healthcare system.[95] For Carter's defenders, Kennedy's plan was "a potential $200-billion-a-year pork barrel" that would have a "shock effect" on the economy and "inevitably result in an arbitrary rationing of health care services." With no compromise in sight, national health insurance disappeared from the congressional agenda in 1980. Congress then turned its attention to the cost increases in existing healthcare entitlements, which, having been ignored for three years, were escalating. Minor "savings" in Medicare and Medicaid were enacted as part of a budget-reconciliation bill, but benefits and coverage were unchanged.

Carter's welfare reform was an ambitious attempt to provide public service jobs and a basic cash benefit for the poor and working poor. Its cash benefit, based on family size and need, would replace several existing programs (Aid to Families with Dependent Children, Supplemental Security Income, and food stamps). The jobs program would create 1.4 million jobs and training positions, with eligibility extended to all low-income families. First-year costs were estimated at more than $30 billion, but net costs, which took into account savings from programs that were to be replaced, were less than $3 billion.[96] Once again, liberal Democrats in Congress were disappointed with Carter, but the most important objections on this occasion came from critics of the cost of welfare. As their attacks intensified, Carter responded with a much more modest proposal two years later, but it too failed to make it through the House and the Senate.

Carter's problems with Congress extended to the tax side of the budget. His targeted 1977 tax cut stimulus was barely recognizable when it finally passed Congress, and its impact was reduced, if not eliminated, by the payroll tax increase enacted in December. The Social Security trust funds were being depleted as benefits outstripped revenues, and Congress was forced to move up scheduled increases in the Social Security tax rate and wage base to cover the shortfall. These increases were nowhere near sufficient to insure the long-term solvency of the trust funds. The administration's recommended benefit reforms, however, were completely ignored by Congress, and, as was predicted at the time, a more balanced "rescue plan" would soon be needed.

Carter's tax reform proposal, submitted to Congress in 1978, combined individual and corporate income tax rate cuts with reduced tax preferences. For individuals, the plan would have concentrated relief on low- and middle-income families. Congress approved instead an increased capital gains exclusion, which primarily benefited upper-income taxpayers, and rejected almost all of the tax preference reforms for individuals and corporations.

The Revenue Act of 1978 was also undercut, in terms of distributive tax relief, by the increased payroll taxes that were taking effect, and accelerating inflation was making "bracket creep" an issue for many taxpayers as well. Despite the wider income brackets Congress added to the 1978 tax cut, taxpayers were being pushed into higher tax brackets without equivalent increases in real income. The combined effect of higher payroll taxes and inflation-generated income tax increases meant that some taxpayers received little or no benefit from the 1978 tax cuts.

Tax reform resurfaced in 1980, when Carter decided that a balanced budget was essential. While the official justification was inflation control, Carter and congressional Democratic leaders hoped that a balanced-budget commitment would provide a needed boost in the November elections. The difficulty was that congressional Democrats had no intention of cutting domestic spending, and Carter had pledged to increase the defense budget. Carter's election year plan was therefore dependent on much higher revenue levels, but the tax "reforms" Congress approved were relatively minor. Given the spending levels being held firmly in place, revenue-GDP ratios would have to be higher than they were during World War II, and an election-year tax increase of this magnitude was impossible.

High taxes were, in fact, already a serious political liability for Democrats. In 1980, the direct tax burden for individuals—individual income and payroll taxes—was 14.4 percent of GDP, considerably higher than when Carter took office and well above even the balanced-budget level in 1969. Individual direct taxes had grown more rapidly than personal income, with the payroll tax burden climbing by 25 percent.[97] The extraordinary proliferation of tax preferences during the 1970s—half of the more than 300 tax preferences added to the tax code from 1909–1981 were made between 1970 and 1981[98]—did little to counter the increases in average income tax rates and marginal income tax rates for all income groups.[99]

Antitax sentiments were also surfacing in the states, with property taxes the usual target. For the federal government, the "tax revolt of the late 1970s" was aimed principally at the income tax, and it reflected the tax rate increases that were affecting so many Americans.[100] The fact that inflation had caused much of the problem was irrelevant, since policymakers had obviously failed to bring inflation under control or compensate for its impact on taxpayers.

The deficit posed yet another problem. The National Taxpayers Union (NTU) had launched a campaign in 1975 for a constitutional balanced-budget amendment. The NTU's strategy was to convince state legislatures to force Congress to call a constitutional convention.[101] Under Article V of the Constitution, Congress could propose amendments, or, "on the Application of the Legislatures of two thirds of the several states, shall call a Convention for proposing Amendments." By 1979, 29 of the needed 34 states had approved this application, and a number of other states were considering doing so too. The Carter administration managed to convince most of these states to reject the convention proposal, but Carter was hard-pressed to defend his deficit record.

Last, but certainly not least, the unprecedented peacetime spending levels of the late 1970s could not accommodate national health insurance, public assistance welfare reform, or the new domestic policy initiatives Democrats had promised. Moreover, the increases in defense spending that Democrats reluctantly accepted could not support the military buildup that defense experts and much of the public believed was necessary. The 1976 Democratic platform had criticized Presidents Nixon and Ford for their "undue emphasis on the overall size of the defense budget."[102] The 1980 platform attacked them for the "steady decline of 33 percent in real U.S. military spending between 1968 and 1976."[103] Equally remarkably, the 1980 platform claimed that Democrats had "restrained the increase in government spending in ways which have steadily reduced the deficit we inherited."[104] The 1980 deficit was $73.8 billion, substantially higher than the deficit when the Carter presidency began.

Policy Choices and Deficit Politics

The budget policy changes during the 1970s meant that the path to a balanced budget would be difficult no matter who won the election (see Table 1.4). Revenue levels in 1980 were still relatively high, when compared to

1969. Spending, however, was much higher than it had been when the budget had last been balanced. The bulk of that additional spending, moreover, was concentrated in the mandatory programmatic category of retirement and healthcare entitlements. Beneficiary populations of these programs were growing, benefit levels were directly or indirectly indexed, and high rates of future growth were automatic. Another obvious difference between 1969 and 1980 was that the budget had gone from surplus to deficit, but the figures here were misleading. If defense cuts after Vietnam had been more measured and responsible, the 1980 deficit would have been even larger.

Looking ahead, the Democratic party's agenda for the 1980s promised more of the same, with the exception of defense. The Democratic platform highlighted comprehensive and universal national health insurance, new welfare benefits and services, and other domestic policy expansions that had failed to pass during Carter's first term. No reservations were expressed about the entitlements already in place. Real spending for Social Security, for example, had doubled during the 1970s, but Democrats insisted that decisions about future benefits should be divorced from "the program's impact on the budget."[105]

Table 1.4 Revenues, Outlays, and Surplus/Deficit, 1969–1980 (as a percentage of GDP)

FY 1969 =	*+$3.2 billion*	*FY 1980 =*	*–$73.8 billion*
Revenues =	19.1	Revenues =	18.5
Outlays =	18.7	Outlays =	21.2
Surplus =	+0.3	Deficit =	–2.6

	FY 1969	*FY 1980*	*Change*
Revenues			
Individual	8.9	8.7	–0.2
Corporation	3.7	2.3	–1.4
Payroll	4.0	5.7	+1.7
Other	2.5	1.8	–0.7
	19.1	18.5	–0.6
Outlays			
Discretionary Defense	8.4	4.8	–3.6
Discretionary Nondefense	3.5	5.1	+1.6
Mandatory Programmatic	6.3	10.1	+3.8
Net Interest	1.3	1.9	+0.6
Offsetting Receipts	–0.8	–0.7	+0.1
	18.7	21.2	+2.5

Source: *Historical Tables, Budget of the United States Government, Fiscal Year 2021* (Washington, D.C.: Government Printing Office, 2020), Tables 1.1, 1.2, 2.3, 8.4.

Since Democrats were also committed to boosting the defense budget, spending-GDP was almost certain to remain high. Future deficit reduction would therefore depend on revenue increases, but Democrats emphasized their tax cut credentials. They took full credit for the 1977 and 1978 tax cuts and looked forward to passing "targeted tax reductions" in the years ahead.[106] Not surprisingly, balanced budgets were not a priority. Instead, the party adopted a less demanding standard: "We support the discipline of attempting to live within the limits of our anticipated revenues."[107]

The 1980 Republican platform, by comparison, promised to cut taxes and spending and to restore balanced-budget discipline. The tax program was forthright and specific—across-the-board reductions in individual tax rates. The 14–70 percent tax rate structure would be lowered to 10–50 percent over a three-year period, and tax brackets would be indexed to protect these reductions from inflation-generated bracket creep.[108] Republicans explained that this unusually large tax cut would "generate increases in economic growth, output, and income which will ultimately generate increased revenues" but emphasized the "greater justification … lies in the right of individuals to keep and use the money they earn."

There was considerably less specificity regarding spending cuts, and indeed some caveats that suggested painful retrenchments could somehow be avoided. Welfare programs, for example, would be transferred "wholesale" to the states but with the "tax sources to finance them."[109] Social Security benefit taxation was "strongly opposed."[110] Commitments to "quality care" in Medicare and Medicaid would be continued.[111] And, of course, defense spending would be raised by amounts that would close the "gap with the Soviets" and "ultimately reach the position of military superiority."[112] Republicans pledged to cut the "21 percent" of federal spending "as a percent of the Gross National Product" but failed to state by how much or by what means.[113]

With both parties deliberately avoiding difficult tradeoffs between spending and taxes, there was no real possibility that deficits could be eliminated anytime soon. The potential fiscal gap for Democrats was considerably smaller, since revenues would be higher and new domestic commitments could be delayed or blocked. For Republicans, the potential gap would be much greater, since revenues would be lowered well in advance of spending cuts that might or might not be possible. But deficit politics, rather than balanced budgets, was now the fiscal framework in which policymakers in both parties would be operating.

Notes

1 Alexander Hamilton, James Madison, and John Jay, *The Federalist Papers* (New York: New American Library, 1961), 53–54.

2 This work started slowly, as it took several weeks for both chambers to assemble the necessary quorums. When the third session of the First Congress ended in

1791, however, much had been accomplished. The principal executive departments—Foreign Affairs, War, and Treasury—had been established, along with the Office of the Attorney General; the judicial court system had been created and judicial court processes set forth; landmark statutes had been enacted; new states had been admitted; and the Bill of Rights had been added to the Constitution.

3 E. James Ferguson, *The Power of the Purse: A History of American Public Finance, 1776–1790* (Chapel Hill: University of North Carolina Press, 1961), 136–137.

4 Alexander Hamilton, "Report Relative to a Provision for the Support of Public Credit of the United States," January 9, 1790. Harold C. Syrett, ed., *The Papers of Alexander Hamilton* (New York: Columbia University Press, 1962), 6:66.

5 The Funding Act of 1790, which incorporated the key recommendations in Hamilton's debt program, was passed on August 4, 1790. Hamilton's proposal for a national bank was submitted to Congress on December 14, 1790. The House and the Senate passed the necessary legislation, but President George Washington's cabinet was divided over its constitutionality. Secretary of State Thomas Jefferson and Attorney General Edmund Randolph submitted a written argument setting forth their constitutional objections. Hamilton's long and detailed rebuttal persuaded Washington to sign the legislation in February 1791.

6 See John Steele Gordon, *Hamilton's Blessing* (New York: Wallace and Company, 1997), 39.

7 See James D. Savage, *Balanced Budgets and American Politics* (Ithaca, N.Y.: Cornell University Press, 1988), 91–97.

8 For the relevant text of Jefferson's letter to John Taylor advocating a constitutional balanced-budget amendment, see Savage, *Balanced Budgets and American Politics*, 106.

9 Davis Rich Dewey, *Financial History of the United States*, 6th ed. (New York: Longmans, Green and Co., 1918), 67.

10 Savage, *Balanced Budgets and American Politics*, 83.

11 Hamilton, Madison, and Jay, *The Federalist Papers*, 359.

12 Louis Fisher, *Presidential Spending Power* (Princeton, N.J.: Princeton University Press, 1975), 11.

13 Fisher, *Presidential Spending Power*, 11.

14 Fisher, *Presidential Spending Power*, 12.

15 See Dennis S. Ippolito, *Why Budgets Matter: Budget Policy and American Politics*, rev. ed. (University Park: Pennsylvania State University Press, 2015), 35.

16 The constitutional question that divided Hamilton and Jefferson was how to interpret the "necessary and proper" clause at the end of Article I, Section 8.

17 See Dall W. Forsythe, *Taxation and Political Change in the Young Nation, 1781–1833* (New York: Columbia University Press, 1977), 30.

18 Forsythe, *Taxation and Political Change in the Young Nation, 1781–1833*, 32.

19 Albert S. Bolles, *The Financial History of the United States from 1789–1860*, 2nd ed. (New York: D. Appleton and Company, 1885), 183–185.

20 Fisher, *Presidential Spending Power*, 19–20, 60–61.

21 Henry Adams, *The Life of Albert Gallatin* (New York: Peter Smith, 1943), 157. Ways and Means was made a standing, or permanent, committee in 1802. Its counterpart, the Senate Finance Committee, was established in 1816.

22 *Historical Statistics of the United States, Colonial Times to 1970, Part 2* (Washington, D.C.: Bureau of the Census, 1975), 1104.

23 Quoted in Lewis H. Kimmel, *Federal Budget Policy and Fiscal Policy, 1789–1958* (Washington, D.C.: Brookings Institution, 1959), 20.

24 Joseph Story, *Commentaries on the Constitution of the United States* (Cambridge, MA: Brown, Shattuck and Co., 1833), 2:14.

25 It took several decades for a formal party system to be established. In the 1790s, for example, many House and Senate members had no known party affiliation. It is generally accepted, however, that "Federalists" won the first three presidential elections and had congressional majorities for much of their tenure. With the 1801 election, however, the Jeffersonian party took the presidency. Democratic-Republicans, Republicans, and, with Andrew Jackson, Democrats then won all but three presidential elections over the next five decades. Electoral results for the House and Senate were similarly one-sided. What we would now call "unified government" was thus the norm. See Erik W. Austin, *Political Facts of the United States Since 1789* (New York: Columbia University Press, 1986), 50–53, 94–95.

26 Ippolito, *Why Budgets Matter*, 57.

27 See Bolles, *The Financial History of the United States from 1789 to 1860*, and Robert T. Patterson, *Federal Debt-Management Policies, 1865–1879* (Durham, N.C.: Duke University Press, 1954).

28 See Patterson, *Federal Debt-Management Policies, 1865–1879*, 186–189.

29 During the 1850s, annual federal spending averaged less than $60 million. In 1860, federal debt totaled just under $65 million. Ippolito, *Why Budgets Matter*, 59.

30 Richard F. Fenno, Jr., *The Power of the Purse: Appropriations Politics in Congress* (Boston: Little, Brown and Company, 1966), 43–44; Dennis S. Ippolito, *Congressional Spending* (Ithaca, N.Y.: Cornell University Press, 1981), 40–44.

31 Fenno, *The Power of the Purse: Appropriations Politics in Congress*, 43.

32 Savage, *Balanced Budgets and American Politics*, 131.

33 Savage, *Balanced Budgets and American Politics*, 131–132.

34 Quoted in Theda Skocpol, *Protecting Soldiers and Mothers: The Political Origins of Social Policy in the United States* (Cambridge, MA: Harvard University Press, 1992), 128.

35 Ippolito, *Congressional Spending*, 43.

36 This extended period of consecutive surpluses is, by far, the longest in U.S. history.

37 Panama Canal construction costs from 1904–1916 totaled $400 million, with roughly one-third funded by borrowing. Savage, *Balanced Budgets and American Politics*, 141.

38 Ippolito, *Why Budgets Matter*, 89–94.

39 Ippolito, *Why Budgets Matter*, 83.

40 Ippolito, *Why Budgets Matter*, 83.

41 Ippolito, *Why Budgets Matter*, 83.

42 Charles Gilbert, *American Financing of World War I* (Westport, CT: Greenwood, 1970), 223–231.

43 Ippolito, *Why Budgets Matter*, 104.

44 Harding's remarks were contained in his budget message to Congress. *Congressional Record*, 67th Cong., 2nd sess., 1921, 62, pt. 1:37.

45 See Ippolito, *Why Budgets Matter*, 112.

46 The corporate tax rate was increased from 10 percent to 12.5 percent in 1921. From 1925–1931, it was changed several times, ranging between 11 percent (1929) and 13.5 percent (1926). In 1932, it was raised to 13.75 percent.

47 *Historical Statistics of the United States, Earliest Times to the Present: Millennial Edition, Vol. 5* (Cambridge: Cambridge University Press, 2006), 5-110.

48 Dennis S. Ippolito, *Deficits, Debt, and the New Politics of Tax Policy* (New York: Cambridge University Press, 2012), 33.

49 Savage, *Balanced Budgets and American Politics*, 158.

50 *Congressional Record*, 72nd Cong., 2nd sess., 1932, 76, pt. 1:84.

51 *Congressional Record*, 76th Cong., 3rd sess., 1940, 86, pt. 1:47.

52 At that time, there were 96 seats in the Senate.
53 *Guide to U.S. Elections*, 2nd ed. (Washington, D.C.: Congressional Quarterly, 1985), 91.
54 Ippolito, *Why Budgets Matter*, 136.
55 Dennis S. Ippolito, *Uncertain Legacies: Federal Budget Policy from Roosevelt through Reagan* (Charlottesville: University Press of Virginia, 1990), 199–200.
56 *Historical Tables, Budget of the United States Government, Fiscal Year 2021* (Washington, D.C.: Government Printing Office, 2020), Table 3.1.
57 This phrase was contained in a special message transmitted to Congress on June 19, 1935, which offered a number of recommended tax law changes to encourage "a wider distribution of wealth" (*Congressional Record*, 74th Cong., 1st sess., 1935, 79, pt. 9:9657–9658).
58 Congressional Budget Office, *Revising the Individual Income Tax* (Washington, D.C.: Congressional Budget Office, 1983), 9.
59 *Historical Statistics of the United States, Earliest Times to the Present: Millennial Edition, Vol. 5*, 5-11.
60 Ippolito, *Why Budgets Matter*, 146.
61 Joseph A. Pechman, *Federal Tax Policy*, 5th ed. (Washington, D.C.: Brookings Institution, 1987), 315.
62 *Congressional Record*, 79th Cong., 2nd sess., 1946, 92, pt. 1:149.
63 Quoted in John F. Witte, *The Politics and Development of the Federal Income Tax* (Madison: University of Wisconsin Press, 1985), 132.
64 *Congressional Record*, 79th Cong., 2nd sess., 1946, 92, pt. 1:155.
65 *Congressional Record*, 81st Cong., 1st sess., 1949, 95, pt. 4:4427–4428.
66 Richard Smoke, "The Evolution of American Defense Policy," in *American Defense Policy*, 5th ed., ed. J. F. Reichart and S.B. Sturm (Baltimore, MD: Johns Hopkins University Press, 1982), 107.
67 *Congressional Record*, 84th Cong., 1st sess., 1955, 101, pt. 1:389.
68 Iwan W. Morgan, *Eisenhower Versus "The Spenders": The Eisenhower Administration, the Democrats and the Budget, 1953–1960* (New York: St. Martin's Press, 1990), 71.
69 *Congressional Record*, 83rd Cong., 2nd sess., 1954, 100, pt. 1:577.
70 See *Foreign Relations of the United States, 1952–1954*, vol. 2: *National Security Affairs* (Washington, D.C.: Government Printing Office, 1984), 514–534.
71 Ippolito, *Uncertain Legacies*, 106–107.
72 Jerry Tempalski, *Revenue Effects of Major Tax Bills* (Washington, D.C.: Department of the Treasury, 2013), 15–16.
73 From 1975–1980, deficit-GDP averaged 2.8 percent. The averages for the 1950s (0.4%), 1960s (0.8%), and 1970–1974 (1.2%) were significantly lower. *Historical Tables, Budget of the United States Government, Fiscal Year 2021*, Table 1.2.
74 John F. Kennedy, *Public Papers of the Presidents of the United States: John F. Kennedy, 1961* (Washington, D.C.: Government Printing Office, 1962), 302.
75 *Budget of the United States Government, Fiscal Year 1964* (Washington, D.C.: Government Printing Office, 1963), 10–11.
76 *Budget of the United States Government, Fiscal Year 1966* (Washington, D.C.: Government Printing Office, 1965), 10.
77 *Budget of the United States Government, Fiscal Year 1966*, 7.
78 Lyndon B. Johnson, *Public Papers of the Presidents of the United States: Lyndon B. Johnson, 1965, Book I* (Washington, D.C.: Government Printing Office, 1966), 540.
79 Lyndon B. Johnson, *Public Papers of the Presidents of the United States: Lyndon B. Johnson, 1967, Book I* (Washington, D.C.: Government Printing Office, 1968), 42.

80 Lyndon B. Johnson, *Public Papers of the Presidents of the United States: Lyndon B. Johnson, 1967, Book II* (Washington, D.C.: Government Printing Office, 1968), 733.
81 Julian E. Zelizer, *Taxing America: Wilbur D. Mills, Congress, and the State, 1945–1975* (New York: Cambridge University Press, 1998), 263.
82 Zelizer, *Taxing America*, 267.
83 Steven A. Bank, Kirk J. Stark, and Joseph J. Thorndike, *War and Taxes* (Washington, D.C.: Urban Institute Press, 2008), 143.
84 Ippolito, *Why Budgets Matter*, 196–197.
85 *Congressional Quarterly Almanac, 1968* (Washington, D.C.: Congressional Quarterly, 1968), 998.
86 See Ippolito, *Uncertain Legacies*, 120–121.
87 Richard Nixon, *Public Papers of the Presidents of the United States: Richard Nixon, 1973* (Washington, D.C.: Government Printing Office, 1975), 34, 36.
88 Richard Nixon, *Public Papers of the Presidents of the United States: Richard Nixon, 1974* (Washington, D.C.: Government Printing Office, 1975), 586.
89 *Budget of the United States Government, Fiscal Year 1979* (Washington, D.C.: Government Printing Office, 1978), 68.
90 U.S. Senate, Committee on Armed Services, *United States/Soviet Military Balance: A Frame of Reference for Congress* (Washington, D.C.: Government Printing Office, 1976), 32.
91 Central Intelligence Agency, *A Dollar Comparison of Soviet and U.S. Defense Activities, 1965–1975* (Washington, D.C.: CIA, 1976), 2, 5.
92 *Department of Defense Annual Report, Fiscal Year 1980* (Washington, D.C.: Government Printing Office, 1979), 5.
93 *Congressional Quarterly Almanac, 1977* (Washington, D.C.: Congressional Quarterly, 1977), 502.
94 *Congress and the Nation, 1977–1980* (Washington, D.C.: Congressional Quarterly, 1981), 630.
95 *Congress and the Nation, 1977–1980*, 639.
96 *Congressional Quarterly Almanac, 1977*, 474.
97 Ippolito, *Uncertain Legacies*, 53–55.
98 Witte, *The Politics and Development of the Federal Income Tax*, 315.
99 C. Eugene Steuerle, *The Tax Decade* (Washington, D.C.: Urban Institute Press, 1992), 24–26.
100 Steuerle, *The Tax Decade*, 26.
101 Iwan W. Morgan, *The Age of Deficits: Presidents and Unbalanced Budgets from Jimmy Carter to George W. Bush* (Lawrence: University Press of Kansas, 2009), 63–65.
102 *Congressional Quarterly Almanac, 1976* (Washington, D.C.: Congressional Quarterly, 1976), 868.
103 *Congressional Quarterly Almanac, 1980* (Washington, D.C.: Congressional Quarterly, 1981), 114-B.
104 *Congressional Quarterly Almanac, 1980*, 92-B.
105 *Congressional Quarterly Almanac, 1980*, 98-B.
106 *Congressional Quarterly Almanac, 1980*, 92-B.
107 *Congressional Quarterly Almanac, 1980*, 93-B.
108 *Congressional Quarterly Almanac, 1980*, 59-B.
109 *Congressional Quarterly Almanac, 1980*, 64-B.
110 *Congressional Quarterly Almanac, 1980*, 64-B.
111 *Congressional Quarterly Almanac, 1980*, 63-B.
112 *Congressional Quarterly Almanac, 1980*, 76-B.
113 *Congressional Quarterly Almanac, 1980*, 76-B.

2 From Deficit to Surplus
The Reagan-Clinton Transition

The Reagan presidency began with an ambitious fiscal program highlighting lower taxes, lower spending (except for defense), and a balanced budget. By the end of his presidency, annual deficits had averaged more than $165 billion, and the public debt had risen from $789 billion to $2.2 trillion. Reagan's Republican successor, George H. W. Bush, took the first major step in scaling back the deficit, signing a nearly $500 billion deficit reduction agreement in 1990. In 1993, the newly elected Democratic president, Bill Clinton, and a Democratic Congress approved a similarly sized deficit reduction package. In 1998, as tax increases and spending cuts took full effect, the budget was balanced for the first time since 1969, and surpluses over the next three years totaled $490 billion.

The Reagan-Bush-Clinton era also resulted in significant electoral changes. Reagan's victory in 1980 ushered in a Republican Senate majority that lasted six years. In the 1994 midterm elections, Republicans gained control of the House and the Senate and maintained control for the rest of Clinton's presidency. With what were now two highly competitive national parties, the partisan divide on budget policy widened, particularly on matters relating to taxation. By the late 1990s, how to balance the budget was, for strong partisans in both parties, more important than whether it was balanced, and the key difference was tax levels.

The Reagan Fiscal Plan

The central importance of the budget in Ronald Reagan's agenda was made clear at the very beginning of his presidency. The outgoing Carter administration had submitted to Congress a comprehensive executive budget for fiscal year 1982—the budget cycle that would begin on October 1, 1981 and end on September 30, 1982. Despite the compressed timetable, the Reagan administration was determined to make major modifications to the Carter plan. On February 18, 1981, Reagan outlined his four-point "program for economic recovery" to a joint session of Congress.[1] On March 10, the spending and tax proposals attached to this program were sent to Congress.

Reagan's "Fiscal Year 1982 Budget Revisions" included "an immediate, substantial, and sustained reduction in the growth of Federal expenditures"

DOI: 10.4324/9781003167266-2

and "a significant reduction in Federal tax rates over the next three years."[2] The objective was a balanced budget in 1984 at precisely 19.3 percent of gross national product (GNP).[3] This revenue level was well below the revenue baseline then in place, and the even larger cuts from the spending baseline were "designed to share the temporary economic burden of constraining the Federal Government to its proper role."[4]

That proper role, for Reagan, assigned principal importance to national defense. During the 1970s, the budget share for defense had been cut by nearly one-half, dropping below 23 percent of total spending in 1980. The defense budget increases Reagan demanded were much larger than those that Carter had endorsed, and they were an integral part of a comprehensive reshaping of the spending side of the budget. The balanced budget Reagan envisioned in 1984 had a defense budget share of nearly one-third. By 1986, Reagan planned to raise that share to almost 40 percent. The combined defense buildup and domestic retrenchment would bring the budget reasonably close to its pre-Great Society priorities.

The fiscal plan unveiled in 1981 had some initial success, but its balanced-budget goal was undermined by inadequate spending cuts and an unexpected economic downturn. In August, Congress passed the largest tax cut since World War II. At that same time, Reagan secured bipartisan support for significant cuts in domestic spending programs, and Congress approved the administration's add-ons to the Carter defense budgets for 1981 and 1982. What the administration had not anticipated, however, was the steep recession that began in the summer of 1981, lasted until the late fall of 1982, and upended its spending and revenue projections. The 1981 and 1982 deficits exceeded administration forecasts by well over $100 billion, and the deficits that followed were even larger.

As the administration explained in its 1982 economic report, the "strategy of reducing taxes in advance of spending cuts implies that it will take some time to achieve the desired level of deficits."[5] That strategy, too, proved faulty. After the initial round of budget cuts in 1981, Congress refused to expand them. Congressional Republicans joined Democrats in protecting the retirement and healthcare entitlements that were the largest and fastest-growing spending programs. With its economic and political assumptions so widely off the mark, Reagan had to decide whether to subordinate his policy priorities—tax cuts and defense budget increases—to his balanced-budget commitment. After agreeing to corporate and Social Security tax increases in his first term, Reagan rejected further compromises in his second term, and the result was the largest accumulation of deficits and debt since World War II.

Tax Policy and Revenue Raising

Federal tax law changes during the 1980s were numerous and sweeping. The Economic Recovery Tax Act of 1981 (ERTA 1981) was, at the time, the largest tax cut in U.S. history. It was followed by three major tax increases from

1982–1984, a comprehensive tax reform in 1986, and a modest tax increase passed as part of a deficit reduction reconciliation bill in 1987. Overall, the net tax reductions from the 1981 tax cut remained quite large, and revenue-GDP never rebounded to pre-ERTA 1981 levels. This was especially the case with Reagan's most important tax priority—individual income taxation.

From Kemp-Roth to ERTA 1981

In 1980, tax cuts were the centerpiece of the Republican party's election year campaign. This was a testament to the work of a junior Republican House member from New York, Jack Kemp. Kemp had long been a proponent of supply-side economics—the theory that reduced income tax rates would stimulate higher economic growth and, over time, increase revenues—but Republicans in Congress had been skeptical of the theory and reluctant to risk higher deficits given the economic problems of the 1970s. Then, as anti-tax sentiments gained greater traction among voters toward the end of the decade, that reticence vanished. The Republican National Committee encouraged the party's House and Senate candidates to make the case for Kemp's economic stimulus tax cuts in the 1978 midterm elections. Two years later, congressional Republicans lined up in support of a three-year, 30 percent cut in individual income tax rates sponsored by Kemp and Senator William V. Roth, a senior member of the Finance Committee.

When Ronald Reagan, the party's presumptive presidential nominee, endorsed the Kemp-Roth plan on June 25, Republicans decided to make congressional Democrats take a stand on a preelection tax cut. The Carter administration strongly opposed tax cuts as fiscally irresponsible and inflationary, but the Senate Finance Committee reported out a scaled-back version of Kemp-Roth in late August. The Senate Democratic leaders never brought the bill to the floor, and their House counterparts kept any tax bill from being considered in committee. The administration and House and Senate Democratic leaders did agree, however, to move forward with an "anti-inflationary" tax cut in 1981.

What occurred instead in 1981 was the passage of a tax cut that was even larger than that which candidate Reagan had supported and newly elected President Reagan had proposed. Costly new provisions were added, including the indexing of individual income tax brackets, the standard deduction, and personal exemption amounts. Business tax incentives, such as more generous depreciation rules, likewise drew increased support as the congressional deliberations on the tax bill stretched out over several months. Concerns about deficits, though widespread in both parties, were in the end overwhelmed by the public support that Reagan was able to galvanize behind the tax cut effort.

The pivotal issue on which Reagan prevailed was across-the-board relief for taxpayers. On July 29, when House Democrats brought to the floor a plan that targeted tax relief to low- and middle-income taxpayers, 48

Democrats joined Republicans in passing the administration-backed substitute that cut tax rates by the same percentage for taxpayers at all income levels. The Democratic bill had included, however, many of the business tax incentives that the administration had proposed, demonstrating the strong bipartisan support for business tax relief. The Senate's Republican majority faced little opposition in passing a tax bill that was almost identical to Reagan's proposal. In the House-Senate conference that followed, agreement was quickly reached on a package of individual and business tax cuts that largely followed Reagan's plan but included numerous tax preferences that members of both parties had sponsored. The conference agreement was then approved by the Senate on a 67–8 vote and by the House on a 282–95 vote. On August 13, President Reagan signed into law both the tax bill and a budget reconciliation bill that he described as bringing "an end to the excessive growth in government bureaucracy, government spending, government taxing."[6]

On the taxing point, Reagan was not exaggerating. The individual income tax rate cuts (23 percent for 1981–1983) and related provisions reduced revenues by an estimated $557 billion over six years (see Table 2.1). Corporate tax law changes, particularly the new depreciation rules (Accelerated Cost Recovery System), totaled more than $150 billion over this same period. With the new estate and gift tax reductions, savings provisions, and energy tax preferences, the total cost of ERTA 1981 was nearly $750 billion. This was $100 billion more than Reagan had proposed, which meant that spending cuts would have to be larger as well to meet his balanced-budget goal.

The budget reconciliation bill that Reagan also signed on August 13 was the first installment of a planned multiyear domestic retrenchment. As with the tax bill, the House Democratic leadership had attempted to block the domestic program cuts proposed by the administration, but once again Democratic defections and a unified Republican bloc managed to prevail on the crucial votes for a budget resolution and related reconciliation bill that narrowed eligibility and cut benefits for Aid to Families with Dependent Children (AFDC), food stamps, housing assistance, and other low-income assistance programs. This highly controversial measure, the final version of which was drafted by a conference committee comprising more than 250 House and Senate members, contained an estimated $130 billion in spending cuts for fiscal years 1982–1984.[7]

The Omnibus Budget Reconciliation Act of 1981 (OBRA 1981) was, at the time, "the deepest and most widespread package of budget cuts in the history of Congress."[8] It did not affect, however, what the administration had criticized as overly generous entitlement programs that benefited "people with middle to upper incomes." The Reagan budget drew a distinction between "social safety net programs"—"mostly begun in the 1930s, that now constitute an agreed-upon core of protection for the elderly, the unemployed, and the poor"—and "newer Federal entitlement programs … that have undergone rapid growth during the last 20 years."[9] It was this latter category that the Reagan administration hoped to shrink.

Table 2.1 Economic Recovery Tax Act of 1981 (P.L. 97–34): Major Provisions

Individual Income Taxes	*(Revenue Loss: –$557 billion)*
Tax Rate	Cumulative across-the-board reduction in individual tax rates of 23% from 1981–1983.
Maximum Rate	The top marginal rate on individual income reduced from 70% to 50%, effective Jan. 1, 1982.
Capital Gains	The 60% exclusion of long-term capital gains maintained. The new 50% top marginal rate, however, reduced the maximum effective tax rate on capital gains to 20%.
Deduction for Two-Earner Married Couples	Reduction of "marriage penalty," allowing couples to deduct 5% of first $30,000 earnings of spouse with lower earnings in 1982. Increased to 10% in 1983.
Indexing	The individual income tax brackets, zero bracket amount, and personal exemption adjusted annually for inflation (measured by the Consumer Price Index), beginning with calendar year 1985.
IRA Exclusion	Eligibility for IRAs broadened to cover participants in employer-sponsored pension plans. The maximum IRA contribution increased.
Corporate Income Taxes	*(Revenue Loss: –$154 billion)*
Accelerated Cost Recovery	Replaced depreciation rules for tangible property used in trade or business. Accelerated Cost Recovery System (ACRS) provided for faster write-off of capital expenditures under simplified and standardized rules.
Leasing	Liberalized rules allowing firms to transfer unused investment tax credits and depreciation deductions on new investments to profitable firms through leasing transactions.
Oil Tax Reductions	Reduced tax on newly discovered oil. Added exemption for independent producer stripper wells from windfall profit taxes.
Estate and Gift Taxes	*(Revenue Loss: –$15 billion)*
Marital Deductions	Surviving spouse permitted to inherit unlimited amount without paying tax.
Estate and Gift Tax Credits	Increased from $47,000 to $192,800 by 1987, exempting from tax all estates of $600,000 or less.
Rate Reduction	Maximum rate reduced from 70% to 50% over 1981–1985 period.
Gift Tax Exclusion	Increased from $3,000 to $10,000 per donee, effective Jan. 1, 1982.
Other	*(Revenue Loss: –$23 billion)*
Savings Provisions	
Energy Provisions	
Administrative Provisions	
Miscellaneous Provisions	
Total Revenue Loss	–$749 billion

Source: U.S. Congress, Joint Committee on Taxation, *General Explanation of the Economic Recovery Tax Act of 1981* (Washington, D.C.: Government Printing Office, 1981), 5–16, 228, 380.

The OBRA 1981 spending retrenchment, however, could not be replicated. Administration proposals for additional public assistance cutbacks were largely ignored by Congress. More importantly, neither party in Congress supported benefit reductions in the much larger middle-class entitlements, such as Social Security and Medicare. According to the administration, the 1981 tax cut was "an essential part of a long-term strategy of reducing the scope of the Federal Government."[10] That strategy never succeeded, and the result was large deficits.

The 1982 Tax Increases

An immediate problem for Reagan was the unexpected collapse in revenues that occurred during the 1981–1982 recession. The administration's balanced-budget program depended on strong economic growth following the 1981 tax cuts. Revenue growth had been estimated at nearly 10 percent annually for the next several years, with the "target deficits" for 1981 and 1982 totaling approximately $100 billion. Instead, revenues remained essentially flat, and actual deficits were more than $200 billion.

Reagan's political standing and approval ratings plummeted as unemployment rates soared and large sectors of the economy came to a virtual standstill. Congressional leaders of both parties soon pressed the administration to increase taxes in order to curb escalating deficits. In his 1982 State of the Union message, Reagan had rejected any "tax increases this year" but signaled his willingness to "plug unwarranted tax loopholes."[11] Shortly thereafter, the administration proposed some $34 billion in revenue "enhancements" over three years from various tax preference reforms, and later proposals raised the revenue total to nearly $87 billion.[12]

Reagan was completely opposed, however, to any delay in the scheduled individual income tax cuts for 1982 and 1983, much less the effort by House and Senate Democrats to cancel some of them. As it turned out, Reagan was less concerned with protecting corporate tax cuts in order to satisfy Congress's revenue-raising demands. Congressional Republicans were even more willing to do so, and it was the Senate Finance Committee bill that established the revenue goals and major business tax increases that Congress then approved.

The 1982 Tax Equity and Fiscal Responsibility Act (TEFRA) contained an estimated $98.3 billion in increased revenues from 1983–1985; the projected increase over a five-year period was almost $215 billion.[13] More than half of this total represented modification or repeal of corporate tax preferences included in ERTA 1981, but there were also increases in excise taxes and social insurance taxes, curbs on individual tax preferences, and major enhancements in income reporting and withholding requirements for individuals.[14]

House and Senate Democrats readily supported TEFRA, despite their preference for rolling back the 1981 individual income tax cuts, and congressional Republicans likewise agreed that a deficit reduction tax increase would help to avert a dangerous collision "between fiscal policy and monetary policy."[15] The Reagan administration had substantially raised the revenue increase it would support and even agreed to provide political "cover" for members of both parties willing to vote for an election year tax increase.[16] Bipartisan compromise, at that point, was still possible given the near-universal fears about large deficits. As a final note, Congress passed a gasoline tax increase in late December 1982 that increased revenues by an additional $10 billion for fiscal years 1983–1985. Reagan had opposed a gas tax increase in September but reversed his position two months later. With TEFRA and the gas tax increase, roughly one-quarter of the revenue losses from ERTA 1981 were recaptured.

The Social Security Tax Increase

In another policy reversal, the Reagan administration supported a Social Security tax increase in 1983 as part of a comprehensive plan to insure the long-term solvency of the program's trust funds. The Social Security tax increase in 1977 had failed to keep pace with the rapid increase in benefit payments, and Reagan officials initially hoped to erase pending trust fund shortfalls with benefit cuts. In May 1981, the administration proposed reduced benefits for early retirement, a less generous benefit formula for future retirees, and tightened eligibility for the Social Security disability program. Additional savings were to be secured by delaying the scheduled 1982 cost-of-living adjustment (COLA) and eliminating entirely minimum benefits for those with a very low earnings history.

The minimum benefit repeal was included in the OBRA 1981 spending bill, but Congress restored the program several months later, and leaders of both parties made it clear that the administration's plan for Social Security reform was unacceptable. Reagan agreed to appoint a bipartisan commission to develop a plan for dealing with the program's immediate and long-term financing problems. The commission's plan, presented after the 1982 midterm elections, resolved the short-term solvency imbalances by accelerating scheduled increases in Social Security tax rates and making Social Security benefits subject to income taxation for high-income retirees. Additional revenues were also provided by extending Social Security coverage to new federal employees, who would previously have been covered by a separate federal employee retirement system. The estimated revenue gain from the 1983 Social Security Amendments was $58 billion for fiscal years 1984–1988, raising the tax increase total for the three 1982 and 1983 deficit reduction measures to $335 billion.[17]

DEFRA 1984

Despite these measures, deficits remained stubbornly high, as the administration and Congress renewed their deficit reduction efforts in 1984. By this time, the Federal Reserve's anti-inflation policies had been relaxed, unemployment was falling, and the economy was showing signs of robust growth. Reagan's approval rating, which had fallen to 35 percent in early 1983, moved above 50 percent in November and continued to rise in 1984. In practical terms, this meant that the third year of the 1981 individual tax rate cuts was now safe; the tax increases in the 1984 Deficit Reduction Act (DEFRA) primarily targeted tax preferences. DEFRA also included some spending reductions, although these were smaller and less binding than the administration and congressional Republicans had hoped.

The DEFRA revenue increases included excise taxes, reduced tax benefits from property leasing and depreciation rules for businesses, and less favorable treatment of interest income and income averaging options for individuals. There were, however, some offsetting tax cuts, such as the new six-month (rather than 12-month) holding period for long-term capital gains and an expansion of the earned income tax credit for low-income working families. The estimated net revenue gains from DEFRA were approximately $72 billion over a five-year period.[18] Notably, the attempt by Senate Republicans, strongly supported by Reagan, to set multiyear caps on discretionary spending was unsuccessful. The House-Senate conference committee on DEFRA instead adopted the nonbinding "goals" that House Democratic conferees had insisted upon, and it was this measure that Reagan was forced to sign.

Reagan's fiscal 1985 budget, which was submitted to Congress on February 1, 1984, reaffirmed his commitment to reducing spending. It conceded that "limited measures to increase receipts" would be needed to reduce deficits but that "substantial reductions" in spending would be "crucial."[19] The Reagan budget pointed out that since projected future deficits were "structural," they would "persist unless determined policy actions are taken to eliminate them."[20] Those policy actions, according to the Reagan budget plan, had to include the domestic spending cutbacks that had thus far been blocked by Congress. After the spending cuts in 1981, virtually all of the deficit reduction over the next three years had been on the tax side. If Reagan truly was adamant that future deficit reduction efforts would have to be similarly skewed toward spending, there was little reason to believe that Congress would cooperate. The 1984 election was therefore a referendum on whether the public would support the core Reagan tax program, regardless of the deficits it had caused and the future deficits it likely would insure.

Tax Policy and Deficits

The Democratic party platform in 1984 pledged to reduce the "intolerable deficits" that the Reagan tax cuts and defense buildup had caused.[21] The latter was dealt with perfunctorily. The call for "rational defense spending" simply meant reducing the rate of increase in the defense budget. The tax reform program that the party outlined was more specific and did not advocate a wholesale repeal of the Reagan tax cuts. Instead, it proposed to cancel the third year of income tax rate cuts, to defer indexation for upper-income taxpayers (those with incomes above $60,000), and to eliminate "preferences and write-offs, exceptions, and deductions which skew the [tax] code toward the rich and toward unproductive tax shelters." For corporations, the major change would be a 15 percent minimum tax. The tax section of the platform repeatedly referenced fairness and progressivity, and these themes were highlighted by the party's presidential nominee, Walter Mondale.

In Mondale's acceptance speech at the Democratic convention, he declared, "Let's tell the truth … Mr. Reagan will raise taxes, and so will I. He won't tell you. I just did."[22] At the domestic policy debate with Reagan on October 7, Mondale stated that Reagan's enormous deficits were "perhaps *the* domestic issue of our times" [italics in the original], and he went on to defend an even broader tax increase than that which the Democratic platform had endorsed. The only group exempt from any tax increase, Mondale explained, would be those with an income of less than $25,000, and indexing would be totally repealed "at some point."[23] The deficit target Mondale set was "below 2 percent of Gross National Product," less than half the deficit for the fiscal 1984 budget year that had just ended.

The Republican platform presented a very different view of taxation. The party reiterated its long-standing commitment to balanced budgets and promised to "work for the constitutional amendment requiring a balanced federal budget."[24] It nevertheless "categorically reject[ed] proposals to increase taxes in a misguided effort to balance the budget." Instead, the party promised to "lower tax rates … and eliminate the incentive-destroying effects of graduated tax rates" in favor of a "modified flat tax." It made it clear too that any attempt "to repeal, modify, or defer" tax indexing was unacceptable.

The clear contrast between Reagan and Mondale on taxes reflected different calculations of voters' views on deficits. In 1982 and 1983, a number of public opinion surveys had found widespread public concern about the economic risks associated with high deficits and correspondingly negative assessments of Reagan's fiscal record.[25] That concern diminished as the economy recovered in 1984, and, in a particularly revealing national poll conducted in January, the level of public support for tax increases to pay for deficit reduction was less than 30 percent.

Reagan's landslide reelection in November was accompanied by minor Republican gains in the House and the loss of just one seat in the party's Senate majority. For Reagan and top administration officials, the election was seen as a mandate to move ahead with tax reform divorced from deficit reduction. Despite second-term deficits that were much higher than the Johnson and Carter deficits that Republicans had deplored, Reagan refused to consider second-term tax increases of any consequence.

Revenue-Neutral Tax Reform

A number of congressional Republicans, particularly in the Senate leadership, did not share Reagan's downplaying of the deficit challenge. In the spring of 1985, Senate Republicans approved a budget resolution that called for major cuts in discretionary spending and a one-year suspension of COLA increases in Social Security and federal retirement benefits. The House then approved an equally large multiyear deficit reduction target that excluded any entitlement retrenchments and instead relied on defense cuts and various economies to achieve the desired savings.

The House-Senate conference that followed provided an opportunity for Republicans to add tax increases to the mix in the hope that the House would then relax its opposition to entitlement changes. Senate Republican leaders were convinced that structural deficits could not be substantially reduced without a compromise on taxes and entitlements. But when congressional leaders of both parties met with Reagan following weeks of conference committee deadlock, he rejected the "grand compromise" that Senate Republicans had envisioned. The president instead dealt directly with House Speaker Thomas P. O'Neill and agreed to protect full entitlement benefits in exchange for Democratic concessions on defense spending and taxes.

With entitlements and revenues off the table, and Reagan's defense spending commitment further narrowing the range of policy options, a serious deficit reduction program could not be pieced together. The default position for antideficit advocates in the Congress thus became a hastily conceived statute that emerged from a truncated legislative process and, somewhat surprisingly, received Reagan's signature. The Balanced Budget and Emergency Deficit Reduction Act of 1985 (or GRH as it became known for its Senate sponsors—Republicans Phil Gramm and Warren Rudman and Democrat Ernest Hollings)—mandated a balanced budget by fiscal year 1991. The bill included a six-year schedule of declining deficit ceilings and provided that automatic spending cuts, or sequestrations, would be enforced at the beginning of any fiscal year when the projected deficit exceeded that ceiling. Exempted entirely were tax increases, as well as cuts in most entitlement programs, particularly Social Security. That left, of course, defense and domestic discretionary spending to absorb virtually all the required cuts, but the generous deficit ceilings of the first few years were not expected to have much of an impact on Reagan's time in office. This GRH constraint was further eased when the Supreme Court struck down its key enforcement provision, and Congress failed to pass a revised statute until 1987.

As members of both parties argued over when and how to reduce deficits, Reagan's tax reform program faced long odds. The administration's "Treasury II" proposal was announced on May 28, 1985 and was immediately attacked by Democrats and Republicans in Congress. The individual tax brackets in Treasury II called for a top marginal rate of 35 percent on ordinary income and a maximum effective rate of 17.5 percent on capital gains. For congressional Democrats, this was even less fair and less progressive than the 1981 tax cut that Reagan had somehow managed to push through Congress. While Treasury II also cut corporate tax rates, it included changes in depreciation schedules, investment credits, and other business tax preferences that raised effective business tax rates—a prospect that House and Senate Republicans found worrisome. In addition, there was bipartisan agreement that a central premise of Treasury II—revenue-neutral tax law changes—was misguided at a time of deficits in excess of $200 billion.

The House Ways and Means Committee reported out a bill in December that contained individual and corporate tax rate cuts but targeted the bulk of tax relief at middle- and low-income taxpayers and small businesses. It nevertheless reflected the overarching tax reform approach—lower tax rates and a broadened tax base—that was Reagan's main goal. The difficulty of drafting a bill that could attract broad Democratic support was evidenced by the nearly three-month markup Ways and Means had conducted, and persuading House Republicans to support the Democratic version of tax reform required Reagan's intervention. But House action was completed by mid-December, and tax reform then moved to a supposedly more sympathetic Republican Senate.

The first obstacle that the Senate had to grapple with was an unexpected revival of the deficit issue. On February 7, 1986, a federal court effectively invalidated the GRH deficit reduction law. With GRH's sequestration enforcement procedure deemed unconstitutional—a holding that the Supreme Court upheld several months later—Senate Republican leaders argued that credible steps toward deficit reduction should be taken prior to any action on Reagan's tax bill. The Senate proceeded to adopt, by a 72–24 vote, a resolution that required approval of a deficit reduction plan as a precondition for Senate consideration of tax reform legislation. Since the resolution was nonbinding, the Reagan administration ignored it and began to work with Finance Committee leaders on a bill that would more closely mirror the Treasury II plan than the House-passed version.

It was especially difficult to reconcile potential tax law changes that could command bipartisan support with the revenue-neutral requirement that Reagan insisted was nonnegotiable. The Finance Committee markup that began in March was suspended one month later by Chairman Robert W. Packwood, and there was some apprehension that the tax reform effort had come to a dead end. Ironically, the Finance Committee's problem was a bipartisan reluctance to curb the tax preferences needed to offset tax rate cuts. Rather than meeting the revenue-neutral standard, the final weeks of Finance Committee markup produced a bill that contained nearly $30 billion in revenue losses.

The breakthrough came after two weeks of private meetings between what Packwood described as a "core group of Democrats and Republicans, liberals and conservatives, and rural and urban senators,"[26] their staffs, and, on occasion, the Treasury Department. The proposed solution was a much greater reduction in tax rates than anyone had contemplated coupled with a more sweeping attack on tax preferences. The overall plan allowed for a net reduction in individual income taxes, a compensating increase in corporate taxes, and, in an important concession to Democrats, the elimination of all income tax liabilities for several million low-income taxpayers.

The Finance Committee bill was reported out by a 20–0 vote on May 7. During Senate floor action, proposed amendments had to meet the revenue-neutral standard, and no major modifications were adopted. On June 24, the 1,489-page bill passed the Senate by a 97–3 vote. The House-Senate conference took an additional month, with the most important features of the Senate-passed bill being retained. In the case of the tradeoff between individual tax cuts and corporate tax increases, for example, the conference approved a larger increase in order to provide additional middle-income tax relief. By the time that the 2,000-page conference report was filed in September, strong bipartisan support in both chambers was assured. The House vote, which came after an extended debate, was 292–136. The Senate also engaged in a lengthy debate, but the final vote was 74–23.

Since conference committee reports cannot be amended, the floor debates on the Tax Reform Act of 1986 (TRA 1986) were, in large part, arguments about principles—whether the wholesale changes in tax policy Congress was considering would increase fairness, promote economic growth, and enhance tax simplification and administrative efficiency. Even its strongest advocates admitted that there was particular uncertainty about the bill's economic impact. Packwood, for example, closed the Senate debate by conceding that not one senator could "tell you for sure" whether this bill would "help the economy or hurt the economy."[27] He insisted, however, that the bill was "fair," and in this he was joined by House Speaker O'Neill who praised TRA 1986 as "the most sweeping tax reform legislation in the history of this nation."[28]

All sides agreed that TRA 1986 would, at best, be revenue neutral and accordingly would do nothing to reduce the enormous gap between spending and revenues. Indeed, the official scoring of revenue effects by the Congressional Budget Office projected higher revenues for two years, lower revenues for two years, and a revenue increase in the fifth year that would be roughly revenue neutral. In any event, there was no expectation that revenues would increase by any appreciable amount.

The most important tax policy change in TRA 1986 was its new tax rates for individuals. The progressive rate structure that had defined income taxation for decades, and had been a core Democratic party principle since the New Deal, was replaced by a 15 percent rate for most taxpayers, a 28 percent rate at a higher income bracket, and a phase-out provision that raised the effective rate for high-income taxpayers to 28 percent on total income (see Table 2.2). On the Republican side, long-standing positions also changed. The preferential rate for capital gains was scrapped entirely, with the same rate now applying to ordinary income and capital gains. The investment tax credit for corporations was repealed, and corporate minimum tax requirements were strengthened. The reductions in corporate tax preferences would more than compensate for the reduced corporate tax rate (from a top marginal rate of 46 percent to 34 percent), producing a net revenue increase of $120 billion over a five-year period. The individual income tax changes, by comparison, were expected to yield a net decrease of a roughly similar amount.[29] A leading tax analyst concluded that TRA 1986 amounted to the "most sweeping change ever in the income tax," as it simultaneously managed "to lower rates and eliminate shelters, remove the poor from the tax rolls, help equalize treatment of individuals with equal income, and even coalesce conservative and liberal support."[30] The new tax law also reversed the long-term decline in the corporate share of total taxes, a change that the Reagan administration explicitly defended.

Federal tax policy was, in many respects, greatly improved by TRA 1986. Left unaddressed, however, was the structural deficit problem. Reagan's budget message to Congress on February 5, 1986 had identified the deficit as a "major threat" to a "sustained era of national prosperity."[31] Failure to bring the deficit "under control," he warned, would "risk losing all we've achieved—and more," but the tax bill he signed later in the year arguably worsened the threat. Despite initial calculations that it was revenue neutral, later estimates reported net revenue losses of more than $23 billion for fiscal years 1987–1991.[32] Still, the Reagan administration continued to insist that the "path to lower deficits" was the "curtailment of unnecessary domestic spending."[33]

Reagan's "no tax increase" pledge was, ironically, reinforced by the Democratic takeover of the Senate in the 1986 midterm elections. With deficit reduction entreaties from Senate Republicans no longer a concern, Reagan sharpened his attacks on Congress for failing to cut domestic spending. With the enactment of Gramm-Rudman-Hollings II in September 1987, Reagan argued that a "budget summit" to address comprehensive deficit reduction was unnecessary. The problem, he reiterated, was excessive spending.

Several weeks later, the "Black Monday" stock market crash forced the administration to retreat. A market decline had actually begun in late August, but the drop of more than 20 percent in the major stock indexes on October 19 and the market volatility that followed convinced the administration and Congress that reducing the deficit could boost investor confidence. Despite a steep decline from its 1986 peak, the deficit in 1987 was still close to $150 billion, a figure that would have been unthinkable during

Table 2.2 Comparison of Tax Rates, Existing Law and Tax Reform Act of 1986

	Existing Law	*TRA 1986, October 1986*
Individual	11%–50% (14 brackets)	15% and 28%[a]
Corporate	15%–46%	15%–34%
Capital Gains	20% top effective rate	Same as ordinary income

Source: *Congressional Quarterly Almanac, 1986* (Washington, D.C.: Congressional Quarterly, 1987), 494–497.

Note: [a] Effective in 1988. Lower rate phased out for high-income taxpayers through surcharge.

the supposedly profligate 1960s and 1970s. Negotiations between the administration and congressional leaders lasted nearly two months, and the result was the Omnibus Budget Reconciliation Act of 1987 (OBRA 1987) that, along with related legislation, reduced baseline deficits by $76 billion over a two-year period.[34] The spending cuts, which affected numerous discretionary programs and even some entitlements, accounted for more than two-thirds of the deficit savings. The tax increases included corporate and individual tax preferences, such as a new limit on interest deductions for home mortgages, and excise tax extensions. Individual and corporate tax rates, however, were unchanged.

Given the deficit levels in place, OBRA 1987 was definitely small scale, but revenue increases still troubled some Republicans. Reagan, for example, made it known that he "did not support either of the budget bills before he signed them," and most House Republicans voted against the conference report on the reconciliation bill.[35] A chief complaint among House Republicans was that compromises on higher taxes did not "reflect the Reagan revolution."[36]

Deficits during Ronald Reagan's second term were larger than during his first, but the administration's response was very different. Rather than

Table 2.3 Revenue Effects of Major Legislation Enacted During the Reagan Presidency, 1987–1991 (in billions of dollars)

	Estimated Direct Effect for Fiscal Year				
	1987	*1988*	*1989*	*1990*	*1991*
First-Term Tax Legislation					
ERTA 1981	–241.7	–260.8	–285.5	–315.7	–350.2
TEFRA 1982	+56.9	+57.3	+55.8	+57.4	+61.6
SSA 1983	+12.1	+24.6	+31.0	+23.9	+23.9
DEFRA 1984	+22.0	+25.3	+27.7	+31.0	+34.0
All Other	+4.2	+4.3	+4.2	+3.7	+3.4
Net Change	–146.5	–149.3	–166.8	–199.7	–227.3
Second-Term Tax Legislation					
TRA 1986	+21.5	-4.5	–17.2	–13.5	–9.5
OBRA 1987	n/a	+9.1	+14.3	+16.2	+15.6
All Other	+7.6	+11.1	+11.3	+10.5	+10.0
Net Change	+29.1	+15.7	+8.4	+13.2	+16.1
Total Revenue Effect					
	–117.4	–133.6	–158.4	–186.5	–211.2

Source: *Budget of the United States Government, Fiscal Year 1989* (Washington, D.C.: Government Printing Office, 1988), 4-4.

supporting deficit reduction tax increases, Reagan and a growing number of congressional Republicans rejected them out of hand. As a result, the revenue losses from the ERTA 1981 tax cuts were quite large during the final years of the Reagan presidency (see Table 2.3). From 1987–1989, revenue-GNP levels had finally rebounded close to the targets that Reagan had set in his 1981 balanced-budget plan, but spending levels were much higher at the beginning and remained so thereafter. Although defense budget increases were blamed by administration critics for contributing to record deficits, the spending "problem" was more complicated. Reagan did succeed in curbing the growth of domestic discretionary spending, but the entitlement programs were another matter. Retrenchment of the major retirement and healthcare entitlements encountered bipartisan resistance in Congress, and the growth in these programs more than offset the discretionary spending cutbacks.

The Spending "Problem"

The last budget message Reagan sent to Congress reiterated his call "to return the Federal Government to its proper role."[37] This meant, according to Reagan, divesting the government of its "improper responsibilities" and bringing back the domestic spending levels of two to three decades earlier. Reagan complained, "Time and again I have proposed measures to help curb Federal domestic program spending. Time and again these proposals have been rejected by Congress."[38] In fact, Congress had approved some cutbacks, and Reagan had blocked any new domestic expansions, so the domestic "role" that remained when Reagan left office was arguably an accurate measure of how "small" a government Americans were willing to accept.

Rebalancing Discretionary Spending

The defense buildup of the 1980s was not as massive as Reagan had hoped. Starting in fiscal year 1983, Congress began to cut his defense budget requests, and the size of those cuts increased over time. By 1987, congressional defense appropriations were more than $30 billion below the president's budget. In 1988 and 1989, additional reductions were negotiated in a deficit reduction agreement, and real growth in defense spending effectively came to a halt. What occurred along the way, however, was a complete reversal of the defense budget trajectory of the 1970s and a singular focus on defense spending as a measure of U.S. commitment and will.

According to Reagan's first Secretary of Defense, Casper W. Weinberger, "the overriding priority" in 1981 had been restoring "military parity with the Soviet Union." For Reagan and his defense planners, parity required investing "roughly as much in our defenses as our primary competitor."[39] By that measure, the Department of Defense was able to report in 1987 that "the annual difference in the cost of the [Soviet and U.S.] military programs was virtually eliminated."[40] In terms of real spending, the defense budget peaks of the mid-1980s were comparable as well to those during the Korean and Vietnam wars (see Figure 2.1).

Given the perceived urgency of remedying shortcomings in U.S. military capabilities, the Reagan administration continued the conventional and strategic programs from the Carter administration but greatly expanded procurement levels and accelerated procurement schedules. Reagan's force level goals were much higher as well, notably a 600-ship naval fleet with 15 deployable carrier groups. The latter was a well-publicized rejection of Carter's plan to reduce the Navy's reliance on new-generation aircraft carriers and expensive carrier battle groups. Another important reversal was the decision to revive and upgrade the B-1 strategic bomber program that Carter had cancelled. Congress approved a stepped-up development schedule for the new B-1B and later authorized full-scale procurement.

For the Reagan administration, strategic modernization was a central priority, and it extended to the entire nuclear triad. But the Reagan administration made major investments in every force category and the operations and training support for all military branches was substantially increased. To the extent that improved levels of readiness and sustainability required ongoing budgetary support, the administration's commitment was unswerving.

In terms of its cost, the Reagan defense program was sharply criticized by liberal Democrats in Congress, and these criticisms intensified as budget deficits soared during Reagan's first term. Nevertheless, a bipartisan majority

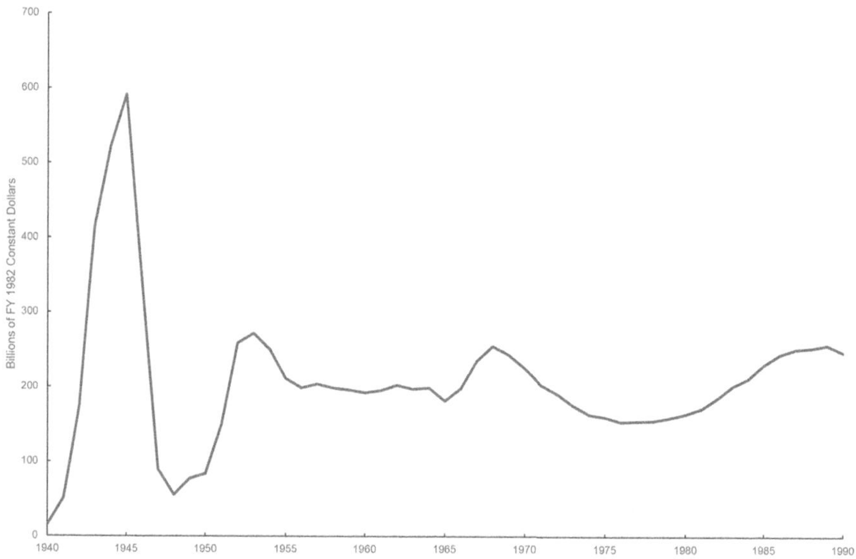

Figure 2.1 Inflation-Adjusted Defense Spending, Fiscal Years 1940–1990
Source: Compiled by author using data from *Historical Tables, Budget of the United States Government, Fiscal Year 1992* (Washington, D.C.: Government Printing Office, 1991), 66–70.

in Congress accepted the administration's argument that the 1970s defense cutbacks had caused a serious and dangerous erosion in U.S. military capabilities, with the major sticking point being just how high the rate of budget increases should be and for how long. The administration's early success in securing long-term budget authority commitments for investment accounts was designed, in part, to insure that spending would continue to rise when Congress's sense of urgency inevitably waned. It was only at the very end of Reagan's presidency that congressional cutbacks affected weapons programs, such as Reagan's controversial Strategic Defense Initiative, and even then the impact was modest.

Reagan's influence on defense policy was one of the most important accomplishments of his presidency. By assigning to defense a level of presidential commitment reminiscent of the early stages of the Cold War, Reagan recaptured the initiative on defense spending that had shifted to Congress in the 1970s. Congressional checks on the administration's defense programs and policies were, in the final analysis, mostly at the margins.

The Reagan defense buildup did contribute to the growing deficits during his presidency, although it is worth noting that the defense budget would have increased even if Carter had been reelected. The damage to the U.S. military from the spending cuts of the 1970s was simply too serious for policymakers to ignore. The rate of increase, and the fate of certain weapons systems, would no doubt have been different, but higher defense spending was inevitable. In addition, the Reagan administration's focus on escalating spending as a demonstration of national commitment was designed to force the Soviet Union to keep pace. While other factors contributed to the end of the Cold War, many would agree that Reagan's "promotion of the largest defense buildup since the Korean War had been a significant factor in bringing the Cold War to the verge of successful resolution by the time he left office."[41]

The fiscal impact of rising defense budgets was also offset by a very significant reduction in nondefense discretionary spending, particularly for domestic programs. Prior to the Great Society, domestic discretionary spending had lagged well behind defense. That disparity continued during the early stages of the Vietnam War, but funding for domestic programs rose sharply during the 1970s. From 1970–1980, domestic discretionary spending nearly quadrupled; more importantly, given the high inflation rate during this period, real spending increased by more than 85 percent. By 1980, discretionary domestic spending-GDP was close to 5 percent, roughly on par with defense.

The Reagan administration's goal of limiting the domestic role of the federal government meant, in part, shrinking this portion of the budget. In some instances, this meant outright terminations. OBRA 1981, for example, eliminated the public service jobs programs authorized by the Comprehensive Employment and Training Act of 1973, abolished the Community Services Administration (an antipoverty agency), and ended certain education benefits for veterans. Several years later, Congress agreed to abolish general revenue sharing, a 1972 program that by the mid-1980s was distributing more than $4 billion in unrestricted funds to thousands of local governments. In general, however, Congress refused to approve the many terminations that Reagan recommended.

The administration was much more successful in attacking funding. In June 1981, Congress approved more than $14 billion in domestic rescissions (canceled appropriations) requested by the administration, an outlay reduction of nearly 10 percent. The annual appropriations cycle then became the mechanism for pursuing additional spending savings, and the results were significant. During the four years of Jimmy Carter's presidency, domestic discretionary spending had increased by almost $45 billion. With the assistance of a Republican Senate, Reagan managed to limit the increase in domestic discretionary spending to less than $10 billion in his first term. A Democratic Senate in the final two years of Reagan's presidency made spending control more difficult, but the second-term increase was still less than $25 billion.

The administration was particularly concerned with some of the relatively new domestic policy expansions. For example, Reagan had called for abolishing the Department of Energy, established during the Carter administration. While Congress refused to eliminate the department, funding for its alternate energy and regulatory programs was scaled back dramatically. From 1981–1989, Department of Energy outlays dropped by more than 50 percent. Funding for community and regional development programs, which Reagan strongly opposed, fell by more than 40 percent. Smaller reductions were made in training, employment, and social services spending and in commerce and housing credit. A number of spending programs, however, increased significantly—science, space, and technology; veterans' benefits and services; health research and public health; law enforcement and administration of justice; and education—reflecting administration priorities or, in some instances, Congress's overriding of proposed cutbacks.

During the 1960s and 1970s, the Democratic party had created numerous domestic discretionary programs, raised funding levels for new and continuing programs, and shifted the balance between defense and domestic spending. The Reagan presidency was strongly committed to a very different vision of the federal government's national security and domestic responsibilities. Moreover, as shown in Table 2.4, total discretionary spending-GDP was substantially lowered under Reagan, despite the higher defense spending levels. Reagan failed to raise defense spending-GDP to its pre-Great Society levels (8–9 percent) but did succeed in restoring the domestic discretionary spending-GDP levels of the early 1960s.

The Entitlement Impasse

In May 1981, the Reagan administration announced its plan for solving the "crisis" facing the Social Security trust funds. Despite the 1977 payroll tax increase, trust fund reserves had continued to dwindle, necessitating an

Table 2.4 Discretionary Spending, 1981–1989 (as a percentage of GDP)

Fiscal Year	*Defense*	*Nondefense*	*Total*
1981	5.0	4.8	9.8
1982	5.6	4.2	9.8
1983	5.9	4.1	10.0
1984	5.8	3.8	9.6
1985	5.9	3.8	9.7
1986	6.0	3.6	9.7
1987	5.9	3.4	9.3
1988	5.7	3.4	9.0
1989	5.5	3.3	8.8

Source: Historical Tables, *Budget of the United States Government, Fiscal Year 2021* (Washington, D.C.: Government Printing Office, 2020), Table 8.4.

emergency reallocation from the Disability Insurance trust fund to the program's main trust fund in 1980. In addition to pending shortfalls between taxes and benefits, much larger post-2000 imbalances were forecast, given the changing ratio between workers and beneficiaries. As a result, there was widespread recognition in Congress that major improvements were needed in Social Security's finances.

The administration's proposed solution relied on benefit reductions—reduced benefits for early retirement (at the age of 62); a less generous formula for calculating retirees' initial benefits; stricter eligibility rules for disability benefits and limits on Social Security benefits for recipients with other pension income; a cap on benefit payments tied to preretirement income; and, for current beneficiaries, a three-month delay in the scheduled COLA for 1982. The administration believed that these benefit cutbacks would allow Congress to reduce Social Security payroll taxes by the end of the decade. Congressional Democrats predictably denounced the plan, with the House Democratic caucus unanimously adopting a resolution promising to protect "a generation of retirees" from the administration's "unconscionable breach of faith."[42] Congressional Republicans used milder language in distancing themselves from what they viewed as a dangerous political miscalculation; the Senate's Republican Finance Committee chairman pointed out he had not been consulted on Reagan's plan.

The retreat that followed was the first of many on entitlement "reform." At the end of May, Reagan wrote to congressional leaders to say that the administration was "not wedded" to any particular plan, and he formally withdrew his proposals in September when announcing the formation of a bipartisan reform commission. He also called on Congress to restore the Social Security minimum benefit that had been terminated by the reconciliation bill that Congress had passed in July, explaining, "It was never our intention to take that support away from those who truly need it."[43]

The administration was stymied as well in its attempts to curb healthcare entitlements. Title XXI of the reconciliation bill contained minor reductions in Medicaid payments to the states but did not include the administration's controversial cap on the federal share of Medicaid payments. Congress voted to increase Medicare deductibles for the hospital insurance (Part A) and optional medical services insurance (Part B) programs but rejected indexing premiums for the latter. In 1982, Congress did limit the general revenue subsidy for Part B insurance costs but the 75 percent subsidy limit it set was well above the less costly subsidy envisioned when the program was created.

There was virtually no support in Congress, however, for limiting Medicare benefits. In response to news reports that the administration would propose restricting Medicare coverage for upper-income retirees, Congress adopted an amendment to a 1982 continuing appropriations bill stating its opposition to "any proposal to impose a 'means test' on eligibility for … or benefits provided by the Medicare program."[44] Beginning in 1983, the administration and Congress strengthened cost controls on payments to healthcare providers, and this same approach was taken in the years that followed, as Medicare spending growth continued to exceed projections. But with eligibility and benefits completely off limits, cost controls on healthcare reimbursements provided only a modest check on spending. In the 1970s, Medicare spending-GDP levels had increased from 0.6 percent to 1.0 percent. Under Reagan, they rose still further, reaching 1.5 percent in 1989.

With Medicaid, the administration was able to secure occasional savings in payment formulas for the states, but Congress rejected a Medicaid "budget" that would limit annual federal cost-sharing. In addition, Congress loosened payment controls by exempting states with high unemployment or with their own cost control programs. Congress gradually increased Medicaid eligibility as well and left intact the medical care services that states were required to cover. As a result, Medicaid spending-GDP levels, which had risen steadily during the 1970s, stabilized but did not decline during the Reagan years.

The Reagan administration also planned to reduce costs and change the philosophy of cash and in-kind public assistance for the poor. Public assistance entitlement cutbacks in the 1981 reconciliation bill included more stringent eligibility criteria that would provide benefits only to the "demonstrably poor"—food stamp eligibility, for example, was terminated for an estimated 1.1 million beneficiaries, and nearly 700,000 households lost some or all of the AFDC cash benefits they were receiving.[45] A second round of reductions proposed by the administration in fall 1981, however, was rejected by Congress, and some of the initial eligibility restrictions were eased in the years that followed. Nevertheless, apart from Medicaid, spending for means-tested entitlements was tightly controlled during the 1980s. The various income security programs for the poor had risen to more than 2 percent of GDP in the mid-1970s but were at roughly half that level by the late 1980s.[46]

The first attempt at programmatic welfare reforms, the administration's 1982 "New Federalism" initiative, failed to progress beyond the discussion phase. Its social welfare component involved a tradeoff of program responsibilities and funding—a federal takeover of the Medicaid program in exchange for the states assuming full control of the AFDC and food stamps programs. The negative response among state governors and the strong opposition of congressional Democrats convinced administration officials that a formal legislative draft would be futile, and none was submitted to Congress. This marked the end of the Republican efforts to shift welfare programs and funding to the states as part of a reordering of federal and state responsibilities.

Welfare reform was revisited in Reagan's second term, and the core issue was Reagan's insistence that mandatory training and work requirements be applied to existing programs. For years, welfare critics had argued that the Great Society's liberalization of public assistance had encouraged dependency and reduced work incentives, and the Reagan administration's "workfare" proposal reflected this critique. In this instance, the states were more receptive than had been the case with the New Federalism plan, and the National Governors Association endorsed work requirements as part of a comprehensive overhaul of cash assistance programs.

A bipartisan compromise was subsequently reached on the first successful welfare reform in decades. While more limited than Reagan had envisioned, the work requirements in the Family Support Act of 1988 marked a philosophical shift away from income maintenance and toward training and employment as the guiding principle of the welfare system. In addition, the legislation bolstered state efforts to strengthen child support enforcement, provided transitional medical and childcare benefits for those families moving from welfare to work, and gave states greater control over benefits for minor parents. For Democrats, and a number of congressional Republicans, the most important legislative expansion was mandated coverage for two-parent families in which the main wage earner was unemployed (AFDC-UP). Roughly half the states had not participated in this program, and the administration finally capitulated to congressional demands for national coverage. The fiscal impact of the Family Support Act was relatively small, but its new focus on the working poor set the stage for more far-reaching changes in cash assistance programs in the 1990s. In addition, the Reagan presidency legitimized debates over dependency and other problematic effects of welfare that had been ignored during the Great Society and 1970s welfare expansion.

The Welfare State

The Reagan administration's bold challenge to the "universalization of social benefit programs" in 1981 clearly failed to shrink the welfare state. The 1983 Social Security rescue plan that Reagan signed left its benefit structure largely intact and insured that ample revenues would be available to support the nation's largest domestic spending program. The Medicare program's eligibility and benefits likewise survived intact. In this case, the less generous healthcare provider reimbursement formulas simply kept the growth of program costs at tolerable levels. The political sensitivity of Medicare was further demonstrated by the failed attempt to add catastrophic illness and prescription drug coverage in 1988. Beneficiaries were expected to pay the full cost of this new coverage, and this self-financing requirement proved so unpopular that Congress repealed its "landmark expansion" the following year. For Medicare's tens of millions of beneficiaries, their "entitlement" extended to the heavy taxpayer subsidies for this cornerstone of the welfare state.

With Social Security and Medicare accounting for some 60 percent of social welfare entitlement spending, significantly reducing the federal government's domestic role would have required an enormous and highly unlikely change in other entitlements. Some of these entitlements, such as federal employee retirement and disability and veterans' benefits and services, were bipartisan commitments and therefore almost certain to continue indefinitely. Medicaid, which nearly doubled in size during the 1980s, had developed a national network of state support. The earned income tax credit, created under Gerald Ford, provided benefits to the working poor, just the kind of work incentive that Republicans envisioned for welfare reform. Spending for the more controversial welfare programs, such as food stamps and cash assistance (AFDC and AFDC-UP) was much too limited to provide major savings in the social welfare budget, and, in any case, full-scale repeal was not a realistic option.

The Reagan administration's impact on the welfare state was, in the end, limited but far from inconsequential. The flurry of new entitlements and entitlement expansions from 1965–1980 came to a halt under Reagan, and the administration's relentless attacks on costs prodded Congress to trim some of the overly generous benefits of the expansionary years (e.g., semiannual COLAs for civil service retirees); to impose stricter controls on healthcare provider reimbursements; and to check the escalating tax subsidy for the Medicare Part B program.[47] Nevertheless, the welfare state survived intact, as did its budgetary share. The "welfare shift" initiated by Lyndon Johnson's Great Society had raised social welfare spending to approximately 45 percent of the budget by 1980. Ten years later, that budget share had not changed.

The Reagan Deficits

Ronald Reagan's original fiscal program was perhaps implausible if not impossible—tax cuts, defense spending increases, domestic program rollbacks, and a balanced budget. When recession and unexpected policy reversals led to soaring deficits in Reagan's first term, bipartisan pressure from congressional leaders persuaded the administration to accept deficit reduction tax increases. The second term was a different matter entirely. Buoyed by a strong economic recovery and a landslide reelection, Reagan successfully blocked tax increases and pursued instead revenue-neutral tax reform. When faced with the choice between continued deficits or tax increases, Reagan chose deficits, and congressional Republicans, particularly in the House, lent strong support to this choice.

In 1984, Reagan had demonstrated the electoral salience of tax cuts, and there was no indication that voters were prepared to punish Republicans for the resulting deficits if the economy was strong. With the possible exception of the 1987 meltdown in the stock market, there was also little to suggest that investors were terribly concerned about deficits either. The remaining concern, that the Federal Reserve would raise interest rates in response to large deficits and growing debt, did not come into play in the mid- and late 1980s.

The growing disregard for deficits among Republicans was reinforced by the decline in deficit levels after 1986. In 1989, deficit-GDP levels had dropped to 2.7 percent, only slightly above the average during the Carter presidency. Of course, Reagan and his fellow Republicans had sharply criticized Carter's deficit record and promised to govern more responsibly. The spending and revenue changes Reagan made reordered budget priorities but did not reduce, much less solve, the deficit problem he inherited (see Table 2.5). Moreover, the economy was quite strong when Reagan left office, which meant that the deficit at that point was almost entirely structural. When a recession took hold the next year, the deficit soared, and Reagan's successor was forced to make the difficult deficit reduction compromise he managed to avoid.

The Bush "Heresy"

In winning his party's nomination for the presidency, Vice President George H. W. Bush promised to preserve the Reagan legacy and, in particular, its defense buildup and tax cuts. In his acceptance speech at the Republican convention, Bush used the uncompromising language on tax increases that had become the defining issue for his party:

> And I'm the one who will not raise taxes... . And, my opponent won't rule out raising taxes. But I will. And the Congress will push me to raise taxes, and I'll say no, and they'll push me again. And I'll say to them: Read my lips. No new taxes.[48]

Just over a year later, President George Bush signed the largest tax increase since 1982 and for the same reason—deficits that were rising to possibly dangerous levels.

The 1990 deficit reduction agreement that Bush reached with congressional Democrats was opposed by many Republicans in the House and Senate. It also contributed to his reelection defeat to Bill Clinton in 1992, who would

Table 2.5 Components of Deficit Reduction, 1981–1989 (as a percentage of GDP)

FY 1981 =	*–$79.0 billion*		*FY 1989 =*	*–$152.6 billion*
Revenues =	19.1		Revenues =	17.8
Outlays =	21.6		Outlays =	20.6
Deficit =	–2.5		Deficit =	–2.7

	FY 1981	*FY 1989*	*Change*
Revenues			
Individual	9.1	8.0	–1.1
Corporation	2.0	1.9	–0.1
Payroll	5.8	6.5	+0.7
Other	2.2	1.5	–0.7
	19.1	17.9	–1.2
Outlays			
Discretionary Defense	5.0	5.5	+0.5
Discretionary Nondefense	4.8	3.3	–1.5
Mandatory Programmatic	10.5	9.5	–1.0
Net Interest	2.2	3.0	+0.8
	22.5	21.3	–1.2
Offsetting Receipts	–0.9	–0.8	+0.1
	21.6	20.5	–1.1

Source: *Historical Tables, Budget of the United States Government, Fiscal Year 2021* (Washington, D.C.: Government Printing Office, 2020), Tables 1.1, 1.2, 2.3, 8.4.

sign a second round of tax increases and spending cuts. The combined effect of the landmark 1990 and 1993 measures would, over the course of a few years, produce the first balanced budget in three decades; however, it would also demonstrate the electoral risks for leaders and parties who raised taxes.

1989: "Painless" Cuts

Under GRH II, the deficit ceiling for fiscal year 1990 was $100 billion, with progressively lower ceilings in 1991 and 1992 and a balanced budget in 1993 (see Table 2.6). The outgoing Reagan administration's 1990 budget did not propose major spending retrenchments but stated that the GRH deficit ceilings would be met without tax increases. Reagan also insisted that higher defense budgets could easily be accommodated within the deficit ceilings. There were concerns, however, that the economic and policy assumptions in the Reagan budget were too optimistic. The Congressional Budget Office (CBO), for example, projected a current policy deficit more than $40 billion above the 1990 deficit ceiling, and the disparities were even greater for 1991–1993.

Table 2.6 The 1987 Gramm-Rudman-Hollings (GRH II) Deficit Ceilings and Congressional Budget Office Deficit Projections (in billions of dollars)

Fiscal Year	*Deficit Ceiling*[a]	*Baseline Deficit Projections*
1988	144	155
1989	136	155
1990	100	141
1991	64	140
1992	28	135
1993	0	129

Source: Congressional Budget Office, *The Economic and Budget Outlook: Fiscal Years 1990–1994* (Washington, D.C.: Congressional Budget Office, 1989), xv.

Note: [a] Plus a $10 billion "margin of error" for all years except 1993 before automatic spending cuts required.

In a speech to a joint session of Congress in February, President Bush offered to "work with the Congress, to form a special leadership group, to negotiate in good faith ... to meet the budget targets."[49] Bush presented compromises that he hoped would facilitate bipartisan cooperation—a one-year freeze in the defense budget, additional spending for domestic programs that Reagan had cut, and full funding for public assistance entitlements. He would not accept, however, any tax increases.

The administration and Congress agreed on a $28 billion deficit reduction goal for 1990, but the negotiations over implementing legislation dragged on for more than two months. The reconciliation bill that finally passed in November fell far short of $28 billion, and other budget-related legislation failed to remedy this shortfall. When the CBO examined the various budget-related legislation enacted for 1990, it estimated a net deficit reduction of only $12 billion.[50] It warned that "without spending cuts or tax increases, the deficit in 1993 is likely to be no lower than in 1990 [$138 billion]."[51]

Bush's hopes for bipartisan cooperation no doubt underestimated the policy frustrations of congressional Democrats facing another four years of a Republican White House. An especially vexing issue for Democrats was the "no new taxes" pledge he had exploited in his campaign and refused to soften in 1989. In fact, Bush proposed a capital gains tax rate cut, claiming that it would increase revenues and contribute to the deficit reduction effort. Democrats rejected the proposal but were also wary of advocating any tax increase that could be used against them in the 1990 midterm elections. Under these politicized circumstances, significant policy compromises were impossible, and the 1989 deficit reduction effort was almost meaningless.

1990: Reality Intrudes

On January 29, 1990, the Bush administration released its fiscal year 1991 budget, and its message was reassuring. The self-described "more complete and balanced perspective on both the present and the future [budget] than has previously been characteristic" promised that the deficit problem was well in hand.[52] The GRH deficit ceiling of $64 billion for 1991 could be met without any major policy changes, and the budget was on track to meet the balanced-budget requirement in 1993 under "plausible and achievable" growth assumptions.[53] The administration's revenue growth estimates, however, were questionable. In 1991 and through the mid-1990s, projected revenue levels as a share of the economy would be higher than at any point since the 1981 Reagan tax cuts, and also higher than during the 1970s.

It did not take long for this entire scenario to fall apart. The CBO's March analysis of the president's budget called into question its economic assumptions and revenue growth estimates and found serious underestimates of debt interest costs and other fiscal obligations.[54] The CBO's fiscal year 1991 deficit estimate, even if Congress were to accept all the president's spending recommendations, was $130 billion, more than double the GRH ceiling. As the economy weakened, the budget numbers continued to worsen in the weeks ahead, and it became abundantly clear the 1990 budget deficit would be much larger than anyone had expected. The CBO's midyear budget update, for example, projected a baseline deficit of more than $230 billion in 1991 and higher deficits in 1992 and 1993.[55]

With shortfalls of this magnitude, it was not feasible to enforce the GRH deficit ceilings. The immediate cuts, or sequesters, of defense and domestic programs would have amounted to 25 percent or more in 1991 with additional cuts needed within the next two years.[56] In early May, President Bush invited congressional leaders to a "budget summit" that would replace what was now an unworkable GRH formula with a more practical and realistic deficit reduction plan. Democrats refused to participate without there being an acknowledgement that tax increases would be part of the negotiations, and Bush announced there would be "no preconditions."[57] Congressional Republicans, however, were not pleased with Bush's concession. Their opposition to tax increases would continue to cause problems for administration representatives, and for Bush, in the months ahead.

The budget summit convened on May 15, but the nearly two dozen administration officials and congressional party leaders could not agree on how to meet their five-year $500 billion deficit reduction goal. The major sticking point was taxes, as might have been expected, and Bush finally issued the explicit acknowledgement that Democrats had demanded. "The size of the deficit problem and the need for a package that can be enacted," he explained, necessitated "tax revenue increases" as well as spending cuts and budget process reforms.[58]

In return, Democratic negotiators offered to discuss entitlement cutbacks, which raised concerns among liberal House and Senate Democrats anxious to protect the programs that had survived the Reagan attacks. There was also rising discontent among rank-and-file Republicans, particularly in the House over the Bush administration's compromise on taxes. In July, House

Republicans adopted a resolution stating their opposition to any tax increases. Republicans were particularly incensed by statements from Democratic leaders that tax increases had to include higher tax rates for upper-income taxpayers. For many Republicans, the most important tax policy legacy of the Reagan presidency was the modified flat tax for individuals. It was a policy on which he had never compromised, and one which they vowed to defend.

On August 2, a crisis in the Middle East erupted, as Iraq invaded Kuwait, and President Bush responded by dispatching U.S. troops to the Persian Gulf. The next day, Congress adjourned for its August recess, and the budget talks did not resume until early September. For Bush, the immediate goal was to avoid the looming GRH sequester that would occur on October 1. In a speech to a joint session of Congress on September 11, he provided a sobering update on the deteriorating situation in the Middle East, and he coupled this with a warning that the "ax of sequester—deep across-the-board cuts that would threaten our military capacity and risk substantial domestic disruption" could only be averted by a quick resolution of the budget talks.[59]

An agreement was finally reached on September 30, but what followed was an unexpected decision by House Republicans to desert Bush during a national security emergency. The negotiated agreement had, as expected, included substantial tax increases—for example, higher Medicare payroll taxes for middle-income taxpayers and limits on deductions for high-income taxpayers—but Reagan's marginal rates remained unchanged. On the entitlement side, increased cost-sharing for Medicare beneficiaries and minor cutbacks in smaller entitlements were included, but Social Security was untouched. Of the roughly $500 billion in savings over five years, the largest share (over 35 percent) was accounted for by scheduled cuts in defense and nondefense discretionary spending; new taxes and user fees represented less than 30 percent of the total, and the entitlement share was approximately 20 percent.[60]

On October 5, the House voted on the budget resolution to implement the agreement. To just about everyone's surprise, a coalition of conservative Republicans opposed to tax increases and Democrats similarly upset by entitlement concessions rejected it by a 179–254 margin. The Republican rebellion was spearheaded by the party's minority whip, Newt Gingrich, who had participated in the budget talks but who then decided to defect and persuaded a substantial majority of his Republican colleagues to join him. Gingrich had split as well with the Republican minority leader, Robert H. Michel, who had strongly defended the agreement as "the only bipartisan basis for attacking the deficit problem."[61]

At this point, it was clear that any budget agreement that Democrats could support would be rejected by House Republicans, and the challenge was to fashion an agreement that could pass with Democratic votes. House and Senate Democratic leaders quickly rewrote the budget resolution, setting spending, revenue, and deficit reduction targets but leaving much of the necessary detail to legislative committees. The revised budget resolution passed the House on a largely party-line vote on October 8 and was approved by a bipartisan Senate majority the following day.

Over the next three weeks, Congress passed the fiscal year 1991 appropriations bills and budget reconciliation bill the budget resolution had authorized. The deficit reduction goal of almost $500 billion included multiyear caps on discretionary spending, revenue increases, entitlement cuts, and budget enforcement rules to protect the mandated deficit savings. On October 27, the House and the Senate passed OBRA 1990. Margins in both chambers were narrow, in large part because an overwhelming majority of House Republicans and a less lopsided majority of Senate Republicans voted "no." A week later, President Bush signed what he defended as "the largest deficit reduction package in history and an important measure for ensuring America's long-term economic growth."[62] On November 6, Republicans lost one Senate seat and eight House seats, which Bush's Republican critics attributed to the squandering of the party's strongest electoral asset—the "no new taxes" pledge with which Bush started his time in office.

These same critics, however, had allowed Democrats to rewrite the deficit reduction agreement to their advantage. The tax increases for upper-income taxpayers now included a high marginal rate (31 percent) and reduced deductions and exemptions. The entitlement cutbacks were greatly reduced, particularly for Medicare, and the discretionary appropriations caps were much more stringent for defense than for discretionary programs. Overall, the revenue increases in OBRA 1990 were more than double the projected reductions in entitlement programs, and nearly as large as the appropriations savings from 1991–1995 (see Table 2.7).

The Bush administration did manage to secure budget enforcement procedures and to institute much stricter budget accounting for the subsidy costs of federal credit and insurance programs. Violations of the discretionary spending caps would trigger automatic spending cuts in budget authority and outlays. "Pay-as-you-go" (PAYGO) limits were applied to revenue and entitlement legislation—for each fiscal year covered by OBRA 1990, any legislative changes reducing taxes or increasing entitlement benefits had to be deficit neutral. The administration also was able to limit the amount of defense cuts that could be transferred to domestic discretionary programs. More importantly, the new deficit reduction policies and enforcement provisions replaced the GRH deficit ceilings with the kind of comprehensive and multiyear plan that GRH's sponsors would have welcomed a decade earlier.

Nevertheless, President Bush had made the politically costly decision to raise taxes. His approval ratings soared with the successful Gulf War he launched in January 1991, and this was followed by the skillful management of the Soviet Union's collapse later that year. Unfortunately, for Bush, those historic foreign policy triumphs were soon overshadowed by a lingering recession and an abysmal deficit record. The fiscal year 1991 deficit reached nearly $270 billion, followed by an election year deficit in 1992 that climbed

Table 2.7 Omnibus Budget Reconciliation Act of 1990: Major Provisions and Deficit Savings (in billions of dollars)

	Fiscal Years 1991–1995
Revenue Provisions[a]	
Tax rates; deduction/exemption limits; AMT; Medicare tax	–67
Excise taxes	–66
Social Security	–9
Business and other	–16
	–158
Spending Provisions	
Discretionary programs (defense and nondefense)	–190
Mandatory programs	–75
Medicare	(–43)
Other	(–32)
	–265
Debt Service Costs	–59
Total Deficit Savings	–482

Source: Congressional Budget Office, *The Economic and Budget Outlook: Fiscal Years 1992–1996* (Washington, D.C.: Congressional Budget Office, 1991), 66–68.

Note: [a] Net changes for FY 1991–1995.

to $290 billion. Of course, those deficits would have been even larger without the spending cuts and tax increases Bush had approved, but trying to explain the difference between structural and cyclical deficits was not helpful when the economy remained in dismal shape.

With OBRA 1990 in place, the Bush administration and Congress were left with low-level budget policy disputes in 1991 and 1992. Bush prevented congressional Democrats from violating the domestic discretionary spending ceilings and was able to limit below-the-cap cuts in defense spending. Congress, in turn, ignored the administration's proposals to means test entitlement programs or to otherwise scale back benefits. Congress passed two middle-class tax relief bills in 1992 that included offsetting increases for high-income taxpayers, but they were successfully vetoed by Bush. The one minor success for Bush was a domestic discretionary spending freeze for fiscal year 1993 appropriations. With the November election only weeks away, Congress complied with the freeze, passed all the regular appropriations bills by the October 1 deadline, and avoided the confrontation that Bush had hoped would mollify his critics.

Bush's Governance

The Bush administration's foreign and domestic policy records were very different. Managing a peaceful end to the Cold War, waging a successful and limited war in the Persian Gulf, and persuading Congress to endorse the new Base Force defense program were major achievements that garnered widespread praise in the United States and among its allies. With domestic policy leadership, Bush's efforts to curb destabilizing deficits and to limit the growth of nondefense spending were stymied by a Democratic Congress and by divisions in his own party. The budget agreement that House Republicans torpedoed in 1990 incorporated a balanced approach to comprehensive deficit reduction—i.e., a rough equivalence between tax increases and entitlement cuts—that was missing in the reconciliation bill that Bush ultimately signed.

Bush's precarious standing with congressional Republicans never improved, allowing Democrats to dominate the budget policy agenda. Bush's compromise on tax increases, coupled with spending controls and budget enforcement procedures, improved the structural deficit problem and was a critical first step in bringing deficit politics to an end. That accomplishment was, not unexpectedly, dismissed by Democrats, but it did deserve support from Republicans proclaiming the virtues of balanced budgets. Instead, Bush would end up apologizing for his "mistake" at the 1992 Republican convention, describing himself as "the candidate who has raised taxes and regrets it."[63]

That apology failed to unify Republicans or appeal to voters. In a three-way race for president against Bill Clinton and Independent Ross Perot, a wealthy Texas businessman, Bush received 37 percent of the vote and lost the Electoral College by a margin of 370–168. Democrats also maintained their 57–43 advantage in the Senate, while their 258–177 House margin was only ten seats fewer than during the 102nd Congress.

The deficit had been a more glaring vulnerability for Bush in 1992, but it was now a Democratic responsibility. And the problem showed no signs of easing—the CBO's January 1993 budget outlook projected $300 billion deficits for several years to come and even higher levels by the end of the decade.[64] What was needed, according to the CBO, was another $500 billion package of tax increases and spending cuts that would bring the deficit under control. The Democratic platform had promised to "relieve the tax burden on middle-class Americans by forcing the rich to pay their fair share" and to "provide long-overdue tax relief to families with children."[65] But it called for "universal access to quality, affordable health care," and the discussion of entitlement reform as a means of "addressing the deficit" was limited to "control [of] soaring health-care costs."[66] Taxes and entitlements had been partisan flashpoints in 1990, and these platform pledges insured another partisan battle in 1993.

The Clinton Presidency: The Deficit Battles

Bill Clinton and congressional Democrats expanded the deficit reduction effort with OBRA 1993. Following the 1990 Bush plan, but with a much greater reliance on tax increases, OBRA 1993 led to a balanced budget in 1998 and growing surpluses in the final years of the Clinton presidency. It also had far-reaching political consequences, contributing to the Republican takeover of Congress in 1994. The 104th Congress that followed featured epic battles between the new Republican majority and the Clinton administration over taxes, spending, and the domestic role of the federal government.

Republican efforts to resurrect Ronald Reagan's balanced-budget program did not succeed, but Republicans still managed to retain control of Congress during Clinton's second term. Once again, they failed to change the fiscal course Democrats had set in 1993. While Republicans often took credit for balancing the budget, the tax and spending policies that actually accomplished the task were far removed from what Republicans had advocated. The balanced budgets of the late 1990s were defined instead by historically high revenue levels and an expansive domestic role for the federal government.

OBRA 1993

In his economic policy speech to Congress on February 17, 1993, President Clinton presented a three-part program: (1) a short-term spending stimulus to fund public works and jobs programs; (2) a multiyear deficit reduction program; and (3) a long-term commitment to public and private investment. The official Republican response, from House Minority Leader Robert Michel, did not offer much hope for bipartisan cooperation. It dismissed economic stimulus as wasteful and long-term investment as "big government spending."[67] Its main target, however, was Clinton's proposed tax increases to reduce the deficit. According to Michel, Clinton had campaigned on higher taxes for "only the super-rich" but was now seeking "more taxes for everyone." If taxes were "a necessary evil," Michel explained, "The difference is that Democrats stress the word 'necessary' and Republicans stress the word 'evil.'"

The Stimulus Filibuster

The legislative vehicle for Clinton's stimulus proposal was a $16.3 billion emergency supplemental appropriations bill for fiscal year 1993. It passed the House in mid-March and was reported out by the Senate Appropriations Committee shortly thereafter. Extended consideration of floor amendments failed to blunt Republican opposition, and Democrats were unable to overcome the Republican filibuster that followed. Republicans unanimously voted against several cloture motions, and Democrats then offered a stripped-down bill limited to extended unemployment benefits. The $4 billion emergency supplemental then passed by voice vote in the Senate on April 21 and was approved by the House the following day.

The Budget Program

The polarization that derailed the stimulus bill intensified with Clinton's announcement in early April of a plan to reduce the deficit by more than $700 billion. The five-year proposal included $375 billion in spending cuts and $328 billion in tax increases. Roughly one-third of this amount, however, was offset by new "investment" spending for infrastructure, education and training, and other domestic programs, as well as business tax incentives. With an estimated $470 billion in net deficit reduction from 1994–1998, the projected deficit in 1998 would be $240 billion.

The Republican response to Clinton's budget program was, as expected, overwhelmingly negative, but there was also considerable unease among congressional Democrats. Clinton's heavy reliance on tax increases was a major concern, and nondefense spending cuts posed problems as well. During the four months of House and Senate deliberations on the Clinton program, Democratic unity would be tested time and time again.

In using reconciliation to avoid a Senate filibuster, Democrats followed the procedure that Reagan had used for his controversial spending cuts in 1981. As with Reagan, the first step was House and Senate approval of a budget resolution with the necessary reconciliation instructions. Under the 1974 Congressional Budget Act, budget resolutions (and reconciliation bills) are protected against Senate filibusters, and both the House and the Senate quickly passed a fiscal year 1994 budget resolution with deficit reduction reconciliation instructions for legislative committees. On March 31, the House approved the budget resolution by a 240–184 vote, with Republicans unanimously opposed. All 43 Senate Republicans voted against it the next day, when the measure passed by a margin of 55–45. In an early sign of the difficulties that would lie ahead, the Senate had been forced to vote on almost four dozen amendments to its original budget resolution, several of which were Republican efforts to eliminate tax increases and expand spending cuts. None was adopted, but it was clear that Senate Republicans, like their House counterparts, were opposed to any tax increases whatsoever.

Given the scope of the deficit reduction effort, multiple House and Senate committees were responsible for drafting sections of the reconciliation bill. Of the 13 House committees involved, the most important work was done by Ways and Means, whose reconciliation instructions totaled nearly $300 billion of the roughly $500 billion deficit reduction goal. In drafting specific tax policies, Ways and Means could ignore recommendations contained in the budget resolution but had to insure that the mandated revenue amount was met. The committee had similar discretion in deciding how Medicare, Medicaid, and other entitlement savings would be secured.

Ways and Means followed the Clinton administration's lead on individual income tax increases—a top marginal rate of 36 percent, and an additional 10 percent surtax, for higher income brackets—along with higher payroll taxes for Social Security and Medicare. Corporate tax changes were smaller than the administration had proposed, and the committee also added exemptions to the new energy taxes that Clinton's budget planners had fashioned. Senior Democrats on the committee hoped that these adjustments would defuse business opposition to what a Republican critic derided as the "biggest tax increase in the history of the world."[68]

The Ways and Means portion of the reconciliation bill was reported out on a party-line vote. Other House committees, which had more modest assignments, completed their work by mid-May, and the crucial House vote on the reconciliation package took place on May 27. An intense lobbying effort by House leaders, White House officials, and Clinton himself finally persuaded enough wavering Democrats to secure the necessary majority. But the margin was thin, 219–213, as over three dozen Democrats defected.

The Senate Finance Committee, like its Ways and Means counterpart, was able to maintain Democratic unity on individual and corporate tax increases, including payroll taxes. The broad-based energy tax, however, proved too divisive, and committee Democrats replaced it with higher gasoline and motor fuel taxes. In order to make up the revenue losses, the Finance Committee trimmed business tax preferences included in the House bill and expanded Medicare and other entitlement savings beyond what the House had approved. On June 18, a party-line vote of 11–9 sent the bill to the Senate floor. The reconciliation package, which included provisions from 11 other Senate committees, was opposed by six Democrats and, of course, by all Senate Republicans. Vice President Al Gore's vote was required to break the tie, as it would be again on the conference report in August.

The House-Senate conference began in mid-July with more than 200 conferees trying to find a compromise that could pass their closely divided chambers. The most important differences were the tax and entitlement provisions. The Senate's gasoline and fuel excise tax increases were adopted, resolving what was probably the most difficult tax issue for Democrats, and the conference also scaled back the Senate's Medicare savings provisions. Compromises were reached as well on small business tax incentives, earned income tax credit (EITC) eligibility, and Social Security benefit taxation. In these and other instances, the tradeoffs between established policy and deficit reduction savings were a constant problem for Democrats across the ideological spectrum.

Those problems resurfaced as the House and the Senate took up the conference report. Once again, administration lobbying was relentless, with Clinton attempting to rally public support with a nationally televised address on August 3. Two days later, the House passed the conference bill by a 218–

216 vote, as 41 Democrats joined the unanimous Republican opposition. The Senate vote on August 6 was 51–50, with Vice President Gore's tiebreaker.

Tax increases provided well over half the deficit reduction in OBRA 1993 (see Table 2.8). The largest share of tax increases was borne by high-income taxpayers, with the new 36 percent and 39.6 percent brackets, changes in alternative minimum tax (AMT) liabilities, and income-based limits on deductions and exemptions. The definition of "high income" was expansive, since the 36 percent marginal rate applied to taxable income above $140,000 (married couple, filing jointly) and the 39.6 rate took effect at $250,000. The Medicare tax increase was similar. It repealed the existing $135,000 limit on income subject to the tax and made all wage and salary income taxable. The percentage of Social Security benefits treated as taxable income was raised from 50 percent to 85 percent for couples with more than $44,000 in post-retirement incomes from other sources.

On the low-income end, the most important changes expanded the EITC. OBRA 1993 raised benefits (refundable tax credits) for families with two or more children and provided eligibility for families without children. Taking into account all federal taxes, families in the lowest income quintile would receive a modest increase in after-tax income as the EITC changes were

Table 2.8 Omnibus Budget Reconciliation Act of 1993: Major Provisions and Deficit Savings (in billions of dollars)

	Fiscal Years 1994–1998
Revenue Provisions	
Tax rates; deduction/exemption limits; AMT; Medicare tax; Social Security benefit tax	–169
Corporate income tax rate	–16
Fuel excise taxes	–31
Business and other	–24
	–240
Spending Provisions	
Discretionary programs (defense and nondefense)	–69
Mandatory programs	–77
Medicare	(–56)
Other	(–21)
	–146
Debt Service Costs	–47
Total Deficit Savings	–433

Source: Congressional Budget Office, *The Economic and Budget Outlook: An Update* (Washington, D.C.: Congressional Budget Office, 1993), 28–31.

phased in over several years. At that point, effective tax rates for low-income taxpayers would fall to their lowest level since the mid-1970s.[69]

The political risk for Democrats was the general public's negative view of the 1993 tax increase. Despite administration efforts to defend it as a tax on the wealthy—which was largely accurate except for the gas tax and the loose definition of wealthy—nearly half the public believed that their taxes had been increased.[70] One of the architects of the Clinton program, Secretary of the Treasury Robert Rubin, later lamented the "mischaracterization of our deficit reduction as a tax increase on the middle class, which proved extremely hard to shake."[71] Equally difficult to counter was the constant reminder by Republicans that Clinton and congressional Democrats had campaigned on a middle-class tax cut.

For Republicans, opposition to the 1993 tax increase was usually couched in economic policy terms—House Minority Whip Gingrich, for example, predicted that it would cause "a job-killing recession."[72] In fact, economic growth surged in the spring of 1994 and remained quite strong for the remainder of the decade. Nevertheless, Republicans never tempered their criticism of the Clinton tax increases and repeatedly promised the middle-class tax cuts that the Democrats had failed to deliver. In 1994, Gingrich's Contract with America, the "national platform" for Republican House candidates, highlighted the American Dream Restoration Act, a package of tax credits and tax relief for a broad swath of taxpayers. The Contract also called for a constitutional balanced-budget amendment with an antitax provision—a requirement that future tax increases would require a three-fifths vote of the House and the Senate.

In many respects, the 1990 and 1993 deficit reduction bills were similar. Both relied heavily on discretionary spending cuts. Tax increases targeted high-income taxpayers, but taxes were raised to a lesser degree for much of the taxpaying population. The ratio of tax increases to spending cuts was higher in 1993 than in 1990, and the marginal rate change for individuals was much greater as well. Still, the unanimous Republican opposition to the 1993 deficit reduction program was surprising.

Most House Republicans had voted against the 1990 bill, but a majority of Senate Republicans provided the crucial votes to send it to President Bush. Included among those Republican supporters was Minority Leader Robert J. Dole, who, as Senate Finance Committee chairman in the 1980s, had helped to craft the 1982 and 1984 deficit reduction tax increases and persuaded Ronald Reagan to sign them. By 1993, however, the politics of taxation had changed completely for Republicans. A "no tax increase" orthodoxy, reinforced by a network of conservative interest groups spearheaded by Americans for Tax Reform, was now embraced by all House and Senate Republicans.

Democrats in Congress could not match this unity. Their intraparty divisions on OBRA 1993 resurfaced on other major parts of the Clinton agenda. The administration's national health insurance proposal, presented to Congress and the public with great fanfare in September 1993, never made it to the floor of the House or the Senate. Welfare reform, another Clinton priority, was undermined by fiscal and policy differences among Democrats and failed to gain committee approval in either the House or the Senate.

Democrats were hampered too by the persistence of large deficits after they passed OBRA 1993. In 1994, the deficit was nearly $90 billion below its 1992 peak but still over $200 billion. Defending deficit reduction tax increases was more difficult given this slow progress, and the 1994 midterm election results confirmed Democrats' worst fears about OBRA 1993.

The Republican party's strategy for November 1994 was to nationalize the election for all of its House and Senate candidates. Defining the election as a referendum on Democratic party governance, House and Senate Republican leaders announced a policy agenda they would act upon if given the majority. Voters responded to an extent that surprised the many experts who viewed a Democratic congressional majority as a permanent feature in electoral politics. Instead, Republicans picked up 54 seats in House elections and ten in the Senate, giving the party control of both chambers for the first time since 1953–1954. In a further indication that the electoral balance between the parties was moving toward much tighter competition, Republicans did unexpectedly well in gubernatorial and state legislative races that November.

When the 104th Congress convened on January 3, 1995, House Speaker Newt Gingrich promised quick action on all the legislative initiatives in the Contract with America. His 100-day deadline saw the House approve all but one of the Contract pledges—the exception being a constitutional amendment setting term limits for House and Senate members. Several minor pledges then made it through the Senate, but others stalled, and the constitutional balanced-budget amendment that the House had easily approved failed to gain the necessary two-thirds majority vote in the Senate. With that failed vote on March 2, Republicans moved ahead with a balanced-budget program that dominated the legislative agenda for the rest of the year. The repeated clashes between Congress and the Clinton administration during these months raised partisan polarization over budget policy to new, and occasionally destructive, levels.

Balanced Budgets and Shutdowns

The centerpiece of the Republican program was a massive reconciliation bill that, unlike its 1990 and 1993 predecessors, promised to balance the budget, not just reduce the deficit. It differed as well in its content—tax cuts instead of tax increases and enormous spending cuts that included major entitlement programs. Republicans also planned to challenge Clinton with domestic spending reductions in the fiscal year 1996 appropriations bills that would be sent to him in the fall. This two-pronged effort began with adoption of a fiscal year 1996 budget resolution on June 29 by essentially party-line votes in both chambers. It ended with vetoes, government shutdowns, debt limit brinkmanship, and a Republican retreat six months later.

Shutdowns

Spending levels for domestic discretionary programs in the fiscal year 1996 budget resolution were well below the president's budget requests. Clinton's offers of a compromise were rejected by congressional Republicans. Instead, the House and Senate Appropriations Committees approved very large cuts in domestic spending bills and raised the stakes by including controversial policy riders.

These policy riders included abortion funding restrictions, environmental policy deregulation mandates, and other constraints on domestic agencies. A number of these were problematic even for Republicans, and only two of the 13 regular appropriations bills were passed by the October 1 deadline. In order to avoid a government shutdown, the administration and Congress agreed to a six-week continuing resolution that contained short-term compromises on funding and on policy restrictions.

That spirit of compromise disappeared in the weeks that followed. The continuing resolution that Congress approved at the November 13 deadline added new policy riders that Clinton found unacceptable, leading to a presidential veto and a six-day government shutdown affecting 800,000 federal workers. This was, at the time, the largest recorded shutdown of the federal government, and Republicans pledged it would continue until Clinton accepted their seven-year deadline for balancing the budget. Clinton finally accepted a watered-down seven-year requirement and signed a new continuing resolution effective through mid-December.

The four-week respite simply escalated tensions. When the December deadline arrived, Clinton offered to sign another continuing resolution, but Republicans demanded he agree to a seven-year balanced-budget plan. Six appropriations bills were still stalled, but Clinton rejected the Republican ultimatum, and a second shutdown began. When Republicans passed three of these measures, Clinton vetoed them, and the shutdown continued. House leaders ignored Senate Majority Leader Dole's plea to end the shutdown. Instead, they approved a narrow measure to fund Washington, D.C. government operations and the processing of welfare checks, before adjourning for the Christmas recess. The agency shutdowns at that point affected some 200,000 federal workers.

This year-end shutdown proved to be politically untenable for Republicans. Public opinion polls revealed an angry public whose ire was directed largely at Republicans. Bill Clinton's approval ratings, which had dipped below 40 percent several months earlier, rose to nearly 50 percent after the third shutdown and remained relatively high until his reelection in 1996. When Republicans returned to Washington in early January, a continuing resolution was quickly enacted that temporarily restored government operations.

The battle over fiscal year 1996 appropriations was not over. Additional continuing resolutions were necessary, until the last of the 1996 appropriations bills was enacted in April. All that Republicans achieved in the end was a modest reduction in domestic discretionary spending: no major programs were terminated, most of the controversial policy riders had disappeared, and no balanced-budget plan had been adopted.

With the fiscal year 1997 appropriations bills, which had to be passed five weeks before the November 1996 election, Clinton exploited Republican fears of another shutdown debacle. The administration insisted that additional funding be provided for its domestic priorities, canceling cuts Republicans had made the previous year, and this time administration-backed policy riders were added to the new spending bills. All the fiscal year 1997 appropriations bills were enacted by the October 1 deadline, with spending levels for domestic programs higher than Republicans had supported before the shutdowns.

The Reconciliation Failure

The government shutdowns in November and December 1995 captured the public's attention, but a far more significant budget policy confrontation took place over reconciliation. In the summer and fall of 1995, 23 House and Senate committees began work on the $894 billion in spending cuts and $245 billion in tax cuts mandated by the budget resolution adopted at the end of June. Both the House and the Senate completed action on separate versions of the reconciliation legislation at the end of October, a compromise conference report was cleared on November 20, and President Clinton vetoed the bill on December 6. No override was attempted.

The Republican reconciliation initiative was a reprise of the Reagan balanced-budget plan—tax and spending cuts. The Reagan plan had failed, since Congress never came close to approving the domestic program cuts that were necessary to balance the budget at low revenue levels, and congressional resistance had been especially strong for entitlement programs. The 1995 Republican program, however, combined tax cuts and spending cuts, and the 104th Congress Republicans were not at all reluctant to cut programs that their predecessors had protected. With the exception of Social Security and defense, both of which Republicans carved out from their budget-balancing formula, the entire range of domestic programs was open for change. The reconciliation bill that passed in November would have set in motion a domestic spending retrenchment of unprecedented size and scope.

Entitlement deficit reduction savings, for example, included $270 billion in reduced Medicare spending over seven years—partly from reduced payments to healthcare providers but also through higher premiums for Part B coverage and a means test for Part B benefits. Beneficiaries would also be offered financial incentives to choose subsidized private health insurance rather than Medicare coverage, in effect scaling back the government's future benefit commitments. For Medicaid and several public assistance programs, block grants would replace open-ended entitlements, lowering federal costs and transferring to states much of the responsibility for determining eligibility and benefits. Supplemental Security Income (SSI), the cash assistance program for low-income aged, blind, and disabled individuals, would remain entirely federal, but tighter eligibility criteria would reduce spending; eligibility would also be narrowed for the EITC. There would still be a welfare state, but its costs and federal guarantees would be very different.

There was much more—including farm subsidies, less generous student loans, increased pension contributions from federal employees, and lower cost-of-living adjustments for disabled veterans and their survivors—in the reconciliation retrenchment. The tax cuts Republicans approved were estimated at $245 billion over a seven-year period. Among the more important provisions were child tax credits for families, a capital gains tax rate cut, expanded individual retirement accounts, and more generous tax preferences for corporations and businesses. Despite disagreements between the House and the Senate on the size and distribution of the tax cuts and drawn-out disputes over some provisions in the Senate, Republican party unity was never seriously threatened. On the final vote, there was only one Republican defection in the House and one in the Senate.

On the Democratic side, there were five votes for the reconciliation bill in the House and none in the Senate. As the reconciliation bill moved through these final stages, House Republicans decided to add the debt limit to the legislative mix. Congress had raised the debt limit to $4.9 trillion, and the Treasury Department reported that another increase would be needed in the fall of 1995. The House and Senate passed a temporary increase in early November, but it contained provisions that would force Clinton to sign the reconciliation bill he would receive later in the month or be faced with a government default. Instead, the Treasury Department used its discretionary authority to circumvent the debt limit, allowing Clinton to veto the debt limit increase on November 13. He then proceeded to veto the reconciliation bill on December 6. The Treasury continued to create new borrowing authorities for several months, until Congress finally capitulated and passed a permanent increase in May 1996.

In his reconciliation bill veto message, President Clinton attacked the "extreme cuts and other unacceptable changes in Medicare and Medicaid," the deep cuts in "student loans, and nutrition programs [and] Earned Income Tax Credit" and the "huge tax cut whose benefits would flow disproportionately to those who are already the most well-off."[73] While Democrats, including Clinton, continued to hold out the possibility of a bipartisan balanced-budget plan, it was difficult to see how that could be accomplished given the fundamental differences over the domestic role of the federal government.

In addition, Clinton had managed to blunt the balanced-budget pressures Republicans had relied upon. He had vetoed the debt limit and reconciliation bills, reopened the government, and avoided a government default without agreeing to any binding budget plan. Another signature Republican issue, welfare reform, was incorporated into the reconciliation bill Clinton vetoed. When Republicans passed it as a separate bill later in December, Clinton vetoed it again.

All these setbacks convinced Republicans that a more cooperative approach might be necessary, particularly in an election year. The appropriations process in 1996 was less confrontational, the debt limit increase was agreed to, and welfare reform negotiations with Clinton and congressional Democrats replaced the unilateral approach of 1995. The welfare reform bill that Clinton signed into law nearly nine months later contained the work requirements and time limits for welfare recipients Republicans had championed in the 1980s. In addition, it replaced the AFDC entitlement with block grants that gave the states much greater control over eligibility and benefits. It did not include the Medicaid block grants that Republicans had wanted, and it eased the more stringent eligibility and benefit restrictions they had included in the two bills Clinton had vetoed. These earlier measures had passed Congress on essentially party-line votes, but the bill Clinton signed was supported by large numbers of House and Senate Democrats. It was also very different from the comprehensive welfare reform that Republicans had promised 18 months earlier.

When the 104th Congress ended, the federal government's domestic role was unchanged. The largest entitlement programs—Social Security, Medicare, and Medicaid—continued to grow, and domestic discretionary spending had dropped only minimally. The only significant spending reduction was in defense, which accounted for most of the decline in total spending-GDP during Clinton's first term. More importantly, the 1990 and 1993 tax increases were beginning to boost revenue levels. Revenue-GDP in 1996 was 18.3 percent, its highest level since the Reagan tax cuts; deficit-GDP was 1.4 percent, the lowest level in more than two decades. Regardless, the Republican platform in 1996 declared, "Raising tax rates is the wrong way to balance the budget… . A balanced budget and lower taxes go hand in hand."[74]

The Clinton Presidency: The Deficit Disappears

Divided government continued after the November 1996 elections. Bill Clinton easily won reelection; Republicans retained control of the House and the Senate. The government shutdowns during the 104th Congress had provided an electoral boost to Clinton, but the public backlash against congressional Republicans had largely dissipated by November. Democrats picked up only a handful of House seats, and the 105th Congress opened with a 227–206 Republican House majority. Senate Republicans had managed to gain two seats, raising their majority to 55–45.

The fiery "Republican Revolution" rhetoric of 1995 was conspicuously absent in this new Congress. Instead, the Clinton administration and Congress quickly reached agreement on a balanced-budget plan in early May, Congress incorporated that plan into a budget resolution on June 5, and reconciliation bills implementing the agreement were signed into law on August 5. According to the CBO, the Balanced Budget Act of 1997 and Taxpayer Relief Act of 1997 would, as promised, balance the budget in 2002 and keep it at or near balance for the next decade.[75]

Bipartisanship was less evident in the appropriations process, where domestic program funding levels and policy riders delayed final action on several spending bills in 1997, and similar problems arose each year thereafter. With Republicans unwilling to risk another government shutdown debacle, Clinton repeatedly used vetoes and veto threats to protect his spending priorities. He succeeded as well in blocking major tax cuts even after the budget unexpectedly moved into surplus. The balanced budget Republicans had long sought was finally achieved, but not on the terms they had expected. Instead, tax increases and defense cuts accounted for nearly all the deficit savings during the 1990s, and the domestic role of government remained intact.

The 1997 Balanced-Budget Accord

The CBO's January 1997 budget outlook reported "considerable improvement" in deficit projections.[76] It nevertheless expected the deficit to grow in 1997 and future years "in the absence of further policies to reduce spending or increase revenues." If current policies were not appreciably changed, the baseline deficit projection for 2002 could be nearly $190 billion.

The Clinton administration's budget was released the next month, and it called on Congress "to help … finish the job" of eliminating the deficit by the 2002 deadline Republicans had set.[77] There were, as expected, Republican critiques of the president's spending and tax program. Nevertheless, Republican House and Senate leaders agreed to work with administration representatives on a deficit reduction plan and timetable.

As these negotiations proceeded, updated projections showed an increasingly favorable deficit outlook, but there remained serious differences over taxes and spending. It was quite possible, for example, that rank-and-file Republicans would oppose any agreement that did not include substantial across-the-board tax cuts. Congressional Democrats, whose leaders were not participants in the budget talks, were concerned that the administration would make compromises on domestic spending they could not support. Conservative Republicans and liberal Democrats had derailed George Bush's "bipartisan" budget agreement in 1990, and the same outcome threatened in 1997.

Instead, the administration and congressional Republican leaders were able to build broad support for an approximately $200 billion deficit reduction package that included tax cuts, discretionary spending cuts, and entitlement cuts. The budget resolution that Congress adopted on June 5, with reconciliation instructions for the tax and spending changes, passed the House (329–97) and Senate (76–22) by comfortable margins. Over the next two months, separate tax reconciliation and spending reconciliation bills were passed by the House and the Senate, and conference committee deliberations were concluded in late July. Once again, the House and the Senate approved the balanced-budget legislation by wide margins, and Clinton held a celebratory signing ceremony on August 5.

While the Taxpayer Relief Act included permanent tax cuts, its size and distributional effects were far removed from what Republicans had demanded just two years earlier. Total tax reductions for 1998–2002 were estimated at $140 billion, with nearly 80 percent of the revenue losses accounted for by the new child tax credit and new education tax credits and preferences (see Table 2.9). Offsetting revenue increases, primarily from additional taxes and fees on air transportation, lowered the net revenue reduction to $80 billion, thereby leaving revenue-GDP at its elevated level for an extended period.

The impact on progressivity was also minimal. The child tax credit, for example, had a fairly high eligibility limit ($110,000 for couples) but was refundable for low-income families with little or no income tax liability. The education tax incentives, such as the Hope and Lifetime Learning tax credits, included income phase-outs. The capital gains tax rate reduction, from 28 percent to 20 percent, was limited to long-term holdings, now defined as 18 months instead of 12 months. More importantly, Republicans failed to index long-term capital gains, which would have substantially benefited high-income taxpayers as well as being much more costly. The estate and gift tax

Table 2.9 Taxpayer Relief Act of 1997: Major Provisions and Revenue Effects (in billions of dollars)

	Fiscal Years 1997–2002
Revenue Reductions	
Child tax credit	–73
Education incentives	–39
Corporate AMT, estate and gift, and other	–28
	–141
Revenue Increases	
Airport and airway taxes	+33
Excise taxes	+6
Other taxes and timing	+21
	+60
Total Revenue Changes	–80

Source: Congressional Budget Office, *The Economic and Budget Outlook: An Update* (Washington, D.C.: Congressional Budget Office, 1997), 36–39.

provisions primarily benefited high-income taxpayers as well, but the changes here were relatively minor.

The spending reconciliation bill—the Balanced Budget Act of 1997—contained similarly balanced tradeoffs. The largest spending savings—an estimated $140 billion over a five-year period—were gained via a straightforward extension of discretionary appropriations caps through 2002.[78] The separate limits for defense and nondefense spending were in effect only for 1998 and 1999. The Medicare and Medicaid changes, which amounted to more than $125 billion, were almost entirely tied to healthcare provider reimbursement cutbacks. The only direct impact on Medicare beneficiaries was an increase in Part B premiums needed to cover 25 percent of Part B program costs. For Medicaid, federal payments to states for hospital and nursing home charges were lowered through state controls on reimbursement rates, but Medicaid eligibility was basically unchanged. In fact, Medicaid eligibility for certain legal immigrants, and for legal immigrant children, was restored, and states were required to extend coverage to disabled children who had lost eligibility under the 1996 welfare reform bill.

Finally, the 1997 Balanced Budget Act created a new federal entitlement—the administration's State Children's Health Insurance Program (SCHIP), which provided coverage for an estimated two million children in low-income households above the Medicaid income eligibility threshold. Some of the 1996 welfare reform restrictions on public assistance benefits were eased as well, particularly for food stamps and SSI. The new and expanded entitlements in the spending reconciliation bill had an estimated cost of more than $45 billion, offsetting a substantial portion of its mandatory spending cutbacks.

What was missing from the balanced-budget accord was arguably more important than what was included. The 1990 and 1993 tax rate increases remained in effect, as did virtually all of the important revenue-raising provisions. Republican proposals to retrench healthcare entitlements with stringent eligibility criteria and caps on federal healthcare spending were never considered. When the budget talks ended, Republican leaders assured their less-than-enthusiastic colleagues that 1997 was just the beginning, and that larger tax cuts and domestic retrenchments were on the way. For the final years of Clinton's presidency, however, that promise proved empty.

The Surplus Budget Agenda

The CBO's January 1998 budget outlook gave no indication that large surpluses would soon be available. Instead, it projected single-digit deficits for several years and small surpluses in 2001 and 2002.[79] The deficit was, in fact, vanishing, and, over the next year, surpluses of more than $100 billion were being projected. With this rapid turnaround, the Clinton administration pledged to block Republican attempts to "spend" these surpluses on tax cuts. Clinton was determined as well to raise domestic discretionary spending above the statutory caps that had been set. In both cases, he succeeded, and the Democratic imprint on budget policy became more pronounced.

In 1998, for example, House Republicans renewed their efforts to redirect budget policy and attempted to hamstring Clinton with a drawn-out impeachment inquiry. Instead, Clinton used veto threats to block tax cuts and also succeeded in pressuring Congress to approve "emergency spending" for domestic spending that circumvented the statutory caps. The impeachment effort backfired, as had the government shutdown years earlier. Once again, Clinton's approval ratings rose, House Republicans lost several seats in the 1998 midterm elections, and the disappointing outcome contributed to the end of the Gingrich speakership. By the time the House voted for impeachment articles in December, it was clear that the Senate trial would end in Clinton's favor.

Republicans fared no better in 1999. With budget surpluses continuing to increase, House and Senate Republicans agreed on a budget resolution with a reconciliation tax cut of more than $800 billion, the largest tax cut since 1981. As Ways and Means Committee chairman Bill Archer dutifully explained, "the defining difference between Republicans and Democrats" is taxation.[80] His committee then reported out an $864 billion tax cut that included a veritable wish list of Republican tax policy changes—lower income tax rates, reduced capital gains and inheritance taxes, and tax preferences of all kinds. The reconciliation tax bill that the House passed was slightly smaller, and the Senate's bill reduced the benefits for high-income taxpayers, but the two chambers settled these differences and proceeded to pass a massive tax cut on party-line votes. The Taxpayer Refund and Relief Act of 1999 was then vetoed by Clinton on September 23, and no override was attempted.

Clinton vetoed four appropriations bills in 1999, and Congress agreed to the additional funding he demanded. In 2000, two more appropriations vetoes produced the same result. In addition, the advent of surplus budgeting encouraged many Republicans to reassess the need for difficult spending cuts. Discretionary spending in 2000 and 2001 was well above the official caps, with additional funding provided for defense and domestic programs. The Medicare "reforms" of 1997 were gradually eased, as reimbursement payments were increased over the next three years. Military retiree healthcare benefits were raised, as were veterans' benefits and SCHIP funding. In a surprising about-face, the Republican House agreed to new prescription drug coverage for Medicare beneficiaries, and it was Senate Democrats who rejected this effort as too limited.

These spending increases, however, were relatively minor given the large surpluses that were available. As a result, most of the surplus funds were used for debt reduction purposes. In 1997, the public debt totaled $3.8 trillion. After four years of surplus, it was $3.3 trillion, just over 31 percent of GDP, the lowest level since the Reagan tax cuts. The federal government now had greater fiscal flexibility to deal with future exigencies, such as war or recessions. It would also be easier to make balanced adjustments in entitlement programs, such as Social Security, whose costs were accelerating rapidly. The Clinton administration and congressional Republicans, for example, could not reconcile their very different approaches to Social Security reform, but falling public debt levels indirectly bolstered the program's finances.

Whose Balanced Budget?

The improvement in federal finances during the 1990s was remarkable. From 1990–1994, deficits averaged well over $200 billion annually. By 2000, the surplus was over $235 billion, by far the largest ever recorded. This turnaround resulted from controversial policy changes in 1990 and 1993, and extremely strong economic growth during the latter part of the decade. Revenues grew much more rapidly than expected, spending grew more slowly, and a balanced budget was achieved years earlier than anyone believed possible.

During the 1980s, by comparison, strong economic growth helped to shrink but could not erase the gap between spending and revenues. The economic recovery that began in 1984 and the accelerating growth that followed substantially reduced deficits—from $221 billion in 1986 to $153 billion three years later. What was missing in terms of actually balancing the budget were the kinds of budget policy changes, particularly tax increases, made during the Bush and Clinton administrations.

The 1980s and 1990s also demonstrated the importance of high revenue levels given the large and firmly established domestic responsibilities of the federal government. With the exception of discretionary programs, Republican retrenchment efforts never progressed very far in the 1980s, and their 1995 budget reconciliation failure ended their efforts in the 1990s. Instead, the path to a balanced budget was marked by tax increases and post-Cold War defense budget cuts (see Table 2.10). In 2000, revenue-GDP was 20.0 percent—its highest level since World War II—and its individual income tax component was actually higher than wartime levels. Defense-GDP was less than 3 percent, its lowest level in six decades. The reductions in discretionary domestic spending and in mandatory programs, by comparison, were relatively small. Despite all the rhetoric about shrinking the domestic role of government, it survived the budget battles of the 1980s and 1990s intact.

Democrats had, in the end, prevailed in the increasingly bitter and highly partisan debate over how to balance the budget. It seemed clear that their domestic policy victories had broad popular support and would be secure for quite some time. Tax policy was another matter.

Opposition to "high taxes" had been a potent campaign issue for Republicans since Reagan's election, and his 1984 landslide victory demonstrated that voters were not terribly concerned with deficits so long as the economy was doing well. When Republicans made tax cuts a central theme in their

Table 2.10 Components of Deficit Reduction, 1990–2000 (as a percentage of GDP)

FY 1990 =	*–$221 billion*		*FY 2000 =*	*+$236 billion*
Revenues =	17.5		Revenues =	20.0
Outlays =	21.2		Outlays =	17.7
Deficit =	–3.7		Surplus =	+2.3
		FY 1990	*FY 2000*	*Change*
Revenues				
Individual		7.9	9.9	+2.0
Corporation		1.6	2.0	+0.4
Payroll		6.4	6.5	+0.1
Other		1.6	1.6	0.0
		17.5	20.0	+2.5
Outlays				
Discretionary Defense		5.1	2.9	–2.2
Discretionary Nondefense		3.4	3.2	–0.2
Mandatory Programmatic		10.3	9.8	–0.5
Net Interest		3.1	2.2	–0.9
		21.9	18.1	–3.8
Offsetting Receipts		–0.6	–0.4	0.2
		21.3	17.7	–3.6

Source: *Historical Tables, Budget of the United States Government, Fiscal Year 2021* (Washington, D.C.: Government Printing Office, 2020), Tables 1.1, 1.2, 2.3, 8.4.

takeover of Congress in 1994, the party's commitment to low taxes became unconditional.

This commitment was more important than the party's long-standing balanced-budget tradition. If balancing the budget at low revenue levels required draconian cuts in popular entitlements, the wiser electoral course was to ignore fiscal realities. Bill Clinton made entitlement protection a major theme in his reelection campaign, and it helped to insulate him from the tax increase backlash that Democrats had suffered two years earlier. That experience convinced Republicans that voters should not be asked to make sacrifices. Instead, the party could offer low taxes, painless spending cuts, and balanced budgets.

With surpluses, this electoral strategy was even more attractive. The 2000 elections featured a Republican pledge to cut taxes and keep budgets balanced through "spending discipline." Democrats hoped to preserve surplus revenues to fund the future expansion of domestic spending programs, but were compelled to promise small tax cuts as well. The defining issue of the 1980s and 1990s—low revenue levels or high revenue levels as a starting point in the budget policy process—was once again in play.

Notes

1 *Congressional Quarterly Almanac, 1981* (Washington, D.C.: Congressional Quarterly, 1982), 15-E–18-E.
2 *Fiscal Year 1982 Budget Revisions* (Washington, D.C.: Government Printing Office, 1981), 1.
3 *Fiscal Year 1982 Budget Revisions*, 11.
4 *Fiscal Year 1982 Budget Revisions*, 10.
5 James Tobin and Murray Weidenbaum, eds., *Two Revolutions in Economic Policy: The First Economic Reports of Presidents Kennedy and Reagan* (Cambridge: Massachusetts Institute of Technology Press, 1988), 420.
6 *Public Papers of the President: Ronald Reagan, 1981* (Washington, D.C.: Government Printing Office, 1982), 706.
7 *Congressional Quarterly Almanac, 1981*, 259.
8 *Congressional Quarterly Almanac, 1981*, 257.
9 *Fiscal Year 1982 Budget Revisions*, 8–9.
10 Tobin and Weidenbaum, *Two Revolutions in Economic Policy*, 420.
11 *Weekly Compilation of Presidential Documents* 18 (February 1, 1982): 78, 79.
12 Dennis S. Ippolito, *Uncertain Legacies: Federal Budget Policy from Roosevelt through Reagan* (Charlottesville: University Press of Virginia, 1990), 68.
13 *Congressional Quarterly Almanac, 1982* (Washington, D.C.: Congressional Quarterly, 1983), 30.
14 Dennis S. Ippolito, *Deficits, Debt, and the New Politics of Tax Policy* (New York: Cambridge University Press, 2012), 124.
15 *Congressional Quarterly Almanac, 1982*, 176.
16 Ippolito, *Uncertain Legacies*, 70.
17 Ippolito, *Uncertain Legacies*, 74.
18 Ippolito, *Uncertain Legacies*, 74.
19 *Budget of the United States Government, Fiscal Year 1985* (Washington, D.C.: Government Printing Office, 1984), M19.
20 *Budget of the United States Government, Fiscal Year 1985*, 2-14.
21 *Congressional Quarterly Almanac, 1984* (Washington, D.C.: Congressional Quarterly, 1985), 78-B.
22 *Congressional Quarterly Almanac, 1984*, 66-B.
23 *Congressional Quarterly Almanac, 1984*, 114-B.
24 *Congressional Quarterly Almanac, 1984*, 42-B.
25 See Iwan W. Morgan, *The Age of Deficits: Presidents and Unbalanced Budgets from Jimmy Carter to George W. Bush* (Lawrence: University Press of Kansas, 2009), 105–106.
26 *Congressional Quarterly Almanac, 1986* (Washington, D.C.: Congressional Quarterly, 1987), 510.
27 *Congressional Quarterly Almanac, 1986*, 524.
28 *Congressional Quarterly Almanac, 1986*, 522.
29 *Congressional Quarterly Almanac, 1986*, 494.
30 C. Eugene Steuerle, *Contemporary U.S. Tax Policy*, 2nd ed. (Washington, D.C.: Urban Institute Press, 2008), 121, 123.
31 *Budget of the United States Government, Fiscal Year 1987* (Washington, D.C.: Government Printing Office, 1986), M-4.
32 *Budget of the United States Government, Fiscal Year 1989* (Washington, D.C.: Government Printing Office, 1988), 4-4.

33 *Budget of the United States Government, Fiscal Year 1988* (Washington, D.C.: Government Printing Office, 1987), M-5.
34 *Congressional Quarterly Almanac, 1987* (Washington, D.C.: Congressional Quarterly, 1988), 615.
35 *Congressional Quarterly Almanac, 1987*, 627.
36 *Congressional Quarterly Almanac, 1987*, 612.
37 *Budget of the United States Government, Fiscal Year 1990* (Washington, D.C.: Government Printing Office, 1989), 1-11.
38 *Budget of the United States Government, Fiscal Year 1990*, 1-5.
39 *Annual Report to the Congress, Fiscal Year 1987* (Washington, D.C.: Department of Defense, 1986), 13, 18.
40 Department of Defense, *Soviet Military Power: An Assessment of the Threat, 1988* (Washington, D.C.: Government Printing Office, 1988), 32.
41 Morgan, *The Age of Deficits*, 118.
42 *Congressional Quarterly Almanac, 1981*, 119.
43 *Congressional Quarterly Almanac, 1981*, 117.
44 *Congressional Quarterly Almanac, 1982*, 474.
45 *Congressional Quarterly Almanac, 1981*, 461.
46 Congressional Budget Office, *The Budget and Economic Outlook: 2019 to 2029* (Washington, D.C.: Congressional Budget Office, 2019), 159.
47 R. Kent Weaver, *Automatic Government: The Politics of Indexation* (Washington, D.C.: Brookings Institution, 1988), 60–61.
48 *Congressional Quarterly Almanac, 1988* (Washington, D.C.: Congressional Quarterly, 1989), 43-A.
49 *Congressional Quarterly Almanac, 1989* (Washington, D.C.: Congressional Quarterly, 1990), 10-C.
50 Congressional Budget Office, *The Economic and Budget Outlook: Fiscal Years 1991–1995* (Washington, D.C.: Congressional Budget Office, 1990), xvii.
51 Congressional Budget Office, *The Economic and Budget Outlook: Fiscal Years 1991–1995*, xiii.
52 *Budget of the United States Government, Fiscal Year 1991* (Washington, D.C.: Government Printing Office, 1990), 21.
53 *Budget of the United States Government, Fiscal Year 1991*, 10–12.
54 Congressional Budget Office, *An Analysis of the President's Budgetary Proposals for Fiscal Year 1991* (Washington, D.C.: Congressional Budget Office, 1990), 1–10.
55 Congressional Budget Office, *The Economic and Budget Outlook: An Update* (Washington, D.C.: Congressional Budget Office, 1990), xiii.
56 Ippolito, *Deficits, Debt, and the New Politics of Tax Policy*, 162.
57 *Congressional Quarterly Almanac, 1990* (Washington, D.C.: Congressional Quarterly, 1991), 130.
58 *Congressional Quarterly Almanac, 1990*, 131.
59 *Congressional Quarterly Almanac, 1990*, 133.
60 The remainder was the estimated interest saving from the reduced federal debt. *Congressional Quarterly Almanac, 1990*, 134.
61 *Congressional Quarterly Almanac, 1990*, 136.
62 *Congressional Quarterly Almanac, 1990*, 166.
63 *Congressional Quarterly Almanac, 1992* (Washington, D.C.: Congressional Quarterly, 1993), 76-A.
64 Congressional Budget Office, *The Economic and Budget Outlook: Fiscal Years 1994–1998* (Washington, D.C.: Congressional Budget Office, 1993), xv–xvi.
65 *Congressional Quarterly Almanac, 1992*, 61-A.
66 *Congressional Quarterly Almanac, 1992*, 60-A.
67 *Congressional Quarterly Almanac, 1993* (Washington, D.C.: Congressional Quarterly, 1994), 13-D.

68 *Congressional Quarterly Almanac, 1993*, 109.
69 Ippolito, *Deficits, Debt, and the New Politics of Tax Policy*, 173.
70 Steuerle, *Contemporary U.S. Tax Policy*, 166.
71 Quoted in Steuerle, *Contemporary U.S. Tax Policy*, 166.
72 *Congressional Quarterly Almanac, 1993*, 122.
73 *Congressional Quarterly Almanac, 1995* (Washington, D.C.: Congressional Quarterly, 1996), D-37.
74 *Congressional Quarterly Almanac, 1996* (Washington, D.C.: Congressional Quarterly, 1997), D-23.
75 *Congressional Quarterly Almanac, 1997* (Washington, D.C.: Congressional Quarterly, 1998), 2-27.
76 Congressional Budget Office, *The Economic and Budget Outlook: Fiscal Years 1998–2007* (Washington, D.C.: Congressional Budget Office, 1997), 17.
77 *Budget of the United States Government, Fiscal Year 1998* (Washington, D.C.: Government Printing Office, 1997), 7.
78 *Congressional Quarterly Almanac, 1997*, 2-48.
79 Congressional Budget Office, *The Economic and Budget Outlook: Fiscal Years 1999–2008* (Washington, D.C.: Congressional Budget Office, 1998), xviii.
80 *Congressional Quarterly Almanac, 1999* (Washington, D.C.: Congressional Quarterly, 2000), 21-11.

3 From Surplus to Deficit

The George W. Bush Presidency

The 2000 national elections gave the Republican party control of the presidency and Congress for the first time since 1953, but its victory was razor-thin. The presidential race was not decided for several weeks, when the U.S. Supreme Court finally ended the dispute over Florida's voting results in George W. Bush's favor. Bush still lost the national popular vote for president, but Florida's 25 electoral votes gave him an Electoral College majority of 271–266. The congressional election outcomes were equally close. Democrats picked up five Senate seats, creating a 50–50 tie in the 107th Congress, and narrowed the Republican House majority to 221.

Bush's signature campaign issue was large, across-the-board tax cuts, and the size of his tax plan eventually reached $1.6 trillion. Bush's opponent, Vice President Al Gore, promised tax cuts as well, but his were much smaller and directed toward low- and middle-income taxpayers. Gore's tax program insured that sufficient revenues would be available to fund Democratic entitlement commitments and other domestic priorities. Bush's more ambitious program was less concerned with budgetary tradeoffs or fiscal consequences. Instead, Bush unconditionally embraced the efficacy of low tax rates in promoting long-term economic growth. He and congressional Republicans were likewise convinced that tax cuts would serve their electoral interests.

Once in office, Bush's "New Approach to Budgeting" was carefully crafted to defuse potential criticism of his tax program, setting forth a prudent, balanced plan for managing future surpluses (see Table 3.1). Its starting point was the Congressional Budget Office's January 2001 budget report, which projected $5.6 trillion in surplus over the next decade.[1] Funding for essential national priorities, "retiring the maximum amount of [government] debt possible," and strengthening Social Security and Medicare would be carved out of this surplus. The remainder ($1.6 trillion) would be reserved for "fair and reasonable tax relief for every American who pays income taxes."[2]

Missing entirely from the Bush budget was the harsh retrenchment rhetoric that Republicans had deployed against Bill Clinton. Instead, Bush called for "moderate growth" in spending to support an expanded federal role in education, healthcare, and environmental protection; an increase in the defense budget; and promotion of his "compassionate conservative" vision

DOI: 10.4324/9781003167266-3

Table 3.1 The Bush Administration's 2001 Budget Program "Highlights"

Moderate Growth in Government and Fund National Priorities:

- Moderates recent rapid growth in spending, while funding national priorities, paying down the debt, and providing tax relief.
- Strengthens and reforms education, granting the Education Department the largest percentage spending increase of any Department (11.5% increase in 2002).
- Saves the entire Social Security surplus ($2.6 trillion) and commits to reforming the program.
- Spends every penny of Medicare tax and premium collections over next 10 years only on Medicare. Modernizes and reforms Medicare.
- Restores commitment to military personnel and begins transition to a twenty-first-century force structure.
- Champions compassionate conservatism by supporting the critical role that faith-based and community organizations play in helping people at the local level.

Debt Reduction: Achieves historic levels of debt reduction, retiring the maximum amount of debt possible over ten years ($2 trillion).

Tax Relief: Lets taxpayers keep roughly one-fourth of the surplus they produced ($1.6 trillion over ten years).

By the Numbers:

- Allocates projected $5.6 trillion surplus over ten years. Breakdown of surplus:

  —Saves all the Social Security surplus ($2.6 trillion) for Social Security.

  —Provides $1.6 trillion in tax relief over ten years.

  —Creates an unprecedented $1.4 trillion reserve for additional needs, debt service, and contingencies.
- Produces a $231 billion total surplus in 2002.
- Reduces historically high income tax burden.
- Moderates recent explosive growth in discretionary spending to 4.0% growth in 2002, an increase of $26 billion over 2001.
- Moderates growth in spending by making reductions in one-time spending, unjustified programs, duplicative programs, and programs that have completed their mission in 2002.

Source: *Budget of the United States Government, Fiscal Year 2002* (Washington, D.C.: Government Printing Office, 2001), 7.

for governing. His debt reduction pledge was specific—$2 trillion over ten years—and its goal was the lowest debt-GDP level since World War I.[3] Also highlighted was "an unprecedented $1 trillion reserve for additional needs and contingencies."

The first budget legislation that Bush signed, however, was a $1.35 trillion tax cut that most House and Senate Democrats strongly opposed. The Economic Growth and Tax Relief Reconciliation Act of 2001 (EGTRRA 2001) was the largest tax cut since 1981 and, as its title indicated, required the filibuster-proof reconciliation procedure to make it through the closely divided Senate. After costly wars in Afghanistan and Iraq were launched in response to the September 11, 2001 terrorist attacks perpetrated on the U.S. mainland (known as 9/11), additional tax cuts were passed in 2003 and 2004. The Bush tax cuts were, as one study noted, "an extraordinary episode in the history of American war finance," since "special taxes [had] supported every major conflict in our nation's history."[4]

With the exception of the Vietnam War, modern wartime finance had also included strong controls on nondefense spending. In 2002, the Bush administration had pointedly criticized this Vietnam exception and vowed not to repeat it. The "guns and butter" budgets of the Johnson presidency, it explained, had caused prolonged inflation and multiple recessions.[5] "Wiser choices" were made during World War II, when "expenditures not related to the war effort" were substantially reduced. Bush expressed confidence that spending discipline and pro-growth economic policies (i.e., tax cuts) would insure that "deficits [would] be both small and temporary."[6]

Deficits during the Bush presidency, however, were neither small nor temporary. From 2002–2005, deficits totaled $1.3 trillion. Revenue-GDP levels during this time were extremely low, averaging just over 16 percent, while both defense and nondefense spending increased significantly. Whether Bush's promises about debt reduction and contingency reserves were sincere was beside the point, since they were quickly abandoned as tax cuts, war, and higher spending transformed the federal budget.

Bush's second term failed to remedy the deficit problem. Bush and congressional Republicans refused to raise taxes, and his plan for cutting "the deficit in half by 2009" depended exclusively on spending cuts.[7] The Republican House and Senate majorities in 2005–2006 were the largest of Bush's presidency but made limited progress in curbing domestic spending. The Democratic-controlled 110th Congress that followed was completely opposed to domestic cutbacks. As a result, there remained a large structural budget deficit when the Great Recession at the end of Bush's tenure completely upended federal finances. Plummeting revenues and massive emergency spending raised the 2008 deficit to almost $460 billion, and those that followed were much, much larger. Deficit politics had returned under Bush and would afterward become increasingly partisan and volatile.

The First Term: "Deficits Don't Matter"

The "bright" budget outlook of January 2001 had almost vanished just one year later. Recession, tax cuts, and increased spending had wiped out more than $4 trillion of the projected ten-year surplus, and the rest quickly disappeared as deficits steadily mounted.[8] Deficits in 2003 and 2004 totaled nearly $800 billion—both well over 3 percent of GDP and the highest since the early 1990s. In just three years, the budget had shifted from a surplus of more than 2 percent of GDP to a deficit of more than 3 percent of GDP—effectively canceling out the hard-fought deficit reduction of the 1990s. At the core of this fiscal reversal was the sweeping change in tax policy that began in 2001.

The Republican Tax Agenda

In 2001, House Republicans quickly passed legislation incorporating the entire $1.6 trillion tax cut, but Senate Republicans eventually persuaded their House colleagues and the Bush administration to settle for a smaller $1.35 trillion package of individual tax cuts. Two years later, the nation was at war and deficits were surging, but congressional Republicans approved another $350 billion tax cut. Once again, Senate Republicans managed to scale back the Bush administration's much larger tax cut proposal but still wound up ignoring the tax cut limit they had insisted on two years earlier. The Bush administration was seemingly unconcerned with the fiscal consequences of burgeoning tax cuts, and most congressional Republicans were eager to follow Bush's lead. The initial rationale for tax cuts—returning to taxpayers a share of the surplus—was no longer useful when deficits suddenly appeared, but a "pro-growth tax policy" was an attractive replacement. Moreover, Republicans apparently believed that the electoral appeal of tax cuts was so compelling that long-standing commitments to balanced budgets and low debt had to be dismissed.

EGTRRA 2001

In early March 2001, the Republican House approved a $960 billion, ten-year reduction in individual income tax rates. The House bill lowered the top marginal rate from 39.6 percent to 33 percent, and a new 10 percent bottom bracket was created for low-income taxpayers.[9] Democrats on the Ways and Means Committee were bypassed, as committee Republicans crafted a bill to provide across-the-board tax rate cuts with a rapid phase-in schedule. The Ways and Means bill was reported out on a party-line vote. It then received unanimous approval from Republicans when the final floor vote took place. House Democrats voted by 197–10 against this first installment of the Bush tax cut plan.

A second House tax bill, reducing taxes for married couples and increasing child tax credits, was passed on March 29. This measure had bipartisan appeal, since benefits were largely confined to middle- and low-income families. It eliminated a disparity in the tax treatment of single and married taxpayers by allowing the latter to claim a standard deduction twice that for single taxpayers, and provided additional relief by expanding the 15 percent income bracket for married couples. The child tax credit increase, from $500 to $600, and expanded earned income tax credit (EITC) benefits, also appealed to Democrats, 64 of whom joined a united Republican bloc in passing the nearly $400 billion, ten-year "marriage and family relief" bill.[10]

In early April, a similar coalition approved a phased-in repeal of estate and gift taxes. Its estimated cost of $185 billion over a ten-year period was based on a gradual reduction in tax rates leading to full-scale repeal in 2011.[11] The fourth and final House tax cut measure was designed to boost retirement savings by raising the limit on tax-free contributions to individual retirement accounts (IRAs) and employer-sponsored defined contribution pension accounts. This was the smallest of the House-passed tax bills, with an estimated ten-year cost of just over $50 billion, and attracted over 400 votes on its final passage in May.[12]

The House passed these tax cuts before a budget resolution was in place. Since the Republican majority remained unified as each bill moved through committee and to the floor, Democrats could not block or even seriously delay Republicans from moving forward. The situation in the Senate was quite different. Vice President Dick Cheney's tiebreaking vote had allowed Republicans to organize the Senate (choosing the majority leader and committee chairmen) and Cheney could also be counted on in the event of a 50–50 party vote on legislation, but Republicans could not overcome Democratic filibusters. Given the strong Democratic opposition to the Bush tax cuts, the only way to circumvent a near-certain filibuster was the reconciliation procedure that Democrats had used in 1993. In order to take advantage of reconciliation, however, Republicans needed to have a budget resolution authorizing its use.

The House Budget Committee had reported out a budget resolution with a $1.6 trillion tax cut provision on a party-line vote on March 17. The House adopted it one week later, again along party lines. The Senate Budget Committee (like all Senate committees at the beginning of the 107th Congress, equally divided between Republicans and Democrats) was deadlocked and unable to report a resolution for Senate consideration on schedule. The Senate Republican leadership drafted its own resolution but could not introduce it until April 1. During this delay, intraparty differences over the size and distribution of tax cuts began to emerge, and more moderate Republicans agreed that the leadership's draft resolution had to be changed. During the lengthy floor debate that followed, these Republicans joined with Democrats to amend the resolution, the most important change being a $1.2 trillion cap on the size of the tax cut.

Special Senate rules regarding reconciliation introduced another complication. A reconciliation tax cut authorized by a budget resolution was limited to the ten-year period covered by the resolution.[13] After 2010, therefore, any reconciliation tax cut would "sunset" or automatically expire, and pre-2001 tax law would again be in effect. The Senate's budget resolution was thus substantially smaller than that of the House regarding both the size and duration of the tax cuts it allowed. Efforts by House Republicans to reinstate their $1.6 trillion tax cut ceiling during conference failed. Instead, the conference committee agreed to a $1.35 trillion compromise, and the conference report was adopted by the House and the Senate in early May. Nevertheless,

House-Senate differences reemerged as the Ways and Means and the Finance Committees subsequently drafted their tax bills.

A major split over marginal rate cuts for upper-income taxpayers, with Ways and Means approving a 33 percent top rate and Finance adopting a smaller reduction to 36 percent, was emblematic of a broader debate about the distribution of tax relief. Progressivity was a minor concern among House Republicans but was taken more seriously in the Senate. The multiple provisions in the Finance Committee's draft bill—from individual income tax brackets to estate and gift taxation—attempted to provide a more balanced distribution of tax relief across income categories than the companion Ways and Means bill. As a result, four Finance Committee Democrats joined its ten Republicans in reporting out the committee's bill on May 15.

During the floor debate, the Finance Committee's bill barely withstood attempts to provide even greater relief to low- and middle-income taxpayers. Another line of attack from Democrats who opposed the bill was its fiscal impact. The complicated phase-ins required to keep its ten-year cost within the $1.35 trillion ceiling meant that many provisions would take effect years later when budget projections were especially uncertain. Democratic Minority Leader Tom Daschle brought up the deficits that had followed the 1981 Reagan tax cuts and warned that Congress was "faced with almost exactly the same circumstances and once again [was] on the threshold of making that same mistake."[14]

Daschle was not the only skeptic. Federal Reserve chairman Alan Greenspan, who had provided a crucial endorsement of tax cuts earlier in the year, now supported adding "triggers" to their implementation. If fiscal circumstances changed—i.e., future surpluses were not available—tax cuts would be delayed or suspended.[15] Bush adamantly opposed adding any conditions to multiyear tax cuts and worked with Senate leaders to defeat the trigger amendment that was offered on May 21. Bush was forced to accept, however, the ten-year "sunset" provision in the Senate bill that passed on May 23.

This time limit was obviously important, but the policy differences between the House and the Senate tax bills were also much greater than Republican leaders and the Bush administration had expected at the outset. House Republicans were clearly more united than their Senate counterparts on the entire tax cut enterprise, and they were especially insistent that marginal rate reductions for high-income taxpayers be much steeper than the Senate had approved. Whether the Bush administration could successfully broker a compromise between the House bill it favored and a Senate bill that was more "moderate" was uncertain, but all sides expected the House-Senate conference scheduled for late May to be contentious and protracted.

On May 24, however, the tax cut odyssey took an unexpected turn. Republican Senator James M. Jeffords, who had just been elected to a third term from Vermont, announced that he was leaving the party and switching his affiliation to Independent. Jeffords went on to explain that he would caucus with the Senate Democrats and vote with them to organize the chamber but would delay doing so until the tax bill cleared Congress and was sent to the president. At this point, Bush convinced House Republicans to act quickly and to accept the key features of the Senate bill. The conference bill they agreed to cut the top marginal rate to 35 percent, which was slightly less than the 36 percent rate the Senate had approved, but the size of the tax cut package, its phase-ins, and other contested provisions hewed closely to what a bipartisan group of 15 senators described as "the delicate compromise that was reached in the Senate."[16] Anything else, they made it clear, would not pass the Senate. The conference report was promptly ratified by the House and the Senate on May 26. The margin in both chambers was fairly comfortable, with a number of Democrats crossing party lines to vote with the Republicans.

The $1.35 trillion cost of EGTRRA 2001 included an estimated $1.26 trillion in individual tax cuts and $92 billion in refundable tax credits. The new marginal rates for individuals accounted for more than 60 percent of the ten-year revenue losses, with roughly equivalent shares for the new 10 percent bracket and the five expanded and reduced brackets (see Table 3.2). Various phase-ins were applied to these bracket changes (and other provisions) that were necessary to keep revenue losses within the $1.35 trillion ceiling, but which also made it more difficult to assess the actual distribution of tax relief among income categories.

The 10 percent bracket and expanded 15 percent bracket took immediate effect in 2001; the 25, 28, 33, and 35 percent brackets were phased in from 2001 to 2006. Marriage penalty relief—the increased standard deduction and the 15 percent tax bracket for couples—was on a 2005–2009 implementation schedule. The estate and gift tax reduction took partial effect in 2001 and continued through 2009, with full repeal in 2010. The deduction and exemption limits for high-income taxpayers were also staged over several years with full repeal in 2010. Retirement savings incentives took effect over several years as well. An increase in the exemption limit for the alternative minimum tax (AMT) was regarded as essential by Democrats and Republicans alike, since it kept the AMT from being applied to taxpayers for whom it was never intended. To minimize its "official" revenue losses, however, the AMT fix was only temporary (2001–2004) and would have to be renewed at that point.

EGTRRA 2001 contained substantial aggregate benefits for low- and middle-income taxpayers, but the average tax relief for upper-income taxpayers was much greater. Since they paid such a disproportionate share of income taxes, their rate reductions significantly increased after-tax income. Reducing estate and gift taxes as well as repealing deduction and exemption limits were similarly skewed in terms of taxpayer benefits. Nevertheless, EGTRRA 2001 provided tax relief for a very broad swath of taxpayers, which brought some Democrats on board and lent it a veneer of bipartisanship.

The fiscal effects of the tax cut, however, were either downplayed or ignored by its supporters. The administration used favorable budget

Table 3.2 Economic Growth and Tax Relief Reconciliation Act of 2001: Estimated Revenue Effects of Major Individual Income Tax Provisions by Income Group* (in billions of dollars)

		Revenue Loss (2001–2011)
Tax Rates		
Low-Middle Income	New 10% marginal rate bracket	–421
Middle-High Income	Expanded 15% bracket; reduced marginal rates to 25%, 28%, 33%, and 35% (phased in 2001–2006)	–421
Child Tax Credit		
Low-Middle Income	Tax credit increased to $1,000 by 2010; refundable credits of 10–15% (phased in 2001–2010)	–172
Married Couples		
Low-Middle Income	Increased standard deduction and expanded 15% bracket (phased in 2005–2009)	–63
Estate and Gift Taxes		
High Income	Reduced estate tax rates and increased exemptions; reduced gift tax rates (phased in 2001–2010)	–138
Deductions and Exemptions		
High Income	Reduced limits on itemized deductions and exemptions (phased in 2006–2010)	–33
Retirement Savings		
High Income	Increased contribution limits on IRAs and other retirement accounts (phased in 2001–2006)	–50
Education Incentives		
Middle Income	New education expense tax deduction; increased education IRA limit; extended employer-provided education assistance income exclusion; new qualified tuition plan earnings exclusion	–29
Alternative Minimum Tax (AMT)		
Middle Income	Increased income exemption limits for AMT (2001–2004)	–14
Other		–8
Total Revenue Loss		–1,349 billion

Source: Congressional Budget Office, *The Budget and Economic Outlook: An Update* (Washington, D.C.: Congressional Budget Office, 2001), 8–11.

Note: *This categorization estimates the exclusivity or primary distribution of benefits by income category for the specific provisions.

projections to justify the tax cuts. As Bush stated, they would simply let "taxpayers keep roughly one-fourth of the surplus they produced."[17] With few exceptions, Republicans in Congress, who supposedly abhorred deficits and debt, were so strongly committed to cutting taxes that fiscal consequences never gave them pause. More important, tax cut advocates refused to consider changing course when deficits returned and surpluses vanished. Instead, the Bush administration and congressional Republicans fought to expand the 2001 tax cut and make it permanent.

President Bush's second budget, submitted to Congress on February 4, 2002, noted that deficits had returned but predicted that the budget would be balanced "by 2005 without endangering the war against terrorism ... and without raising taxes."[18] In order to counter the recession that had begun in the spring of 2001 and deepened after the September 11 attacks, Bush proposed a stimulus package that included extended unemployment benefits and funding for job training. He also called upon Congress to speed "up the tax reductions ... passed last year," provide "tax refunds to lower- and moderate-income individuals and families," lower "the alternative minimum tax on businesses," and offer "better tax treatment" for business investment.[19] The administration's budget explained that ten-year budget forecasts had proved "unreliable and ultimately futile" and would no longer be used for fiscal planning. It failed to mention that Bush's original tax cut program had been based on ten-year surplus projections.

Not to be outdone, the House passed separate bills to make the 2001 estate tax repeal, marriage penalty reductions, and retirement savings initiatives permanent. In October 2001, House Republicans had voted to accelerate scheduled tax rate reductions and cut capital gains taxes as part of a $100 billion economic stimulus package. None of this legislation made it through the Democratic-controlled Senate. What was approved, and signed into law by President Bush on March 9, was a much narrower package of extended unemployment benefits, tax incentives for development recovery projects in New York City, and increased business investment incentives.

JGTRRA 2003

Senate Republicans picked up two seats in the 2002 midterm elections, giving them a 51–49 majority for the 108th Congress, and House Republicans increased theirs to 229–206. President Bush's budget for fiscal year 2004 conceded that "we now face a period of budget deficits" but attributed that to a "recession and a war we did not choose."[20] His administration was committed, he emphasized, to "controlling the deficit and reducing it as the economy strengthens and our national security interests are met."

His legislative priority was nonetheless another large tax cut. Bush's "growth and jobs package" renewed his 2002 proposal for accelerating the 2001 tax cuts—the tax rate reductions, marriage penalty tax relief, child tax credit increase—and introduced a new dividend exclusion for individuals.

Other major provisions included a one-year AMT "fix" and increased deductions for small businesses. According to estimates by the Joint Committee on Taxation, the multiyear cost of the Bush plan was more than $725 billion, the most costly provision being the dividend exclusion for individuals that accounted for almost $400 billion of this total.[21]

Despite Bush's insistence that the 2001 tax cut was not responsible for the negative deficit outlook—"In fact, if the tax cut of 2001 had never become law ... the outcome would have been worse because the economy would have been even weaker"[22]—there were widespread concerns that another large tax cut would indeed make matters worse. Regardless, in early March the House Budget Committee reported out a budget resolution that authorized reconciliation for the entire $725 billion tax cut that Bush had proposed. The House then proceeded to approve the resolution by a 215–212 vote.

The Senate Budget Committee also reported out its budget resolution with the entire tax cut allowance, but the full Senate proceeded to cut it by more than half. A Democratic amendment setting a $350 billion revenue ceiling on any reconciliation tax cut attracted three Republicans and passed by a 51–48 margin. Deficit estimates for 2003 and 2004 were continuing to rise, and the administration's request for a $75 billion Iraq War supplemental funding bill in the spring of 2003 was larger than expected. Nevertheless, Senate Republican leaders, like their House counterparts, had no hesitation on moving ahead with a massive wartime tax cut, but their narrow majority would not support the House's $725 billion goal.

In the budget resolution conference, House Republicans succeeded in convincing Senate conferees to accept a compromise $550 billion ceiling—$350 billion for the reconciliation tax cut and an additional $200 billion that could be added after the House and the Senate went to conference on the actual tax bill. The Senate approved the conference agreement after Republican leaders pledged to enforce the Senate's original $350 billion ceiling in the upcoming conference on the tax bill. With that assurance, the Senate voted 51–50, as Vice President Cheney cast the tiebreaking vote.

With a budget resolution finally in place, the Ways and Means and the Finance Committees began to draft their tax bills. The policy differences between the two were numerous, and one of the more important differences was the jettisoning by Ways and Means of the dividend exclusion that Bush had proposed. Ways and Means opted instead for cutting capital gains and dividend tax rates, while the Finance Committee supported a modified dividend exclusion and did not address capital gains taxes. The bottom-line difference was unresolved—Ways and Means reported out a $550 billion tax cut compared to $350 billion for Finance. The House adopted the Ways and Means bill without amendment by 222–203 on May 9. The Finance bill was passed by the Senate by a 51–49 vote on May 15, after being amended to include an expanded dividend exclusion.

As in 2001, the Bush administration feared that a long and divisive conference might result in no tax bill at all, and the president called on both sides to send him a bill before Congress's scheduled recess on May 24. The Senate "won" the contest over the cost of the tax cut, as the conference bill's revenue losses were officially scored as $350 billion. The House prevailed on the capital gains and dividend tax rate reductions, with a 15 percent rate for both effective in 2003. In order to keep within the $350 billion ceiling, short-term "sunsets" were attached to major provisions. The multiyear cost of the capital gains and dividend tax rate cuts, for example, was less than $150 billion, because they would only be in effect through 2008. The conference tax bill was approved by the House on a party-line vote of 231–200. The Senate vote was 51–50, as Vice President Cheney weighed in once again.

The Jobs and Growth Tax Relief Reconciliation Act of 2003 (JGTRRA 2003) contained an estimated $319 billion in individual tax cuts for fiscal years 2003–2013 (see Table 3.3). Temporary corporate depreciation and expensing allowances and fiscal assistance for state governments brought total revenue losses to $349 billion. The capital gains and dividend tax rate reductions were new, but other provisions stepped up the effective dates of various phase-ins from 2001. The end result was a substantial increase in revenue losses above the $1.35 trillion "ceiling" that Bush agreed to accept in 2001. With JGTRRA 2003, the Bush tax cuts now totaled $100 billion more than his original $1.6 trillion goal.

The 2004 Tax Cuts

President Bush decided that tax cuts would be the economic policy centerpiece of his reelection campaign in 2004. In his January 20 State of the Union Address, Bush called on Congress to complete "some unfinished business" by making its earlier tax cuts permanent.[23] The 2003 deficit had climbed above $375 billion, the 2004 deficit was on track to be even higher, and balanced budgets were nowhere in sight. Bush pledged to "cut the deficit in half over the next 5 years," but the administration's deficit reduction plan consisted entirely of nondefense spending cuts.

House Republicans were eager to follow Bush's lead. In late April and early May, the House voted to extend through 2010 any prior tax cuts scheduled to expire before that date. The House passed separate legislation that made the 2001 and 2003 tax cuts permanent. Republicans were, not surprisingly, united behind the tax cut agenda, and election year pressures convinced many Democrats to support parts of that agenda.

Legislation making the 2001 and 2003 tax cuts permanent stood no chance in the Senate, and the Senate also voted to include pay-as-you-go (PAYGO) offsets in its budget resolution to insure that any new tax cuts would be revenue neutral. When the House rejected any PAYGO restrictions, the Senate was forced to move ahead without the procedural protections of a budget resolution. A bipartisan measure was then negotiated that included the "middle class" tax breaks the House had approved—an extension of the 10 percent bracket, marriage penalty tax relief, and AMT exemption limit. It

Table 3.3 Jobs and Growth Tax Relief Reconciliation Act of 2003: Major Provisions and Estimated Revenue Effects, Fiscal Years 2003–2013 (in billions of dollars)

		Revenue Loss (2003–2013)
Individual Income Taxes		
Capital Gains and Dividends	Reduced capital gains and dividend tax rates (15%/5%) for 2003–2007 and (15%/0%) for 2008	–148
Previously Enacted Tax Reductions	Accelerated phase-ins of expanded 10% bracket and reduced marginal rate brackets to 2003; accelerated increase in standard deduction and expanded 15% bracket to 2003; expanded child tax credit to $1,000 for 2003 and 2004	–153
Alternative Minimum Tax (AMT)	Increased exemption limits for AMT (2003–2004)	–18
Corporate Income Taxes		
Depreciation and Expensing	Increased first-year depreciation deduction for qualified property and increased deduction for immediate expensing (2003–2005)	–10
Outlays		
State Fiscal Relief Fund	Temporary fund to increase federal share of Medicaid spending and support government services	–20
Total Cost		−349 billion

Source: Congressional Budget Office, *Cost Estimate: H.R. 2, Jobs and Growth Tax Relief Reconciliation Act of 2003* (Washington, D.C.: Congressional Budget Office, May 23, 2003).

also incorporated Democratic priorities, such as expanded child tax credits for low-income working families.

The House-Senate conference that followed was quickly concluded. The individual income tax extensions and refundable tax credit in the conference bill had an estimated revenue cost of nearly $135 billion.[24] Business tax preference extensions, such as research and development tax credits, raised the total revenue losses above $145 billion. With Democratic presidential nominee John Kerry having endorsed the bill, the Working Families Tax Relief Act easily passed the House and Senate in late September. More than two-thirds of House Democrats and all but one Democratic senator joined Republicans in approving the third major tax cut of George Bush's first term. As with the first two, there were no offsets or other deficit reduction provisions.

The American Jobs Creation Act of 2004, which passed in early October, was the fourth. This bill had its origin in a World Trade Organization ruling that a U.S. subsidy for export businesses was illegal. This subsidy—the Extraterritorial Income Exclusion—had an estimated annual cost of approximately $5 billion, but Congress used its repeal to enact the largest corporate tax cut since 1981. The numerous business tax preferences that were adopted had an estimated revenue cost of $137 billion over ten years, and full offsets were included that made the bill officially revenue neutral.[25] Many of these offsets were considered questionable, and the net revenue loss estimates ranged up to $80 billion, but Congress overwhelmingly passed a tax cut about which even the Bush administration had reservations.

Tax Cuts and Deficits

The $1.6 trillion tax cut that George Bush sponsored in 2001 was the largest since 1981. Republicans in Congress, with few exceptions, were eager to follow Bush's lead, but the dissenters managed to reduce its cost to $1.35 trillion. Even with the onset of war and the abrupt return of deficits, however, the tax cut agenda never paused. Rather, the Bush administration pressed for additional tax cuts each year and succeeded in passing an additional $350 billion measure in 2003 and a nearly $150 billion cut in 2004. Bush was unable to make the tax cuts permanent but otherwise succeeded in securing cumulative cuts that went well beyond the ambitious goals he set originally.

The Bush administration's disregard for deficits was unusual, particularly for an ostensibly conservative Republican administration. Administration officials dismissed the theory that deficits would lead to higher interest rates or curb economic growth.[26] In the lead-up to the 2003 tax cut, Vice President Cheney reportedly declared, "Reagan proved deficits don't matter… . We won the midterms. This is our due."[27]

If Cheney was referring to Reagan's landslide reelection in 1984, his claim was justified. However, it ignored the fact that Reagan had bowed to deficit reduction tax increases in 1982 and 1984 and that congressional Republicans had made balanced budgets the centerpiece of their budget policy program in the mid-1990s. Moreover, in both cases, balanced budgets had provided the rationale for domestic spending cuts to pay for tax cuts. The Bush administration, by comparison, never seriously challenged domestic program commitments during its first term and even pressured congressional Republicans to fund a major new entitlement. With spending, as with taxes, the Bush administration's fiscal program had no modern counterpart with regard to deficit consequences. The result was a deficit record that Republicans would once have denounced but now accepted as the cost of building an electoral majority.

Guns and Butter Redux

During the early years of the Vietnam War, spending for domestic programs continued to grow but generally lagged behind the increases in defense spending. The Bush administration's wartime budgets were even more generous in funding discretionary domestic programs and entitlements. From 2001–2005, defense spending-GDP increased from 2.9 percent to 3.8 percent, but the increase in domestic spending—discretionary and mandatory—over this period was even greater. Nevertheless, Bush ignored the latter, as well as tax cuts, in defending his deficit record.[28] The administration's "war on terrorism" was costly, but there was no real attempt to "maintain overall spending discipline" and to keep deficits "small and temporary," as Bush had promised.[29]

The Defense Budget

During the Clinton presidency, congressional Republicans sharply criticized the lack of adequate funding for the military. The Republican platform in 2000 pointed out that the Clinton "administration has cut defense spending to its lowest percentage of gross domestic product since before Pearl Harbor," and the result was "a shrunken American military … that has eroded its military readiness."[30] President Bush's first budget called for strengthening and modernizing the military but did not project an expensive defense buildup. Real defense spending would increase, but at a modest rate, and defense spending-GDP would continue to decline through the mid-2000s.

The wars in Iraq and Afghanistan required much larger defense budgets than the administration had initially planned. Even so, wartime defense budgets were less than some military officials believed necessary. In particular, the Bush administration assumed that the wars in Afghanistan and Iraq would be relatively brief and did not plan to increase active-duty force levels. As the wars dragged on, however, defense spending continued to rise each year from 2001–2005.

By 2005, defense spending had climbed to 20 percent of the budget and to 3.8 percent of GDP. While somewhat higher than when Bush took office, neither was close to Vietnam War levels and both were below the post-Cold War defense budgets of the early 1990s. While defense spending contributed to the abrupt change from surpluses to deficits under Bush, its fiscal impact was much smaller than that of the tax cuts before and after war had begun. In addition, domestic spending—discretionary and mandatory—rose steadily during Bush's first term, despite the rhetoric about "overall spending discipline."

Domestic Spending

The discretionary spending caps that Congress had adopted in the 1990s were bypassed when the budget moved into surplus. In 2002, the caps officially expired, and no attempt was made to renew them as part of another deficit reduction program. From the outset, Bush administration budgets supported increased funding for politically popular domestic programs, and Congress usually approved even more generous funding. From 2001–2005, domestic appropriations climbed steadily, as both parties in Congress avoided prolonged appropriations battles.

From 2000–2002, for example, the growth in discretionary domestic spending outpaced the increase in defense spending. This reflected reconstruction assistance and other emergency spending after the September 11 attacks, but "regular" programs such as education, energy and water development, and conservation and environmental protection also benefited from broad bipartisan support for additional funding.[31] In numerous cases, Congress raised spending above the president's budget requests, and the administration's occasional threats to veto excessive spending were never enforced.

With the Democrats in control of the Senate from mid-2001 through 2002, for example, the administration could not enforce a nondefense spending freeze. In 2003, with Republicans in control of both chambers, Congress adopted discretionary spending limits in line with the administration's budget, but enforcement again proved difficult. Appropriation bills were delayed, continuing resolutions were necessary, and the omnibus appropriations bill approved in January 2004 contained numerous congressional add-ons for domestic programs.

A more concerted push by the administration and House Republicans to tighten discretionary spending limits in 2004 again stalled the appropriations process. The House and the Senate did not enact final appropriations for fiscal year 2005 until after the November election. Most domestic appropriations were funded within the overall cap that Bush and congressional Republicans had agreed to earlier in the year, but Congress then approved disaster relief and other emergency spending that raised actual spending well above the cap. Discretionary domestic spending in 2005 amounted to $436 billion, roughly $45 billion higher than in 2003. The increase in defense outlays during the 108th Congress—approximately $88 billion over a two-year period—was about double the increase in domestic spending, but the latter still grew by more than 10 percent with a Republican Congress.

Despite occasional protests from fiscal conservatives, Republican House and Senate leaders, as well as the Bush administration, showed little interest in "spending austerity." There was no appetite in Congress for program terminations, although the administration dutifully recommended some every year, nor was there widespread support for spending caps or strict spending discipline. In 2004 and 2005, for example, congressional earmarks, which directed funds toward specific districts and states, continued to proliferate at an estimated cost of more than $90 billion.[32]

Entitlements

The Bush administration's "guns and butter" fiscal program was even more evident in the case of social welfare entitlements. Ronald Reagan failed to retrench entitlements but did block their expansion. Bush sponsored the biggest increase in the Medicare program since its inception, and he was much more supportive of public assistance entitlements than Reagan or the "tax cut/spending cut" Republicans of 1995–1996. Even the few minor entitlements the administration slated for "reform," such as farm subsidies, managed to survive.

The Bush administration's 2001 Social Security reform plan, for example, conceded that the program's long-term financing problems were serious but claimed that they could be resolved without benefit cuts or tax increases.[33] Bush promised that there would be no change in "existing benefits for current retirees or near-retirees" or "disability or survivors' components." Instead, he pledged to "save" Social Security surpluses to bolster the system's finances and to introduce "individually controlled, voluntary personal retirement accounts … [to] augment the Social Security safety net." With the disappearance of budget surpluses, Social Security's financing challenge was more urgent, but the administration carefully avoided any discussion of benefit adjustments or cost savings in what was at the time the federal government's largest spending program.

The Medicare Prescription Drug, Improvement, and Modernization Act of 2003 had an estimated ten-year cost of $400 billion and represented a remarkable change in the Republican party's approach to the welfare state. Republicans had opposed the Clinton administration's efforts to add prescription drug coverage to the Medicare program and indeed had tried to scale back the entire program as part of their balanced-budget reconciliation plan in 1995. In 2001, however, President Bush had proposed "better coverage options … and higher quality of care" for Medicare beneficiaries, the most important change being the addition of prescription drug coverage.[34] The estimated ten-year cost of Bush's Medicare "modernization" plan was $153 billion, an amount Democrats criticized as grossly inadequate. In 2002, House Republicans approved a costlier version of the Bush plan that relied on private insurers, which Senate Democrats blocked.

In 2003, Bush announced that prescription drug coverage was his domestic legislative priority, and Republicans included a $400 billion Medicare allowance in their budget resolution. At this point, wartime spending was mounting as was the deficit, which gave some Republicans pause about moving ahead but also persuaded key Democrats that costlier options would not be available any time soon. On June 12, the Senate Finance Committee reported out a bill that had bipartisan backing, and the Senate approved it by a 76–21 margin two weeks later.

The Senate-passed measure could not provide coverage for all prescription drug costs given the $400 billion limit. Instead, it included premiums and deductibles for beneficiaries, along with a complicated coverage formula. The new prescription drug subsidy would be applied to annual expenses up to a certain threshold, but beneficiaries would then be responsible for all costs up to a second threshold. Above this second threshold, "catastrophic coverage" would apply, with the federal subsidy covering nearly all costs. The compromise was criticized by conservatives for its high costs and by liberals for its limited coverage, but majorities in both parties found it acceptable.

In the House, a new $400 billion entitlement did not appeal to Republicans hoping to narrow, rather than expand, the federal government's role in healthcare. Democratic opposition was also more widespread than in the Senate, given the coverage limitations in the bill drafted by the Ways and Means and the Energy and Commerce Committees. Close party-line votes in committee were mirrored on the floor, and the Republican leadership barely managed to hold together a 216–215 majority.

These intraparty tensions nearly derailed the conference committee that followed. After four months, the conference reached agreement on a coverage formula and included some "free market" options, such as health savings accounts, to placate conservatives. Conferees also provided $25 billion in additional funding for hospitals and healthcare providers in rural areas. Despite an endorsement from the AARP, the conference bill was nearly defeated in the House. The initial tally showed a 218–216 majority voting against the bill, but House leaders refused to close the vote. After nearly three hours, a number of Republican opponents were persuaded to switch sides, and the bill passed by a 220–215 margin. The Senate vote, three days later, was 54–44, Democratic support having dropped because of the privatization options added to the conference bill.

President Bush signed the bill into law on December 8, hailing it as "the greatest advance in health care coverage for America's seniors since the founding of Medicare."[35] It was also a costly addition to the nation's second-largest entitlement program and a further indication that the Republican party's challenge to popular entitlements was over. Fiscal conservatives in the party would continue to complain about big government and unchecked domestic spending, but the Bush administration's unwavering commitment to tax cuts placated even these critics.

Bush's "compassionate conservatism" also benefited public assistance entitlements that Republicans had sought to curtail in the past. The EITC was expanded in 2001, federally funded extensions of unemployment benefits were approved in 2002 and 2003, retirement and disability benefits for veterans were increased in 2003, and a new veterans' healthcare benefit was added as well. The Medicare prescription drug benefit in 2003 augmented Medicaid, providing coverage for so-called dual eligibles qualifying for both programs. As a result, spending-GDP for Medicare, Medicaid, and other means-tested entitlements climbed to its highest level in decades during Bush's first term.

The Second Term: Temporary Deficits Prove Permanent

In 2004, George Bush was reelected and Republicans increased their House and Senate majorities. Unlike 2000, Bush managed to win the national popular vote, but his Electoral College majority was only slightly higher, and the

Republican congressional majorities were nowhere close to that which Democrats had enjoyed during the 1960s and 1970s. For those anticipating a permanent Republican majority, 2004 was a disappointment, and fiscal conservatives now complained that Bush's deficit record had blurred the party's electoral message.

Neither Bush nor these Republican critics, however, had any interest in raising taxes. Instead the deficit reduction goal that Bush announced at the beginning of his second term was feasible—cutting the deficit in half by the end of his presidency—but depended entirely on unspecified cutbacks in domestic spending. On the revenue side, Bush renewed his push to make the 2001 and 2003 tax cuts permanent and proposed a new round of individual and business tax credits.

The Republican-controlled 109th Congress agreed to curb the growth of discretionary domestic spending but was no more willing than its predecessors had been to cut entitlements. In addition, the nearly $1.3 trillion in deficits from 2002–2005 had strengthened Senate opposition to new tax cuts. As a result, tax and spending policy changes in 2005 and 2006 were relatively minor, and the Democratic takeover of Congress in the 2006 mid-term elections meant that tax increases would have to be part of any deficit reduction program. To no one's surprise, bipartisan deficit reduction that included taxes was rejected outright by the Bush administration, and the structural deficit problem remained in place. The Great Recession that began in December 2007 then raised deficits to new heights. The 2008 and 2009 deficits totaled nearly $1.9 trillion, and debt-GDP at the end of the Bush presidency was at its highest level since the early 1950s.

Taxes: The "Unfinished Business"

In 2005, President Bush presented Congress with another tax cut plan, this one totaling $1.5 trillion for fiscal years 2005–2014.[36] The 2001 and 2003 tax cuts were scheduled to expire in 2010, and Bush was determined to make these cuts permanent. Bush was also asking Congress to approve an array of new tax preferences affecting retirement savings, healthcare costs, and private sector research and development.

This time, the House-Senate Republican split gave the president little of what had been requested. The budget resolution that Congress adopted in April included an allowance of just $70 billion for a reconciliation tax cut, and disagreements between the House and the Senate over what this allowance would be used for stalled final action until the spring of 2006. In the interim, the Republican House passed several permanent estate tax measures that did not have reconciliation protections, and none of these managed to reach the floor of the Senate.

Another House priority was preventing a scheduled increase in capital gains and dividend tax rates. These rates had been reduced to a 15 percent maximum in 2003, but the revenue losses from this reduction were so substantial that Congress had limited their duration. Unless Congress approved an extension, a 20 percent capital gains tax rate would be reinstated in 2009, and dividends would then be taxed at higher ordinary income rates. Given that reconciliation protection would almost certainly be needed to move this extension through the Senate, House leaders decided to spend the $70 billion reconciliation allowance on a two-year, 15 percent tax rate extension.

Another extension was needed for the AMT. Again, Congress had used temporary increases in the AMT exemption level to keep "official" revenue losses within prescribed limits. These AMT "patches" had been included in the 2001, 2003, and 2004 tax cuts, with the last of these scheduled to expire at the end of 2005. An estimated 19 million taxpayers would then be subject to higher income taxes under the AMT, compared to 3.6 million in 2005.[37] The vast majority of those affected would be "middle-class" taxpayers, and both parties agreed that these taxpayers should be protected against an unwarranted tax increase. House Republicans therefore planned to raise the AMT exemption level in a freestanding bill, in effect adding $30 billion to the $70 billion reconciliation tax cut.

Senate Republicans, however, decided that the $70 billion reconciliation limit would apply to any new tax cuts, and the AMT exemption increase was included in their reconciliation tax bill. After months of deadlock, a conference committee compromise was agreed in the spring of 2006. In order to accommodate both the tax rate reductions and the AMT exemption reductions, $20 billion in "revenue raisers" was added to keep the net tax cut within the $70 billion reconciliation ceiling. These revenue offsets, which included new tax withholding and tax paying requirements, were not officially classified as tax increases.

In any case, the Tax Increase Prevention and Reconciliation Act of 2005, which was actually signed into law on May 17, 2006, was a very limited measure by Bush standards, and the 109th Congress came to a close with none of the permanent tax relief Bush had hoped to secure. In 2007, Bush faced Democratic majorities in the House and the Senate but still renewed his call for permanent tax cuts. At this point, estimated revenue losses from income tax rate cuts and repeal of the estate tax had increased substantially and other tax cuts in the Bush package raised the total to $1.75 trillion.[38] In fact, the true cost was considerably higher, since the AMT exemption increase was for only one year. Making this provision permanent would have added $875 billion to what was already the biggest tax cut Bush had proposed.

The only tax cut Democrats would consider was the AMT exemption increase. The House and the Senate adopted a budget resolution in May providing for a temporary AMT exemption increase but also requiring tax increases to offset its roughly $50 billion cost. The House then passed the AMT exemption increase and extended a number of expiring individual and business tax preferences. In order to comply with the revenue-neutral, or

PAYGO, requirement, the House raised taxes on private equity firms, hedge funds, and multinational corporations. House Republicans unanimously opposed the AMT bill that included these tax increases, and Senate Republicans then blocked it from coming to the Senate floor. Democrats were forced to drop the PAYGO offsets, and a stripped-down AMT bill of more than $50 billion was passed in December.

The AMT was back in 2008, as was the attempt by Democrats to revive PAYGO controls. Democrats succeeded in attaching $40 billion in revenue offsets to a $150 billion package of popular tax extenders, including the AMT, that passed in October.[39] Earlier in the year, however, a bipartisan economic stimulus bill had been approved that included refundable tax credits for individuals and families and increased depreciation and expensing deductions for businesses. This bill contained no offsets and was expected to add more than $150 billion to an already soaring 2008 deficit.[40]

The Great Recession was so severe that short-term tax cut stimulus overrode any deficit considerations, and its duration precluded any consideration of deficit reduction tax increases long after Bush left office. More importantly, the Democratic party had adopted a tax policy strategy designed to compete in elections rather than balance the budget. Its 2004 platform promised to cut taxes for "98 percent of Americans" and "99 percent of American businesses."[41] The 2008 platform included "additional tax cuts for middle class families" and the elimination of "federal income taxes for millions of retirees."[42] The tax rates of the 1990s that had done so much to help to balance the budget would be reinstated for high-income taxpayers only. Of course, Republicans could be counted on to oppose any tax increases for any group, which pretty much guaranteed that structural deficits would continue indefinitely.

Spending: Cuts and Retrenchment

In 2005, President Bush reversed course and revived the domestic retrenchment theme of the Reagan presidency. The budget he submitted to Congress on February 7 was described as the "most austere fiscal blueprint of his presidency to date."[43] It included more than 150 program terminations and reductions and the "tightest" discretionary domestic spending limits "since the Reagan Administration."[44] Bush also called for cuts in Medicaid and other entitlements totaling more than $60 billion over a five-year period.[45]

A supportive Republican Congress delivered some of what Bush requested in 2005, but these savings were dwarfed by disaster relief and other emergency spending that raised actual outlays well above spending targets. One year later, this brief experiment in spending restraint came to an end as House and Senate Republicans battled over domestic spending cuts. Congress failed to pass a budget resolution, Bush's second round of entitlement program cutbacks was completely ignored, and final action on appropriations bills was delayed until the following year.

Bush mounted an even more aggressive effort to reduce domestic spending with the Democratic-controlled Congress in 2007. Protracted conflicts over domestic appropriations yielded mixed results, and entitlement "reforms" were rejected out of hand by Democratic leaders. The 2007 deficit was the smallest since 2002, but domestic spending-GDP remained well above pre-Bush levels, and this improvement quickly came to an end with the economic collapse in 2008.

The Entitlement Stalemate

In 2001, President Bush had endorsed "individually controlled, voluntary personal retirement accounts that will augment the Social Security safety net" and appointed a commission to study financing options.[46] A reform plan was submitted to Congress in 2005, and its core proposal was to allow younger cohorts of workers to invest a portion of their Social Security payroll taxes in private retirement accounts. The investment returns on these accounts would presumably be sufficiently high to fund retirement incomes well above what Social Security alone could provide. The "guaranteed" benefits from Social Security could then be reduced.

Bush's Social Security plan was aimed at long-term financing issues and had nothing to do with short-term deficit reduction. Indeed, the transition costs of diverting payroll taxes would have required additional borrowing, an obvious concern given the already substantial deficit problem. The intense Democratic opposition to partial privatization went well beyond transition costs, but Republican support for Bush's plan was shaky from the outset. Sporadic attempts to engage the Ways and Means and the Finance Committees were unsuccessful in 2005, and Social Security reform was missing entirely from the congressional agenda in 2006.

Bush's efforts to curb the growth of other entitlement programs were a major part of his deficit reduction plan, but Congress approved only a fraction of his proposed cuts in 2005 and nothing of consequence thereafter. Bush's entitlement savings target of more than $60 billion in 2005 was gradually lowered as House and Senate Republicans struggled to reach agreement on specific program cuts. Reconciliation instructions mandating $35 billion in entitlement program savings over a five-year period were included in the budget resolution that Congress adopted in late April. It then took nine months to put a reconciliation bill together, and the end result was disappointing.

The Deficit Reduction Omnibus Reconciliation Act of 2005 contained net savings of $38.8 billion.[47] Its reductions in Medicaid, agriculture subsidies, and student loans were much smaller than Bush had recommended. In addition, approximately $11 billion of the estimated savings had nothing to do with social welfare entitlements—over $7 billion in revenues from broadcast spectrum auctions to television broadcasters was designated as a deficit reduction saving, as was an additional $3.6 billion in increased private employer premiums for federal pension insurance. A projected saving of more than $6 billion in Medicare was also suspect, since existing benefits were unchanged. Still, this less-than-heroic measure barely made it through Congress. The Senate vote on December 21 was 51–50, as Vice President Cheney cast another of his tiebreaking votes on controversial budget legislation. The House vote, which was delayed until February 1, 2006, was 216–214. In both chambers, Democratic opposition was unanimous.

Bush's second round of entitlement reforms in 2006 largely targeted Medicare. The savings goal in this instance was more than $70 billion over a five-year period, but the proposed Medicare changes did not include benefit cuts.[48] Instead, the administration's plan relied on management initiatives to improve "productivity and efficiency" and "program integrity" and to foster greater competition among healthcare providers. Whether any of this was serious did not really matter, since Congress was not about to revisit entitlement policy in an election year. The House managed to pass a budget resolution with mandatory program reconciliation instructions, but the required savings were less than $7 billion and both Medicare and Medicaid were exempted from any changes. The Senate's budget resolution did not include entitlement savings of any kind. Other disagreements over domestic spending kept the House and the Senate from passing any budget resolution for fiscal year 2007.

In 2007, the Bush administration's entitlement "reforms" were even more ambitious, with a proposed $95 billion in five-year savings, nearly two-thirds of which involved Medicare.[49] House and Senate Democrats responded with a budget resolution that included $70 billion in increased entitlement spending, most of which was designated for expanding the State Children's Health Insurance Program (SCHIP) the Clinton administration had established a decade earlier. Bush vetoed two SCHIP authorization bills that provided increased funding, both of which Democrats failed to override. In December, Bush signed a third bill that maintained spending at baseline levels and suspended scheduled reimbursement cuts in Medicare payments to physicians. Congress had mandated these a decade earlier but never allowed them to take effect. These latest suspensions, while costly, had bipartisan support.

The 2008 Bush budget renewed the call for Medicare and Medicaid program reforms, but Congress predictably ignored these along with lesser entitlement changes Bush had proposed. Democrats then went on to pass an increase in agriculture subsidies over Bush's veto in June and a Medicare physician reimbursement increase over a veto in July. Congress also established additional funding for veterans' education programs. The administration opposed this increase, which had an estimated cost of more than $60 billion over ten years, but it was added to an emergency war supplemental funding bill that Bush signed on June 30.[50]

Discretionary Spending

With tax increases off the table and very little, if any, success in curbing the growth of entitlement programs, the Bush administration focused its deficit reduction efforts on discretionary spending. With defense, the hope was that the large supplementals that funded the Afghanistan and Iraq wars from 2002–2004 would gradually decrease as these wars wound down.

Unfortunately, the military situation in Iraq deteriorated during 2005 and 2006, and President Bush ordered additional troops to be deployed in 2007. Spending for the Iraq and Afghanistan wars fell from $88 billion in 2004 to $70 billion in 2005 but more than doubled, to $152 billion, over the next two years.[51] Defense spending-GDP levels had fallen below 3 percent in 2001, rose to 3.8 percent in 2004–2007, and then climbed above 4 percent in 2008.

A second obstacle the administration faced in curbing discretionary spending was the enormous increase in emergency appropriations for national disaster relief after Hurricane Katrina struck in late August 2005. During Bush's first term, regular disaster relief appropriations totaled $3.6 billion and supplemental appropriations accounted for an additional $14.7 billion.[52] Regular and supplemental appropriations in 2005 were more than $68 billion, and nearly $27 billion in additional funding was provided from 2006–2008. Moreover, these figures understate the full cost of disaster relief, since a number of departments and agencies supply funding out of separate appropriations.

In 2005, for example, the budget resolution adopted by the House and the Senate included the $843 billion discretionary spending limit that the president had requested. In order to keep the appropriations process on track, Republicans agreed to shift additional funds to domestic programs but final appropriations remained within the $843 billion ceiling.[53] The defense appropriations bill, however, did not include funding for the Iraq and Afghanistan wars. An emergency war supplemental of $82 billion was approved in May, and emergency funding bills were also enacted for veterans' healthcare and hurricane relief. None of these supplementals counted against the discretionary spending caps. In total, emergency supplemental appropriations exceeded $200 billion, with most of this funding added to the fiscal year 2005 budget and the remainder to 2006.

In 2007, neither the House nor the Senate could agree on a discretionary spending limit or the level of domestic appropriations. The Senate's discretionary spending limit was $9 billion higher than the $873 billion in the Bush administration and House budget plans, and the Senate also provided for additional funding through advance appropriations if necessary.[54] With the House and the Bush administration demanding domestic spending cuts and Senate Republicans insisting on increases, none of the regular appropriations bills was passed by the September 30 deadline and only the defense and homeland security bills cleared Congress by the end of the year. With their intraparty disagreements unresolved, it was left to the incoming Democratic Congress to pass the continuing resolution that provided funding for the remainder of fiscal year 2006. Republicans did approve, however, a $94.5 billion war and disaster relief supplemental for 2006 that was entirely separate from their battle over discretionary spending limits.

Ironically, the Bush administration was able to cut domestic spending in 2007, when Democrats took control of the House and Senate. The first skirmish was a Bush veto on May 1 of an emergency war supplemental, which included deadlines for withdrawing troops from Iraq as well as additional funding for domestic programs. Democrats failed to override the veto, and a revised supplemental Bush signed on May 25 eliminated troop withdrawal deadlines and most of the domestic add-ons.

Bush then turned his attention to domestic appropriations bills, threatening to veto any that exceeded his budget requests. The House proceeded to add funding anyway, but Senate Republicans helped to stall the appropriations process, and a continuing resolution was needed to provide temporary funding after September 30. In November, the House and the Senate finally cleared a Labor, Health and Human Services, and Education appropriations bill that exceeded Bush's budget by $10 billion, and a veto quickly followed. When the override attempt failed, Democrats agreed to an omnibus appropriations bill that complied with Bush's spending limits in mid-December. For the first time in Bush's presidency, discretionary domestic spending was reduced, from $461 billion in 2006 to $459 billion in 2007.

The final year of Bush's presidency was marked by emergency spending and related financial initiatives to combat the Great Recession. Only a fraction of these massive financial commitments was reflected in discretionary spending totals. Loans and credit subsidies, for example, were not included, and the Federal Reserve's emergency measures were of course entirely outside the regular budget. It was necessary, however, to raise the statutory debt limit to accommodate the substantial borrowing necessary to stabilize the housing and financial markets, and House and Senate Democrats moved this legislation forward in a timely fashion. Notably, much of the sharpest criticism of the soaring deficit and debt obligations came from congressional Republicans, particularly in the House.

In the spring of 2008, Democrats adopted a budget resolution that set discretionary domestic spending limits well in excess of the president's budget. With Bush again threatening vetoes, a six-month continuing resolution was enacted in the fall that funded domestic programs at current levels. The final decisions on domestic appropriations for 2009 were left to the president and Congress chosen in the November elections.

When the Bush administration singled out domestic spending as its deficit reduction target in 2005, it was echoing the Republican retrenchment themes of the 1980s and 1990s. With entitlements, it encountered the same problems that Reagan had faced—strong Democratic opposition and weak Republican support in Congress. Reagan's efforts to cut discretionary domestic spending were much more successful. Given the steep rise in spending during the 1970s, with discretionary domestic spending-GDP levels climbing to nearly 5 percent, there was ample room to cut spending, and Reagan proceeded to do so.

When Bush took office, by comparison, discretionary domestic spending was just above 3 percent, and the 2003–2004 peaks under Bush were approximately 3.5 percent. There were certainly deficit reduction savings available in this part of the budget, but since it accounted for less than 20 percent of total spending, the feasible cuts were relatively small. As a senior Budget Committee Democrat complained at the time, "No one can argue that these programs are the source of the deficit, because they've barely increased over the last several years. Cuts like this hurt, but in the end they barely make a dent in the deficit."[55]

In 2005 and 2006, deficits did decline, but discretionary domestic spending cuts had little to do with this improvement. As Table 3.4 shows, the most important policy component of the fiscal reversal from 2000 to 2007 was the tax cuts that lowered revenue-GDP levels by two percentage points. This decline would have been even greater without the increase in corporate revenues. Republicans generally agreed that corporate tax rates were too high, but the 2001 and 2003 tax cuts left these rates unchanged. The increase in spending-GDP levels from 2000 to 2007 was substantial for defense but also for domestic programs, with the growth in entitlements alone equaling the wartime defense surge. The only spending category that declined over this period was interest payments. The very low interest rates in effect from mid-2001 through the fall of 2005 greatly reduced the cost of rising debt levels and kept total spending-GDP levels from rising above 20 percent.

Table 3.4 The Surplus to Deficit Reversal, 2000–2007 (as a percentage of GDP)

FY 2000 =	*+$236 billion*		*FY 2007 =*	*–$161 billion*
Revenues =	20.0		Revenues =	18.0
Outlays =	17.7		Outlays =	19.1
Surplus =	+2.3		Deficit =	–1.1

	FY 2000	*FY 2007*	*Change*
Revenues			
Individual	9.9	8.1	–1.8
Corporation	2.0	2.6	+0.6
Payroll	6.5	6.1	–0.4
Other	1.6	1.2	–0.4
	20.0	18.0	–2.0
Outlays			
Discretionary Defense	2.9	3.8	+0.9
Discretionary Nondefense	3.2	3.5	+0.3
Mandatory Programmatic	9.8	10.7	+0.9
Net Interest	2.2	1.7	–0.5
	18.1	19.7	+1.6
Offsetting Receipts	–0.4	–0.6	–0.2
	17.7	19.1	+1.4

Source: *Historical Tables, Budget of the United States Government, Fiscal Year 2021* (Washington, D.C.: Government Printing Office, 2020), Tables 1.1, 1.2, 2.3, 8.4.

The Return of Deficit Politics

In 2001, George W. Bush inherited the most positive budget numbers of any president in the modern era. Surpluses had totaled more than $430 billion over the previous three years, the 2001 surplus was expected to reach $280 billion, and baseline surpluses were estimated at several hundred trillion dollars over the next decade. Publicly held debt had already been lowered by more than $430 billion and an additional $260 billion reduction was projected for 2001.

Eight years later, the federal budget was in dismal shape, and the budget outlook was even worse. The Bush deficits from 2002–2008 were more than $2.1 trillion, the 2009 deficit was on track to reach $1.4 trillion, and debt-GDP was climbing to the highest level since the early 1950s. The deficit that developed during the first year of the Bush presidency was the result of recession and war and the 2001 tax cut. As the economy recovered in 2002, fairly limited changes in taxes and spending would have curbed, or even eliminated, deficits in the years that followed. Instead, the new tax cuts that Bush and congressional Republicans chose to implement widened the deficit gap, their deficit reduction spending cuts never materialized, and Bush's fiscal legacy was the return of deficit politics.

Quite remarkably, the Republican party's support for Bush's "pro-growth tax cuts" had become stronger as the deficit consequences mounted. For Republicans in Congress, particularly fiscal conservatives, Bush's failure to shrink the federal government's domestic role was the sole cause of deficits. Looking ahead, this myopic view of budget policy left little room for bipartisan compromises on deficit reduction. The Bush administration's promise of low taxes financed by painless domestic spending cuts would prove to be especially unhelpful in keeping deficits and debt at tolerable levels.

The 2008 Republican platform, for example, laid out an unapologetic defense of the Bush tax cuts: "Republicans lowered taxes in 2001 and 2003 in order to encourage economic growth… . It worked."[56] In order to "grow the economy" moving forward, more tax relief was needed. In addition to making the 2001 and 2003 tax cuts permanent, corporate tax rates should be cut and new tax benefits provided for individuals and families.

In fact, there had been a roughly six-year economic expansion under Bush. In the period between the 2001 recession and the economic collapse in 2008, the annual rate of GDP growth had averaged 2.6 percent, and total civilian employment had increased by 6.6 percent.[57] The Bush expansion, however, was shorter and less robust than the "high tax" expansion under Clinton that produced annual average GDP growth of 3.7 percent and job growth of 15.5 percent. It was equally unimpressive when measured against other "high-tax regimes" in the post-World War II period.[58] There are obviously many factors that affect economic growth, including monetary policy, and the impact of stand-alone tax cuts on long-term growth is more complicated and uncertain than Republican tax cut advocates are willing to admit.[59]

In addition, the Bush tax cuts were not "financed" by spending cuts but rather by borrowing. An objective assessment of the Bush tax cuts must take into account fiscal consequences, particularly when the deficit and debt effects are substantial and prolonged. In retrospect, it seems reasonably clear that the Bush administration, along with most House and Senate Republicans, squandered the hard-won budgetary equilibrium of the late 1990s for a tax agenda whose economic benefits were comparatively meager. Nonetheless, Republican support for tax cuts, and opposition to tax increases, was more fervent at the end of Bush's presidency than at the beginning.

As for deficits, Republicans continued to claim that budgets could be balanced by cutting domestic spending despite three decades of evidence to the contrary. The Reagan administration's ambitious domestic retrenchment plans had failed to gain congressional support, even among Republicans. In the mid-1990s, House and Senate Republicans passed a far-reaching entitlement retrenchment plan to finance future tax cuts. Bill Clinton's veto blocked that effort, and the public's negative response discouraged Republicans from trying to resurrect it.

Under Bush, the Republican congressional majorities from 2003–2007 had ample opportunity to scale back entitlements and domestic spending, and the readily available budget reconciliation process to assist them, but never came close to taking meaningful action. They did, however, approve a new Medicare prescription entitlement in 2003 and a variety of smaller entitlement expansions around the same time. When Bush unveiled his domestic spending reform agenda in 2005, House and Senate Republicans found it difficult to agree on minor savings from discretionary programs, much less meaningful cutbacks in popular entitlements like Social Security, Medicare, and Medicaid. After four years of unified Republican control, spending-GDP for domestic programs—entitlements and discretionary—was well above pre-Bush levels. Indeed, the domestic spending increase over this period was roughly comparable to the change in defense spending after 9/11.

After the 2008 elections, the immediate challenge for Barack Obama and congressional Democrats was the Great Recession. In planning an economic stimulus program, they faced some formidable constraints. Since the Bush tax cuts were still in effect, the cyclical fall in revenues was so steep that broad-based tax stimulus was not a realistic option. With the structural deficits and debt increases Bush had accumulated during his tenure, the budgetary margin for an aggressive spending stimulus was considerably smaller than it otherwise might have been.

In terms of political consequences, Vice President Cheney's assertion that "deficits don't matter" was probably accurate at the time. Deficits did not hinder Bush's reelection, and the plummeting approval ratings during his second term had more to do with feckless government performance at home (Hurricane Katrina) and abroad (Iraq) than the state of federal finances. Deficits did matter, however, for Bush's successor, just as they had for Reagan's.

Notes

1 Congressional Budget Office, *The Budget and Economic Outlook: Fiscal Years 2002 to 2011* (Washington, D.C.: Congressional Budget Office, 2001), xiii.
2 *Budget of the United States Government, Fiscal Year 2002* (Washington, D.C.: Government Printing Office, 2001), 3, 7.
3 *Budget of the United States Government, Fiscal Year 2002*, 3, 7.
4 Steven A. Bank, Kirk J. Stark, and Joseph J. Thorndike, *War and Taxes* (Washington, D.C.: Urban Institute Press, 2008), xii, 164.
5 *Budget of the United States Government, Fiscal Year 2003* (Washington, D.C.: Government Printing Office, 2002), 13.
6 *Budget of the United States Government, Fiscal Year 2003*, 13, 39.
7 *Budget of the United States Government, Fiscal Year 2006* (Washington, D.C.: Government Printing Office, 2005), 2.
8 Congressional Budget Office, *The Budget and Economic Outlook: Fiscal Years 2003 to 2012* (Washington, D.C.: Congressional Budget Office, 2002), xiii.
9 *Congress and the Nation, 2001–2004* (Washington, D.C.: Congressional Quarterly, 2006), 92.
10 *Congress and the Nation, 2001–2004*, 92–93.
11 *Congress and the Nation, 2001–2004*, 93.
12 *Congress and the Nation, 2001–2004*, 93.
13 The Byrd Rule allows a point of order to be raised in the Senate when a reconciliation bill increases deficits or reduces surpluses in fiscal years beyond the period covered by the budget resolution. The point of order objection can only be waived by a three-fifths (60) majority vote.
14 *Congress and the Nation, 2001–2004*, 94.
15 The so-called trigger provision apparently originated with Bush's first Treasury secretary, Paul O'Neill, who had long advocated for balanced budgets. See Iwan W. Morgan, *The Age of Deficits: Presidents and Unbalanced Budgets from Jimmy Carter to George W. Bush* (Lawrence: University Press of Kansas, 2009), 223–224. O'Neill's disagreements with Bush policies led to his dismissal at the end of 2002.
16 *Congress and the Nation, 2001–2004*, 98.
17 *Budget of the United States Government, Fiscal Year 2002*, 7.
18 *Budget of the United States Government, Fiscal Year 2003*, 8.
19 *Budget of the United States Government, Fiscal Year 2003*, 6, 33.
20 *Budget of the United States Government, Fiscal Year 2004* (Washington, D.C.: Government Printing Office, 2003), 1, 25.
21 *Congress and the Nation, 2001–2004*, 105.
22 *Budget of the United States Government, Fiscal Year 2004*, 27.
23 *Public Papers of the President: George W. Bush, 2004, Book 1* (Washington, D.C.: Government Printing Office, 2007), 86.
24 *Congress and the Nation, 2001–2004*, 114.
25 *Congress and the Nation, 2001–2004*, 114.
26 Morgan, *The Age of Deficits*, 217–218.
27 As quoted in Morgan, *The Age of Deficits*, 219.
28 *Budget of the United States Government, Fiscal Year 2004*, 1.
29 *Budget of the United States Government, Fiscal Year 2003*, 39.
30 "2000 Republican Party Platform, July 31, 2000," The American Presidency Project, www.presidency.ucsb.edu/documents/2000-republican-party-platform.
31 *Congress and the Nation, 2001–2004*, 51–56.
32 *Earmarks in Appropriations Acts: FY1994, FY1996, FY1998, FY2000, FY2002, FY2004, FY2005* (Washington, D.C.: Congressional Research Service, January 26, 2006), 2, 7, 10, 12, 14, 17, 23, 28, 30, 32, 37, 41, 44, 49.
33 *Budget of the United States Government, Fiscal Year 2002*, 116–117.

34 *Budget of the United States Government, Fiscal Year 2002*, 107–108.
35 *Congress and the Nation, 2001–2004*, 501.
36 *Congress and the Nation, 2005–2008* (Washington, D.C.: Congressional Quarterly, 2010), 69.
37 *Congressional Quarterly Almanac, 2006* (Washington, D.C.: Congressional Quarterly, 2007), 15-3.
38 *Congressional Quarterly Almanac, 2007* (Washington, D.C.: Congressional Quarterly, 2008), 4-4.
39 *Congressional Quarterly Almanac, 2008* (Washington, D.C.: Congressional Quarterly, 2009), 4-11–4-14.
40 *Congressional Quarterly Almanac, 2008*, 7-17–7-19.
41 "2004 Democratic Party Platform, July 27, 2004," The American Presidency Project, www.presidency.ucsb.edu/documents/2004-democratic-party-platform.
42 "2008 Democratic Party Platform, August 25, 2008," The American Presidency Project, www.presidency.ucsb.edu/documents/2008-democratic-party-platform.
43 *Congress and the Nation, 2005–2008*, 67.
44 *Budget of the United States Government, Fiscal Year 2006*, 5.
45 *Congress and the Nation, 2005–2008*, 67.
46 *Budget of the United States Government, Fiscal Year 2002*, 116–117.
47 *Congress and the Nation, 2005–2008*, 81.
48 Office of Management and Budget, *Major Savings and Reforms in the President's 2007 Budget* (Washington, D.C.: Government Printing Office, 2006), 165–166.
49 *Congress and the Nation, 2005–2008*, 110.
50 *Congress and the Nation, 2005–2008*, 593.
51 Congressional Budget Office, *The Budget and Economic Outlook: Fiscal Years 2008 to 2018* (Washington, D.C.: Congressional Budget Office, 2008), 7.
52 *The Disaster Relief Fund: Overview and Issues* (Washington, D.C.: Congressional Research Service, November 13, 2020), 35.
53 *Congress and the Nation, 2005–2008*, 72.
54 *Congress and the Nation, 2005–2008*, 98.
55 *Congress and the Nation, 2005–2008*, 67.
56 "2008 Republican Party Platform, September 1, 2008," The American Presidency Project, www.presidency.ucsb.edu/documents/2008-republican-party-platform.
57 Morgan, *The Age of Deficits*, 247–248.
58 Jane G. Gravelle and Donald J. Marples, *Tax Rates and Economic Growth* (Washington, D.C.: Congressional Research Service, January 2, 2014), 5.
59 William G. Gale and Andrew A. Samwick, "Effects of Income Tax Changes on Economic Growth" (Washington, D.C.: Tax Policy Center and Brookings Institution, 2016), 14–18.

4 Stabilizing the Deficit

The Obama Presidency

In 2008, Democrats gained control of the presidency and Congress for the first time since 1994. Barack H. Obama's victory in the presidential race was decisive, and Democratic majorities in the House (257–178) and the Senate (58–41) were the largest since 1992.[1] The Obama administration also inherited the most serious economic crisis since the Great Depression, record deficits that would almost certainly grow larger, and an opposition party that attacked its fiscal program from the beginning.[2] The administration's first priority—an economic stimulus bill passed by Congress in February 2009—was unanimously opposed by House Republicans and received only three Republican votes in the Senate. From that point on, partisan rancor in Congress intensified, and budget policy was a constant target.

In 2010, Democrats succeeded in enacting healthcare reform but failed to pass a second round of economic stimulus or to keep the appropriations process on track. The Republican takeover of the House in the 2010 midterms, abetted by a Tea Party insurgency that moved the party further to the right, upended the budget process. The remainder of Obama's presidency was marked by an extreme version of divided party control that featured government shutdown threats (and an actual 16-day shutdown in 2013) and debt limit brinkmanship that would once have been unthinkable.

The fragile compromises that ended these recurring crises did little to remedy the structural deficits that predated the Great Recession. Discretionary spending caps enacted in 2011 eventually proved unworkable, most of the Bush tax cuts became permanent in 2013, and entitlements continued their inexorable growth. A sharp decline in deficit levels—from nearly 10 percent of GDP in 2009 to 2.4 percent in 2015—resulted from improved economic conditions rather than deficit reduction initiatives. By 2016, the final year of Obama's presidency, the deficit was rising once again, as was the level of public debt. The core fiscal problem of the Bush presidency—a narrow tax base and an expansive welfare state—was now measurably worse because of a bitter partisan stalemate his successor could not break.

DOI: 10.4324/9781003167266-4

The Limits of Party Government

Economic stimulus planning began shortly after the November 2008 election. President-elect Obama's policy team and congressional Democratic leaders crafted a package of spending and tax stimulus that could be introduced when Congress convened on January 3 and quickly taken up by the House and the Senate. Prior to his inauguration on January 20, Obama attempted to build bipartisan support for the measure, but the Republican response to his overtures was not encouraging.

The negative response from House Republicans was not unexpected, but it soon became clear that Senate Republicans would also be a problem. The Republican party's postmortem of the Bush presidency had reinforced the belief that excess spending, not tax cuts, caused deficits; with Democrats now in charge, even more spending could be expected, and the debt spiral would continue. Since dire warnings about soaring debt resonated with many voters, not just Tea Party activists, House and Senate Republicans made opposition to the Democratic spending agenda the centerpiece of their 2010 midterm election strategy. From the outset, this created serious problems for Democrats, who were not nearly as united on new spending as Republicans were on tax cuts. The result was a stimulus bill that fell short of what Obama had envisioned and House Democrats had hoped to pass.

The Stimulus Challenge

Signs that Obama would face serious difficulties with Senate Republicans emerged even before he took office. The 2008 Troubled Asset Relief Program (TARP) had authorized the Bush administration to provide up to $350 billion in loans and equity purchases to assist struggling financial institutions. Congress had also reserved the right to block the release of a second $350 billion authorization if and when the president requested additional funding. After meeting with Obama in early January, Bush agreed to send the second TARP authorization request to Congress. The next day, Senate Republicans introduced a disapproval resolution, and Obama representatives spent the next week lobbying senators to defeat the resolution. They succeeded, as the measure failed on a 42–52 vote, but only six Republicans lined up behind Obama, and a handful of Democrats deserted him as well.

Speaker Nancy Pelosi and Democratic House leaders released a draft economic stimulus bill on January 15, and House committees completed legislative markups over the following week. The Appropriations Committee approved over $360 billion in spending for infrastructure, education, income security, healthcare, and related domestic programs.[3] The Ways and Means Committee was responsible for the tax stimulus initiatives—a $500 refundable tax credit for workers, increased child tax credits and earned income tax credits, expanded business tax deductions—and fiscal assistance for state Medicaid programs. The Energy and Commerce Committee handled the remainder of the bill, which included funding for energy projects, healthcare, and electronic medical records. The combined bill, totaling $819.5 billion, was passed by a 244–188 margin on January 28, with all 177 Republicans voting "no" and 11 Democrats also opposing it.

The Senate process was lengthier, and the outcome less certain. A Republican filibuster was seen as inevitable, which meant that at least two Republicans would eventually have to vote for cloture. In addition, the cost of the House bill, and its high ratio of new spending to tax relief, was expected to raise objections from some moderate Democrats. When the Appropriations and the Finance Committees completed their work on January 27, a nearly $70 billion alternative minimum tax (AMT) exemption increase was included in the Senate bill that the House had expected to handle through separate legislation. The net funding for what would be considered new stimulus in the Senate package was therefore below the level approved by the House.

The Senate then spent a week debating floor amendments to the committee bills, but behind-the-scenes discussions between moderate Democrats and several key Republicans produced the substitute bill that the Senate approved on February 10. This bipartisan compromise had a substantially lower cost than the House-passed bill—approximately $780 billion versus $820 billion[4]—and included a larger share of tax relief. Cloture was, as expected, necessary to bring an end to floor debate and to allow the Senate to vote on the substitute bill. The cloture vote was 61–36, and the vote to pass the bill was 61–37. In both cases, three Republicans joined with the Senate's 58 Democrats.

The three Republicans—Susan Collins, Olympia Snowe, and Arlen Specter (he would switch parties several months later)—then helped to shape the conference bill that the House and Senate adopted on February 13. House Speaker Nancy Pelosi had criticized the spending cuts in the Senate bill as "very dangerous," and stated that she was "very much opposed to the cuts proposed in the Senate."[5] Only minor adjustments were made in conference, however, and the Congressional Budget Office (CBO) estimated the total cost of the American Recovery and Reinvestment Act of 2009 (ARRA 2009) at $787 billion over the next decade with more than 90 percent of the stimulus in fiscal years 2009–2011 (see Table 4.1).

The spending provisions in ARRA 2009 were heavily weighted toward fiscal assistance to state and local governments whose budgets had been upended by the recession. Federal funding was provided to insure continuity in public education programs, law enforcement, and healthcare (primarily Medicaid). Additional spending and tax credits were provided for individuals and families—primarily low-income working families, but also retirees, unemployed workers, and college students. The third stimulus category was direct spending for various energy and infrastructure programs, especially highway construction. The funding levels for fiscal assistance to state governments and for education programs were below what the House had originally planned, but the conference committee was, in effect, bound by the

Table 4.1 Spending, Revenue, and Deficit Impact of the American Recovery and Reinvestment Act of 2009 (in billions of dollars)

	Fiscal Years		
	2009–2011	*2009–2019*	
Total Spending Increase	465.6	575.3	
Total Revenue Losses	253.1	211.8	
Deficit Impact	+718.7	+787.2	
Major Provisions:			
Making Work Pay Refundable Tax Credit			116.2
State and Local Fiscal Assistance (Education, Law Enforcement, Job Training)			86.8
Medicaid Assistance to States			86.6
AMT Exemption Increase			69.8
Energy Modernization, Conservation, Development			51.2
Highway and Other Transportation			45.2
Unemployment Benefits			39.2
Pell Grants and Tuition Tax Credits			29.5
COBRA Health Insurance Subsidy (Unemployed Workers)			25.1
EITC and Child Tax Credits			19.5

Sources: Congressional Budget Office, *Estimated Cost of the American Recovery and Reinvestment Act of 2009* (Washington, D.C.: Congressional Budget Office, February 13, 2009), Table 1; *Congressional Quarterly Almanac, 2009* (Washington, D.C.: Congressional Quarterly, 2010), 7-7–7-9.

spending ceiling the Senate had adopted in order to get Republican support for cloture.

Republicans in the House unanimously voted against the conference bill, as did all the Senate Republicans except Collins, Snowe, and Specter. Republicans' complaints about the bill targeted its cost, but they also objected to the limited amount and targeted distribution of tax relief. In particular, virtually all the individual tax relief—the numerous refundable tax credits—was phased out for high-income taxpayers. There was no broad-based tax cut, in the form of reduced tax rates at all income levels, that Republicans insisted was the only proven way to boost economic growth.

The Republicans' strongest denunciations, however, were reserved for the impact of the stimulus bill on the deficit, a task made easier by the $789 billion debt limit increase included in the bill. Projected deficits for 2009 and 2010 were already close to $2 trillion, and ARRA 2009 was expected to increase them by more than $580 billion.[6] For the many Democrats who believed that a much larger and more ambitious stimulus effort was needed, these attacks were patently hypocritical given the deficit record of the Bush presidency. Indeed, the slow pace of economic recovery after 2009 was interpreted by some as evidence that the stimulus bill was too timid a response to an emergency situation for which there were no recent precedents.

The unfortunate reality, however, was that House and Senate Republican leaders were not interested in substantive arguments about the purpose, scope, and timing of stimulus legislation. According to one account, Republican members of the House Appropriations Committee rejected an invitation to help to draft the committee's portion of the stimulus package.[7] As Jerry Lewis, the committee's ranking Republican, explained, "I've simply got my instructions. We can't play." With the exception of the three Republican senators who were willing to break with their leadership, efforts to write a bipartisan bill were doomed from the outset.

This unyielding opposition had not been anticipated, since Democrats had repeatedly supported President Bush's requests for emergency relief legislation. His most controversial proposal, the TARP, would never have passed the House without that support. Bush's Treasury secretary, Henry M. Paulson, had negotiated the TARP authorization with congressional leaders of both parties, Federal Reserve chairman Ben S. Bernanke had endorsed it, and President Bush had personally lobbied for it with Congress and with the public. In a nationally televised address, Bush had stated, "The government's top economic experts warn that, without immediate action by Congress, America could slip into a financial panic … businesses would close their doors, and millions of Americans would lose their jobs."[8]

Despite Bush's plea, the TARP bill was defeated in the House by a vote of 205–228. Although a majority of Democrats voted for the bill, Republicans opposed it by a 2:1 margin. The stock market's Dow Jones industrial average then dropped by 777 points, the biggest one-day decline in its history. The House quickly reversed course and passed the TARP authorization, but a majority of Republicans still voted "no." In 2009, with a Democratic president seeking their support, Republicans in Congress refused to cooperate at all.

In March, Democrats wrapped up the pending appropriations bills for 2009 with an omnibus package that included domestic spending increases Bush had threatened to veto six months earlier. Republicans dutifully complained about excess spending and earmarks, but their main focus had shifted to the Obama budget plan for fiscal year 2010 and the budget resolution that Democrats were drafting to implement that plan. Obama had proposed major increases in domestic spending programs, including a new healthcare insurance plan, and several major revenue increases. The latter included repeal of the Bush tax rate cuts for high-income taxpayers and an environmental initiative that included the sale of emission allowances as part of a greenhouse gas reduction plan.

By the time that the House and the Senate adopted a budget resolution in late April, Obama's domestic spending requests had been trimmed, and the "revenue raisers" had mostly disappeared. The budget resolution did include, however, authorization for Obama's healthcare plan and much of his domestic policy agenda. Republicans in the House and the Senate unanimously voted against the budget resolution, and domestic spending was their main target. As described by House Minority Leader John A. Boehner, the Democratic program was "nothing short of an audacious move to a big socialist government in Washington, D.C."[9] Relentless Republican attacks on domestic spending would continue to test Democratic unity time and time again over the next year and set the stage for a near-breakdown of the budget process in 2010.

Healthcare Reform

The initial framework for healthcare reform was provided by the Obama administration in early 2009. Its primary goal was to insure healthcare coverage for low- and middle-income individuals and families who did not have employer-provided health insurance and who did not qualify for Medicaid. The first remedy was expanded eligibility for the Medicaid program. The second was subsidized health insurance for those who would still not qualify for Medicaid. The administration specified that total costs for these and related healthcare initiatives, including more generous Medicare prescription drug benefits, would be capped at $900 billion over a ten-year period. Healthcare reform would also be deficit neutral, with all costs offset by taxes, fees, and savings from healthcare efficiencies and improvements. While the last of these was dismissed by Republican critics, the administration was determined to reduce healthcare cost inflation. Previous attempts to control costs by limiting federal payments to healthcare providers, such as hospitals and physicians, had achieved limited success at best, so it was unclear whether less costly but more effective healthcare might be possible. The budgetary implications, however, were serious. In 1990, Medicare and Medicaid had accounted for roughly one-tenth of the federal budget. Two decades later, that share had doubled and would continue to grow even without the added costs of healthcare reform.

Obama's deficit-neutral pledge did little to mute Republican protests about runaway spending and made it difficult for House and Senate Democrats to find common ground on the types of taxes and fees that should be imposed. On the benefit side, one of the more divisive issues facing Democrats concerned the so-called public option, namely whether a federal health insurance plan as well as private plans would be available to those qualifying for the new subsidized coverage. There was disagreement as well about seeking Republican participation in drafting what inevitably would be an enormously complex legislative measure.

A number of Senate Democrats, including the chairman of the Finance Committee, Max Baucus, believed that a bipartisan bill could be negotiated with Republicans. Other senior Democrats went further, insisting that bipartisan reform would provide the necessary stability and predictability as new policies were implemented. For example, Kent Conrad, chairman of the Senate Budget Committee, had argued against using the reconciliation process to pass healthcare reform for this very reason, and the Senate's original budget resolution did not include reconciliation instructions. When it was added by the House-Senate conference committee, Conrad made it clear that he had opposed it "at every step of the way, publicly and privately."[10] House Democratic leaders, including the committee chairs who would be directing the legislative markups, took the opposite view. They were convinced that bipartisan outreach would be futile and decided to proceed accordingly.

Based on discussions conducted entirely within the Democratic caucus, the House leadership released a 1,000-page draft bill in mid-July. It included the government-run health plan, or public option, and individual and employer insurance mandates. For individuals, health insurance coverage would be required; mid- to large-sized companies would have to provide health insurance for their employees. Failure to comply with these mandates would, in both cases, result in a financial penalty. Funding for the leadership bill was primarily tax-based, with new excises, fees, and surtaxes on high-income taxpayers. The public option, mandates, and tax provisions in the leadership bill would prove to be completely unacceptable to Republicans, but they also generated a surprising level of controversy among Democrats.

Three House committees—Ways and Means, Education and Labor, and Energy and Commerce—handled separate parts of the bill. Committee markups were completed by the end of July, but disagreements among Democrats on these committees signaled trouble ahead for House leaders. Ways and Means, for example, had approved the public option and insurance coverage mandates in the leadership bill, and the committee's proposed surtax on high-income taxpayers followed the leadership's guidance as well. Republicans had, as expected, unanimously opposed the committee bill, but three Democrats also voted against it. Education and Labor, which voted to broaden eligibility for subsidized health insurance coverage, had an identical split. Energy and Commerce moved in the opposite direction, as moderate Democrats belonging to the fiscally conservative Blue Dog Coalition demanded more stringent income eligibility tests for subsidized coverage and broader small business exemptions from the employer mandate as the price for moving ahead. Finally, Education and Labor had turned back attempts to limit abortion coverage in subsidized health insurance plans, but this issue would prove to be a major stumbling block in the floor debate that followed.

It took several months for the leadership to reconcile the intraparty divisions that had emerged during committee deliberations. In the end, the public option and income tax surcharge were retained with slight modifications—for example, the income threshold at which the surtax applied was raised, the Medicaid income eligibility test was loosened, and the subsidies for private health insurance were increased. A last-minute abortion compromise was the only serious exception to the liberal "tilt" of the House bill.

Speaker Pelosi reluctantly agreed to allow the House to consider an amendment offered by Democrat Bart Stupak that barred federal funding for abortion services and prohibited abortion services from being covered in any insurance plan that received a federal subsidy. The amendment was then adopted by a vote of 240–194, with all 176 Republicans joining 64 Democrats. A threatened mass defection of pro-choice Democrats on the amended bill never materialized, but the final vote margin was still an uncomfortably narrow 220–215, as 39 Democrats voted "no."

In the Senate, two committees had jurisdiction over the healthcare bill. The Health, Education, Labor, and Pensions (HELP) Committee began its deliberations in June and completed its markup on July 15. The HELP bill, reported out on a 13–10 party-line vote, was similar to the House leadership's plan. It provided a public option and included the individual and employer mandates. The Finance Committee, however, spent several months trying to put together a bipartisan plan that would attract some Republican support on the floor. The Finance chairman, Max Baucus, offered to scrap the public option, ease the employer mandate, and curb the use of federal funds for abortions, in a bid to secure votes from committee Republicans; however, the results were disappointing.

To assist Baucus, President Obama met with him and the senior Finance Committee Republican, Charles E. Grassley, to discuss the form a bipartisan bill might take. As recounted by the former president years later, Grassley was asked, "[I]f Max took every one of your latest suggestions, could you support the bill?"[11] When Grassley did not respond, Obama repeated, "Are there any changes—any at all—that would get us your vote?" Grassley eventually answered, "I guess not." After all of Baucus's efforts and a delay of several months, only one committee Republican, Olympia Snowe, voted to report out the committee's bill. Snowe also stated that her support could be withdrawn if the committee's bill was changed on the floor.[12]

Senate Majority Leader Harry Reid then faced the difficult task of combining the very different HELP and Finance Committee bills into a measure that all 60 Senate Democrats would support, since a Republican filibuster would otherwise kill it. After several weeks of meetings that included Obama administration representatives, Reid released what was, in effect, the first of a series of intraparty compromises that would be negotiated over the following month. On November 21, the Senate invoked cloture on the Healthcare "Shell Bill" by a 60–39 vote.

The cloture vote allowed the Senate to begin floor consideration of the bill, but its practical effect was to allow Reid and other Democratic leaders to begin discussions with individual senators on contested provisions within the measures. The core disputes were the public option, which liberals demanded and conservatives deemed unacceptable, the taxes and fees to provide the necessary revenues for healthcare expansion, and abortion funding restrictions. In some cases, Reid had to deal with more parochial questions, such as federal funding for Medicaid expansion in specific states. The stretched-out timeline needed to reach a consensus, and the "deals" that some senators demanded amplified Republican attacks on the entire healthcare reform enterprise and threatened to undermine public support for it as well.

In mid-December, as Reid pressed for a conclusion, the White House weighed in. President Obama met with the entire Democratic caucus on December 15 and followed up with individual conversations and meetings with wavering Democrats over the next few days. With administration backing, Reid agreed to delete the public option and to include a more stringent restriction on abortion funding as part of the substitute amendment he offered on December 18. On December 21, the Senate voted by 60–40 to invoke cloture on the Reid amendment, but Republicans refused to give up. Minority Leader Mitch McConnell, who had taken advantage of Senate rules to require the Senate clerks to read the entire text of the bill before the first cloture vote, now used procedural loopholes to force two more cloture votes. Finally, on December 24, the Senate voted by 60–39 to pass the bill.

The hard-fought victory in the Senate came with a cost—major differences with the House-passed bill that would be difficult to resolve. Given how fragile the 60-vote Democratic Senate compromise had been, it would be difficult for a House-Senate conference committee to accommodate the House in a meaningful way. At the same time, the vast majority of House Democrats, as well as Speaker Pelosi and the party leadership, were expecting more concessions than the Senate had delivered on the stimulus bill.

In the meantime, Republican obstructionism was becoming more encompassing. Democrats had included a debt limit increase in the February 2009 stimulus bill, but another increase was needed at the end of the year. Initially, Democrats planned to raise the limit by $1.8 trillion, an amount that would cover projected Treasury borrowing for at least another year. Republicans, on the other hand, wanted an election year vote on the debt limit that would underscore their attacks on "tax, spend, *and borrow*" Democrats [italics added]. In late December, the House barely managed to pass a $290 billion debt limit increase, the minimum needed for the next few months. Senate Democrats, in turn, had to come up with 60 votes in order to clear the measure. In both the House and the Senate, Republican opposition was unanimous.

Then, on January 19, 2010, Democrats lost their filibuster-proof majority in the Senate. Republican Scott P. Brown unexpectedly won a special election for the Massachusetts U.S. Senate seat that had been filled by an interim Democratic appointee after the death of Edward M. Kennedy in August 2009. With Brown now added to the Republican ranks, Senate Democrats lacked the votes to overcome a certain Republican filibuster on a conference committee healthcare bill. With the conference option foreclosed, and House Democrats demanding changes in the Senate's healthcare bill, the Obama administration and Democratic leaders turned to the reconciliation option that had been included in the 2010 budget resolution. First, House and Senate leaders would agree to the necessary changes in the Senate-passed bill, and incorporate these into a healthcare reconciliation bill. Second, the House would pass the Senate's bill, along with the reconciliation agreement. Third, the Senate would promptly pass the reconciliation bill and complete the two-part healthcare package. Both pieces of legislation would then be sent to the president for his signature.

On March 21, the House narrowly passed both measures, with nearly three dozen Democrats breaking with the leadership on the two votes. The Senate then passed the reconciliation bill by 56–43 on March 25. Over several days of debate, Republicans failed to amend the measure, but two relatively minor provisions had to be dropped after the Senate parliamentarian ruled that they violated the germaneness requirement for reconciliation legislation. This last problem was resolved when the House passed the amended reconciliation bill later that day.

On March 30, President Obama signed the reconciliation bill, having signed the underlying healthcare legislation a week earlier. With the months-long ordeal finally at an end, Obama had a healthcare policy victory that had eluded Democratic presidents from Truman through Clinton. If not quite the universal healthcare that liberal reformers had sought for decades, approximately 32 million uninsured Americans were now expected to qualify for subsidized private health insurance or Medicaid.[13]

The Patient Protection and Affordable Care Act of 2010 together with the Reconciliation Act of 2010 had an estimated cost of $938 billion over ten years (see Table 4.2). The most costly provisions in terms of new spending were the health insurance subsidies and Medicaid and Children's Health Insurance Program (CHIP) expansions that would take effect in 2014. Costs for subsidized health insurance came in the form of tax credits that would offset more than 95 percent of premiums paid by households whose income was between 133 percent and 150 percent of the federal poverty level. The subsidy rate would then be reduced for households with higher income levels up to 400 percent of the poverty level. The CBO estimated the average cost of federal tax credits in 2015 at approximately $5,200 per household.[14]

In 2010, federal matching funds for Medicaid provided slightly less than 60 percent of total program spending, with the matching rates for individual states based on their per capita income. The matching formula for the CHIP was slightly higher, again with more generous federal support for low-income states. The 2010 healthcare bill broadened income eligibility for state Medicaid and CHIP programs; it also increased the federal matching formula to finance this additional coverage. The federal government would cover 100 percent of a state's costs for newly eligible families and individuals from 2014 to 2016, with a gradual reduction to 90 percent in 2020 and to 90 percent thereafter. Estimated total costs for the Medicaid and CHIP expansions over a ten-year period were $434 billion.

The taxes, fees, and savings to cover these costs—to provide an estimated $143 billion in deficit savings over ten years—were equally as complicated in terms of phase-ins and program interactions. The single largest revenue raiser was the increase in Medicare taxes for high-income families and individuals.

Table 4.2 Spending, Revenue, and Deficit Effects of the Patient Protection and Affordable Care Act of 2010 (in billions of dollars)*

	Fiscal Years 2010–2019
Spending Provisions	
Health Insurance Premium Support	464
Medicaid and CHIP Expansion	434
Other	40
	938
Offsetting Penalties/Fees	149
Net Spending Costs	788
Revenue Increases and Savings	
Medicare Hospital Insurance Tax	210
Pharmaceutical and Health Insurance Company Fees	107
Other Revenues	103
Reductions in Healthcare Spending (Savings and Related Provisions)	511
Net Revenue Increases and Savings	931
Net Deficit Effects	–143

Source: Congressional Budget Office, "Enacted Legislation, Item 1: Final Cost Estimate, March 20, 2010," *Selected CBO Publications Related to Health Care Legislation, 2009–2010* (Washington, D.C.: Congressional Budget Office, December 2010), Tables 1, 2.

Note: * Includes the Reconciliation Act of 2010.

Beginning in 2013, these taxpayers would be subject to a Medicare surtax on wage and salary income and a new Medicare tax on investment income above certain income thresholds. Estimated revenues from the additional Medicare taxes were $210 billion through 2019. Additional revenues were also expected from annual fees paid by pharmaceutical firms (beginning in 2011), health insurance companies (beginning in 2014), and various tax law changes affecting individuals and businesses that would be phased in at different times as well. Total revenue increases for the ten-year estimating period were $420 billion.

More than $510 billion in deficit savings, however, was based on new Medicare and Medicaid provisions designed to reduce spending below baseline levels. Among these were lower payments for the Medicare Advantage program, decreased Medicare and Medicaid reimbursements for certain healthcare services and institutions, and various cost controls and productivity efficiencies. Substantial savings were expected as well for changes in

Medicaid and Medicare that would affect interactive coverages and other federal health programs.

Whether savings of this magnitude could in fact be realized was obviously uncertain, which simply added to the Republican indictment of the Affordable Care Act (ACA—or what they derisively termed Obamacare) as a fiscal and regulatory nightmare. They argued that its costs would inevitably be much higher than estimated and that new taxes and fees, in addition to being objectionable as tax policy, would never come close to covering these costs. In sum, they argued that the ACA of 2010 would make it even more difficult to control deficits and debt, adding to what the ARRA had done one year earlier.

For House and Senate Democrats, the growing unease over spending was not an isolated problem. Democrats could not agree on the fate of the expiring Bush tax cuts (including the estate tax, which was scheduled to expire in 2010); whether to reinstate strict pay-as-you-go (PAYGO) requirements on tax and entitlement policy changes; or how to proceed on routine domestic appropriations. The House and the Senate failed to pass a budget resolution for fiscal year 2011, and continuing disputes over discretionary spending deadlocked the appropriations process. None of the 12 appropriations bills for fiscal year 2011 was passed on time, and Congress was forced to settle for a temporary continuing resolution to fund agencies through the midterm election break.

In December 2009, the House had passed a $154 billion jobs bill providing nearly $50 billion for infrastructure projects, over $25 billion in state and local fiscal assistance to preserve public sector employment, and additional funding for extended unemployment benefits and healthcare assistance. When the Senate took up the bill in February, virtually all of this spending disappeared. The jobs bill that Congress then cleared in March provided only $13 billion in payroll tax relief for businesses that hired unemployed workers, extended expensing rules for small businesses, and authorized minor highway programs and infrastructure investment initiatives. Attempts by the House to include full offsets for the tax relief in this $17.6 billion package were blocked in the Senate, and those that were included were limited to accounting rules and tax payment schedules.

The House also failed to gain Senate approval for meaningful deficit-neutral PAYGO controls as part of a $1.9 trillion debt limit increase in February 2010. The PAYGO provision that was included was essentially symbolic, since it exempted most of the 2001 and 2003 tax cuts, provided a two-year AMT exemption increase, extended 2009 estate tax rates and rules for two years, and postponed for five years scheduled Medicare reimbursement program reductions. Senate Democrats were then unable to pass legislation authorizing a bipartisan debt commission to provide Congress with a long-term deficit reduction plan.

When the congressional debt commission was blocked by Senate Republicans, President Obama created one by executive order. On February 18, an

18-member commission was established, with six of its members—including the co-chairmen Erskine Bowles and former Senator Alan K. Simpson—appointed by the president and the others by the majority and minority leaders in the House and Senate.[15] The National Commission on Fiscal Responsibility and Reform was charged with making recommendations to "bring the budget into primary balance (balance excluding interest costs) in 2015, and to meaningfully improve the long-run fiscal outlook."[16] Its report was to be submitted in December, after the midterm elections.

In the meantime, President Obama proposed a three-year freeze on non-defense discretionary spending beginning in 2011, but this did little to defuse Democratic disagreements over spending. With the unemployment rate at nearly 10 percent, long-term unemployment (27 weeks or more) at its highest level in decades, and the disappointingly slow pace of economic recovery, some Democrats argued that additional spending to support private and public sector employment was needed immediately. When the House attempted to add $23 billion in domestic spending to a war funding supplemental in July, however, these funds were deleted by the Senate. In August, Congress approved a $26 billion supplemental that provided fiscal assistance to state and local governments to prevent public school teacher layoffs and to maintain Medicaid services. Various offsets were included, none of which involved tax increases, but Republicans still filibustered the bill. Two Republicans, Susan Collins and Olympia Snowe, then provided the votes that Democrats needed to invoke cloture and pass the bill.

This victory aside, congressional Democrats were clearly on the defensive during 2010. President Obama's approval ratings, which had generally remained well above 50 percent for much of 2009, dropped to 47 percent in the spring of 2010 and remained below 50 percent for the rest of the year.[17] Politically risky votes for the ACA in the House and Senate had produced an enormously complicated program about which the public was, at best, ambivalent and in any case would not provide any benefits until 2014. The Republican party's mounting attacks on spending and deficits were rarely challenged, even though most of the new spending was for entitlements and defense.

In 2009, for example, discretionary domestic spending had increased by nearly $60 billion, but this accounted for only a fraction of the increase of more than $535 billion in total outlays from 2008.[18] The bulk of the additional spending was accounted for by Social Security ($66 billion); Medicare and Medicaid ($89 billion); unemployment benefits ($81 billion); and defense ($44 billion). Moreover, in 2010, so-called runaway spending came to an abrupt halt, as total spending fell by $60 billion, the first year-on-year decline since 1965. Revenue shortfalls, however, kept deficits at elevated levels. In 2009 and 2010, revenue-GDP was only 14.6 percent, the lowest level since 1950. Revenues would rebound when the economy recovered, but the fate of the Bush tax cuts would determine how great that rebound would be. For example, during the Bush presidency revenue-GDP peaked at 18 percent in

2007. If the Bush tax cuts were made permanent, extremely large domestic spending cuts would be needed to curb the structural deficits those tax cuts had created in the first place. Since failures to retrench domestic programs extended back several decades, the prospects for massive future retrenchments were not promising.

Nevertheless, the Republican party's message for the 2010 midterms was the tax cut/domestic retrenchment rhetoric that had surfaced in the 1980s and that had been amplified in the 1994 Contract with America. It was resurrected with the "Pledge to America" that House Republicans unveiled in September 2010.[19] The Republican agenda included the permanent extension of all the Bush tax cuts and an additional tax cut for small businesses. As far as future tax policy was concerned, Republicans pledged to oppose any tax increases. Their spending plan promised a smaller government—immediate termination of the TARP and stimulus programs, a rollback of nondefense spending to pre-Great Recession levels, and "hard" budget caps that would continue to limit spending in the years ahead. To reverse the government "takeover" of healthcare embodied in the ACA, Republicans would "repeal and replace" it by lowering healthcare costs and improving access to affordable private insurance. In sum, the Republicans vowed to balance the budget and reduce the public debt.

The Pledge's language reflected the fierce criticism of Democratic "big government" that had resonated with Republican primary voters earlier in the year. A number of Tea Party-backed candidates had been nominated, but the movement's appeal had an impact on "traditional" Republican candidates as well. Added pressure had come from groups such as Americans for Tax Reform, an antitax advocacy group founded in 1985. Its Taxpayer Protection Pledge, a written promise to oppose tax increases for individuals and businesses, had become a litmus test for Republican legislators and candidates over the years. By 2010, very few Republicans were willing to dissent.[20]

Republican gains in the 2010 midterms were sweeping. The party took control of the House, picking up 63 seats, and narrowed the Democratic Senate majority to 53–47. Republicans also did exceptionally well in state gubernatorial and legislative elections, which proved to be a major advantage when U.S. House districts were redrawn after the 2010 census. In the lame-duck session that followed the election, Republicans scored major victories on spending and especially on taxes. When House Democrats passed a continuing resolution to fund domestic programs and agencies for the remainder of fiscal year 2011, Republicans blocked its consideration in the Senate. Democrats had to accept a short-term resolution that postponed final action on 2011 appropriations until March, when the new 112th Congress would be in place.

The tax victory for Republicans was even more decisive. On December 6, President Obama reached an agreement with Senate Republicans to continue the Bush income tax cuts for two years in their entirety. The president also accepted the Republican plan for extending estate tax rate cuts and exemptions over this two-year period. The final tax cut package included another AMT exemption extension, a one-year Social Security payroll tax reduction, a variety of other extensions for child and tuition tax credits, and new business tax credits. In return, Republicans agreed to a continuation of federal funding for extended unemployment benefits through 2011. House and Senate Democrats publicly criticized Obama's concessions on tax policy, but their attempts to amend the agreement failed. The Senate ultimately accepted it by an 81–19 vote on December 15. House Democrats then attempted to change the estate tax provisions in the Senate-passed bill, but when this effort was unsuccessful, the House cleared it for the president's signature two days later.

On nonbudgetary matters, President Obama fared much better. First, the administration gained Senate approval for the nuclear arms reduction treaty it had negotiated with Russia. The first strategic arms reduction treaty (START I) had been signed by President George H. W. Bush in 1991 and remained in effect through 2009. In the spring of 2010, President Obama had signed a new agreement, and START II was submitted to the Senate for ratification. Senate Republican leaders strongly opposed the treaty and forced repeated delays in bringing it to the Senate floor for a vote. After the midterm elections, the Obama administration recognized that Republican gains would likely doom the treaty in the upcoming Congress and moved to take it up in December. Senate Minority Leader Mitch McConnell then mounted a filibuster, but 11 Republicans voted with the Democrats to end the debate on December 21. The Senate ratified the treaty by 71–26 the next day, with 13 Republicans and 58 Democrats providing more than enough votes to meet the two-thirds ratification requirement.

Senate Republican votes were also needed to secure the passage of another controversial administration initiative—a repeal of the 1993 legislative ban on openly gay persons serving in the military. The House had included the "don't ask, don't tell" repeal in the defense authorization bill that it approved in May 2010, but a Republican filibuster forced Senate Democrats to remove it. A separate bill was then passed by the House in December, and a second filibuster took place in the Senate. Six Republicans then joined 57 Democrats to invoke cloture, and the Senate cleared the bill shortly thereafter. As with START II, the "don't ask, don't tell" repeal would likely have been impossible in the upcoming 112th Congress, so the Obama administration's bipartisan outreach worked on these national security matters. On taxes and spending, however, the partisan lines had held firm. In the 112th Congress, they would prove to be nearly insurmountable.

Divided Government Dysfunction: 2011–2012

With deficits having totaled more than $2.7 trillion in 2009 and 2010 and debt-GDP climbing above 60 percent, deficit reduction was a bipartisan priority for the 111th Congress. In his State of the Union Address on

January 25, 2011, President Obama called for "a principled compromise … to rein in our deficits" and "make sure we aren't buried under a mountain of debt."[21] As a first step, Obama offered to freeze discretionary domestic spending for five years but cautioned that serious deficit reduction would have to extend beyond this small piece—"a little more than 12 percent"—of the budget. Echoing the presidential fiscal commission's report issued in December, Obama insisted that tax increases and entitlement reform would have to be a major part of any long-term solution.

House Republicans, however, were focused entirely on spending cuts, and they threatened to shut down the government unless Obama agreed to immediate cuts in discretionary domestic programs. In April, with the shutdown threat still unresolved, they adopted a budget plan that broadened the cutbacks to include healthcare and public assistance entitlements. Republicans also reiterated their commitment to lower taxes by including a new round of income tax rate cuts. The stalemate that then ensued over deficit reduction was predictable. More surprising was the extent to which Republicans were willing to upend the budget process for the next two years in pursuit of a "small government" vision divorced from the political realities of divided government.

The Simpson-Bowles Comprehensive Plan

On December 3, 2010, the President's National Commission on Fiscal Responsibility and Reform issued its long-awaited deficit reduction report. Its official title was "The Moment of Truth," but it was rechristened by the media as Simpson-Bowles in recognition of the co-chairmen who served as its principal planners and public spokesmen. The report outlined an ambitious and comprehensive deficit reduction program for 2012–2020, along with Social Security reforms to bring benefits and revenues into long-term balance.

Like the deficit reduction plans of 1990 and 1993, the Simpson-Bowles plan included discretionary and mandatory spending cuts and increased revenues (see Table 4.3). The discretionary spending savings—approximately $1.7 trillion over nine years—were divided between defense and domestic programs. The report did not specify where cuts should be made but recommended instead annual discretionary spending caps and enforcement mechanisms for the appropriations process.

Revenue increases provided the second largest deficit reduction component—approximately 25 percent of total deficit savings—and Simpson-Bowles did propose specific changes in individual and corporate tax policy. These included lower tax rates, along with the wholesale elimination of tax preferences and a more progressive distribution of tax burdens. The net effect of these changes would be revenue-GDP levels in 2020 that matched those of the late 1990s.

The mandatory program reforms in the commission's report were specific as well, with a number of proposed changes in healthcare provider

Table 4.3 The Simpson-Bowles Comprehensive Deficit Reduction Plan (in billions of dollars)

	2012	*2013*	*2014*	*2015*	*2016*	*2017*	*2018*	*2019*	*2020*	*2012–2015*	*2012–2020*
Discretionary Spending	49	102	141	172	194	215	236	261	291	464	1,661
Mandatory Spending	1	32	47	54	64	70	88	97	104	134	556
Spending in the Tax Code/ Tax Reform	0	20	40	80	90	105	120	150	180	140	785
Other Revenue	1	5	11	18	27	32	36	39	43	34	210
Net Interest Savings	1	5	16	33	58	87	119	155	199	56	673
Total Deficit Reduction*	52	164	255	357	433	509	599	702	817	828	3,885
Projected Deficit Under Plan (*excluding* Social Security Reform)	–943	–655	–469	–440	–456	–404	–332	–343	–333		
	–6.0%	–3.9%	–2.7%	–2.4%	–2.4%	–2.0%	–1.6%	–1.6%	–1.5%		
Projected Deficit Under Plan (*including* Social Security Reform)	–949	–646	–455	–421	–432	–372	–294	–298	–279		
	–6.0%	–3.9%	–2.6%	–2.3%	–2.2%	–1.8%	–1.4%	–1.3%	–1.2%		

Source: *The Moment of Truth: Report of the National Commission on Fiscal Responsibility and Reform* (Washington, D.C.: The White House, December 2010), 15.

Note: * Excludes Social Security.

reimbursement formulas, dual Medicare and Medicaid coverage, and repeal of the long-term care insurance program established under the ACA. Equally as important, the commission proposed limits on total federal healthcare spending after 2020 in order to stabilize overall spending levels. Its Social Security proposals, which included increased payroll taxes and reduced benefits for high-income retirees, were primarily directed toward long-term trust fund solvency rather than deficit reduction but reinforced the message that "everything must be on the table."

The scope of the Simpson-Bowles plan, and the fact that virtually all of its individual proposals were controversial, produced an interesting voting split within the commission.[22] The report was endorsed by 11 of the commission's 18 members—five Democrats, five Republicans, and one Independent. Six of the nonsigners—three Democrats and three Republicans—had been appointed by House and Senate party leaders. The split within the commission was not unexpected, given the partisan divide in Congress over deficit reduction. Nevertheless, the report served a useful purpose in highlighting the fact that long-term deficit reduction required revenue increases and entitlement reform.

Unfortunately, bipartisan compromises on taxes and entitlements were not possible during the 111th Congress. In the summer of 2010, negotiations between the Obama administration and House Republicans on a "Grand Bargain" failed, and Congress's "supercommittee" initiative that fall became deadlocked as well. What remained instead was a deficit control agreement limited to discretionary spending cuts that soon proved to be unworkable.

Budget Brinkmanship

The first of several unusually rancorous conflicts over spending was instigated by House Republicans in early 2011. The continuing resolution for fiscal year 2011 approved by the previous Congress expired on March 4, and House Republicans threatened to trigger a government shutdown unless pending appropriations bills were cut by $60 billion below 2010 funding levels. Temporary funding extensions over the next several weeks allowed the Obama administration, Senate Democrats, and House Republican leaders to negotiate an omnibus appropriations agreement that included $40 billion in discretionary spending cuts and was cleared by Congress on April 14.[23] Most of these cuts, however, were spread out over several years. The impact on fiscal year 2011 spending was minimal—slightly more than $350 million, according to the CBO.[24]

The House Speaker, John A. Boehner, had seen his party's shutdown strategy fail against the Clinton administration and was anxious to avoid a similar outcome with President Obama. Many House Republicans, and particularly the several dozen members of the Tea Party caucus, were less concerned about the potential backlash and concluded that Boehner and other House leaders had not taken full advantage of the shutdown threat to secure a better agreement. As a sign of the dissension within the party's ranks, 59 Republicans voted against the compromise Boehner had negotiated, and his relationship with Tea Party Republicans never fully recovered.

These disputes were overshadowed, however, by the starkly different budget plans that President Obama and House Republicans unveiled in April. The deficit reduction proposal Obama outlined on April 13 followed the Simpson-Bowles prescription of discretionary spending cuts, entitlement reductions, and tax increases. Obama's goal was $4 trillion in deficit reduction over 12 years, with $2 trillion provided by spending savings, $1 trillion from tax increases, and $1 trillion in reduced interest payments.[25]

Obama invited party leaders in Congress to appoint representatives to a bipartisan deficit reduction working group, headed by Vice President Joseph Biden. The Biden-led panel would draft the spending and tax policy legislative changes to meet Obama's deficit reduction goal, and Congress would then approve this legislation by the end of July. The timetable was not arbitrary. It was understood that the Treasury would reach the limits of its borrowing by the end of July, at which point an increase in the statutory debt limit would be needed to insure the timely payment of the federal government's financial obligations.[26] House Republicans had threatened to block any increase that did not include offsetting spending cuts, and Obama's deficit reduction initiative was intended to avert that threat.

The budget resolution that House Republicans adopted on April 15, however, left no room for the type of comprehensive deficit reduction that Obama had endorsed. Paul Ryan, chairman of the House Budget Committee, was the principal drafter of a Republican budget plan that took domestic retrenchment well beyond anything the party had endorsed in the past.[27] In addition to very large cuts in discretionary domestic programs, the Ryan proposal featured comprehensive rollbacks in healthcare entitlements and a long-term reduction in the size and role of the federal government. Titled the "Path to Prosperity," the budget blueprint that House Republicans adopted was a radical departure from long-established federal policy.

In 2013, for example, the Ryan proposal called for converting Medicaid into a block grant program. In 2023, the Medicare eligibility age would be raised and, more importantly, Medicare payments for healthcare services would be replaced by insurance premium support payments—financial subsidies for the purchase of private insurance plans by beneficiaries. As with Medicaid block grants, Medicare private insurance subsidies would allow the federal government to set annual healthcare spending budgets in line with spending-reduction targets.

These Medicaid and Medicare proposals ignited a firestorm of controversy, but the spending trajectory in the Republican plan had much broader implications for the welfare state and domestic responsibilities the federal government had taken on since the New Deal. In 2010, total federal spending-GDP (excluding interest payments on the debt) was approximately 22 percent. The CBO's analysis of the long-term implications of the Ryan budget plan projected a reduction to 17 percent by the early 2020s and to 14 percent by 2050 (see Table 4.4). With the exception of Social Security, where current policy would remain in effect, House Republicans were looking to shrink the size and role of the federal government to pre-World War II levels.

House Republicans overwhelmingly supported (by 235–4) the budget resolution that Ryan's committee had drafted. The Senate majority leader, Harry Reid, allowed the Senate to vote on the House-passed budget resolution, presumably to force Republicans to cast a difficult vote. Difficult or not, 40 Republicans voted for it, and only five joined Democrats in rejecting it by 57–40. With a Democratic Senate and White House, the governing philosophy of the Path to Prosperity budget plan was easily dismissed. Moreover, it was questionable whether Republicans would have been willing to follow its prescriptions even if they had unified control. Nevertheless, its singular focus on spending cuts as the only acceptable path to deficit reduction—tax increases were excluded—made bipartisan compromise close to impossible.

In mid-May, for example, a Senate working group of three Democrats and three Republicans abandoned its effort to negotiate a comprehensive deficit reduction plan, and the Biden-led panel reached a similar impasse at the end of June. In early July, President Obama stepped in and met with House and Senate leaders of both parties to discuss a "grand bargain" to resolve the growing deadlock over deficit reduction and the debt limit. Entitlement reforms were part of these discussions, but the necessary tradeoff for Democrats was increased revenues. When House Speaker John Boehner announced that tax increases were off-limits, these talks collapsed. House Republicans passed a debt limit increase on July 29, but it required both chambers to approve a constitutional balanced-budget agreement and to enact offsetting spending cuts. The Democratic Senate rejected the House plan but could not adopt an alternative.

Table 4.4 The Long-Term Path of Federal Spending Under the Ryan Budget Plan (as a percentage of GDP)

	Actual	*Projected*			
	2010	2022	2030	2040	2050
Major Mandatory Health Care Programs	5½	5½	6	5¾	4¾
Social Security	4¾	5¼	6	6¼	6
Other Mandatory and Defense and Nondefense Discretionary Spending	12	6	5¼	4¼	3½
Spending Excluding Interest	22½	17	17½	16¼	14

Source: Congressional Budget Office, *Long-Term Analysis of a Budget Proposal by Chairman Ryan* (Washington, D.C.: Congressional Budget Office, April 5, 2011), 16.

A last-minute legislative compromise was then negotiated by Senate Minority Leader Mitch McConnell and Vice President Biden. McConnell had promised when he reached out to Biden that "Our country is not going to default for the first time in history."[28] The Budget Control Act of 2011 (BCA 2011) that the House and the Senate cleared for the president's signature on August 2 provided for an immediate increase of $400 billion in the debt limit.[29] Additional increases of $500 billion and $1.2 trillion were also authorized, subject to a joint resolution of disapproval. Since the president could veto the disapproval resolution, its inclusion was little more than a face-saving check for Republicans.

BCA 2011 did include, however, deficit reduction provisions that were more consequential. There were three components: (1) discretionary spending caps (like those of the 1990s) provided an estimated $917 billion in deficit savings for fiscal years 2012–2021; (2) $1.5 trillion in additional deficit reduction over this period from a deficit reduction package passed by Congress; or (3) automatic spending cuts, or sequesters, that would take effect if Congress failed to approve such a package.[30]

The spending caps in BCA 2011 limited the total discretionary appropriations that Congress could enact each year, with exceptions only for emergency spending—notably disaster relief or war funding (Overseas Contingency Operations). The caps would have the greatest impact from 2012–2014, with lesser reductions thereafter. The net effect, if these caps were enforced, would be a roughly one-third reduction in discretionary spending—from 9 percent in 2011 to 6.1 percent in 2021.[31]

BCA 2011 also established a Joint Select Committee on Deficit Reduction to draft legislation that would provide an additional $1.5 trillion in deficit reduction in fiscal years 2012–2021. The parties in the House and the Senate would be equally represented on the committee, which was given an end-November reporting deadline. Congress would then vote on the committee's proposal using expedited procedures.

If this committee option failed, which not surprisingly turned out to be the case, the fallback procedure was an automatic reduction in spending below the discretionary spending caps. These reductions, or sequesters, would be applied each year beginning in 2013 and ending in 2021. For defense, the sequesters would amount to approximately $55 billion annually.[32] Nondefense reductions would be roughly equal, with discretionary programs primarily affected but nonexempt mandatory programs affected as well. Given the stringent limits on discretionary spending from the annual caps, there were widespread concerns in both parties that these additional cuts would seriously damage defense capabilities and essential domestic programs. It was hoped that these concerns would encourage Republicans and Democrats to replace an admittedly blunt and probably unfeasible procedure with a more balanced and workable deficit reduction program. It was equally possible that Congress would simply cancel future sequestrations as the programmatic damage mounted.

Finally, the August budget agreement required Congress to vote on a constitutional balanced-budget amendment, a House Republican priority. In November, the House approved an amendment that prohibited outlays from exceeding revenues during a fiscal year, unless three-fifths of the House and the Senate voted to allow a temporary deficit. It also contained a wartime waiver that only required a majority approval of the House and Senate. The 261–165 vote fell well short of the required two-thirds majority for constitutional amendments. In December, the Senate considered two different versions—one sponsored by Republicans and the other by Democrats—neither of which attracted even a majority of votes.

Given the protracted disputes over deficit reduction and the debt limit, none of the 12 appropriations bills for fiscal year 2012 had been passed as the October 1 deadline approached. When the House leadership brought up a continuing resolution in September, conservative Republicans in the newly formed Freedom Caucus demanded that it adhere to the discretionary spending total in the fiscal year 2012 budget resolution ($1.019 trillion) rather than the $1.043 trillion Congress had agreed to in the BCA agreement.[33] They also insisted that spending offsets be required for a pending disaster relief bill. Caucus members then voted with Democrats who had very different objections to defeat the leadership measure. When a revised continuing resolution was passed by the House on September 23, the Senate refused to consider it. With a government shutdown only a week away, Senate leaders of both parties agreed on a continuing resolution compromise that was approved by 79–12 on September 26. After some procedural maneuvering, it was passed by the House, but three more continuing resolutions were needed before Congress finally approved the remaining spending bills in December. Congress also agreed to extend the expiring Social Security payroll tax cut for an additional year, but the House allowed only a temporary extension of unemployment benefits pending a more thorough review of the program in January.

Full enforcement of BCA 2011's caps and sequesters would provide $2.1 trillion in deficit reduction over the next decade, but it was extremely unlikely that this would occur. Massive defense budget cuts would inevitably pose problems for congressional Republicans, and congressional Democrats could not be expected to allow the evisceration of domestic programs their party had championed for decades. Moreover, the deficit reduction that BCA contained was roughly half of what the Simpson-Bowles plan had provided and what President Obama had proposed to Congress in April. The unusually hard-line and reckless tactics that House Republicans adopted in 2011 produced a great deal of drama but delivered very little of the deficit reduction they considered absolutely essential.

Nevertheless, House Republicans renewed their attack on domestic spending in 2012. In late March, the House approved a budget resolution that called for even steeper reductions in domestic appropriations than those agreed to in BCA 2011 and also contained reconciliation instructions for

$260 billion in ten-year entitlement savings from healthcare and public assistance entitlements.[34] In addition, they proposed canceling the upcoming defense budget sequester and offsetting it with additional cuts in domestic spending.

Senate Democrats refused to allow a vote on the House plan and decided to forego passing a Senate version. Instead, the Budget Committee provided guidelines for a deficit reduction plan modeled on Simpson-Bowles as the basis for future bipartisan discussions, and it advised the Appropriations Committee to proceed under the defense and nondefense spending caps agreed to in BCA 2011. In September, with none of the fiscal 2013 appropriations bills having been cleared, a six-month continuing resolution was passed that rejected the defense-domestic tradeoffs the House had proposed and extended virtually all programs at slightly higher funding levels.[35] Resolving House-Senate differences was then left to the next Congress.

The November 2012 elections, however, simply extended the partisan deadlock that had caused so much turmoil during the 112th Congress. Barack Obama won election to a second term by a comfortable margin, and the Senate Democratic majority increased by two seats to 55–45. House Republicans also retained control with a 234-seat majority, slightly below their 2010–2011 strength.

The Fiscal Cliff Agreement

In a post-election session that began on November 9, the Obama administration and Senate Democrats faced off once again with House Republicans. The core dispute in this instance was the Bush tax cuts that were scheduled to expire on December 31. For two years, House Republicans had rejected anything other than the permanent extension of all the 2001 and 2003 tax cuts, while Democrats had insisted on a partial extension that would exclude high-income taxpayers. Tax politics aside, there was a compelling fiscal policy consideration. Allowing the Bush tax cuts to expire would raise taxes substantially and immediately at a time when the nation's economic recovery was halting and fragile. The spending sequestrations for 2013 were also scheduled for January, adding to this looming fiscal policy contraction.

Federal Reserve chairman Ben Bernanke had used the term "fiscal cliff" in urging the president and Congress to take timely corrective action, but the lame-duck Congress struggled for weeks to reach the necessary compromise. Finally, on January 1, 2013, Congress cleared the American Taxpayer Relief Act of 2012 (ATRA 2012) that avoided the fiscal cliff, but set the stage for rancorous disputes over spending, deficits, and the debt limit for the next two years.

ATRA 2012 was, by any objective standard, an enormous tax cut, since it reduced federal revenues by an estimated $3.9 trillion over a ten-year period.[36] Its most costly provision was a permanent "fix" for the alternative minimum tax problem that Congress had been grappling with since 2001. ATRA 2012 raised the exemption limit and indexed it annually for inflation at an estimated cost of $1.8 trillion. This AMT reform drew strong bipartisan support, but the estate tax exemption and estate tax rate provisions in ATRA 2012 were more contentious. In the end, Democrats made major concessions on what had long been a highly partisan issue. They agreed to an estate tax exemption of $5.1 million for 2012 and annual indexing of the limit thereafter, essentially in line with what Republicans had proposed. They also agreed to a top estate tax rate of 40 percent, well below the pre-Bush rate of 55 percent. The estimated revenue loss from these estate tax changes was nearly $370 billion; another $210 billion in temporary extensions under ATRA 2012 affected businesses as well as individuals and was supported by both parties.

The core dispute between Democrats and Republicans involved income tax rates. Democrats had for years agreed to maintain the Bush tax cuts for "middle class Americans," and the party's 2012 platform had defined this group to include the "98 percent of American families who make less than $250,000 a year."[37] ATRA 2012, however, extended the Bush tax rate cuts for taxpayers whose taxable income was less than $450,000 (for joint filers), and it also continued the reduced rates for capital gains and dividend income for these taxpayers. Above the $450,000 income threshold, however, the top marginal rate was raised to 39.6 percent and the capital gains and dividend rates were increased to 20 percent. Limits on itemized deductions and the amount of personal exemptions claimed by high-income taxpayers were also reinstated. The net effect of these income tax provisions was a revenue loss of $1.5 trillion over the ten-year estimating period.

Regardless, many House Republicans considered ATRA 2012 to be a violation of their "no tax increase" pledge and voted to reject it by an 85–151 margin. However, overwhelming support from House Democrats (172–16)—and a lopsided bipartisan vote of 89–8 in the Senate—cleared the fiscal cliff agreement for the president's signature on January 2. One day later, the 113th Congress convened, and having "lost" the battle over taxes, House Republicans were determined to renew their attacks on domestic spending.

The Second Term Stalemate

Barack Obama's second term featured battles over budget policy every single year—domestic spending was bitterly contested, government shutdown threats and debt limit impasses were routine, and Republican warnings about deficit and debt verged on the apocalyptic. Missing entirely, however, was bipartisan agreement on comprehensive deficit reduction. BCA 2011 remained in place, but its planned spending cuts were proving to be much too severe. The bipartisan budget agreements that were reached in 2013 and 2015 restored the funding needed for defense and domestic programs but also erased much of the deficit reduction that Congress had mandated.

Entitlement reform, which could have facilitated long-term deficit reduction, was another casualty of the partisan divide over budget policy. With tax increases off-limits for Republicans, the Obama administration and congressional Democrats had no incentive to retrench entitlements. In addition, Republicans were deeply divided over entitlement policy. The budget plans that they adopted left untouched the single largest entitlement, Social Security, but proposed enormous rollbacks in healthcare and public assistance entitlements. Since Republicans never advanced legislation to implement these cuts—with the exception of an ACA repeal, which they knew would be vetoed—it was apparent that many within the party had serious misgivings about the policy and political consequences of entitlement reform. If deficits and debt truly posed a serious problem, the 113th and 114th Congresses failed to take corrective action.

Bipartisan Budget Act of 2013

In January, President Obama notified Congress that an increase in the debt ceiling was urgently needed. The Treasury Department had reached the $17.1 trillion limit and had been using "extraordinary measures" to support continued borrowing. In order to placate House Republicans, the debt ceiling legislation included an unusual provision that deferred the payment of congressional salaries unless the House and Senate passed fiscal year 2014 budgets by the April 15 deadline.[38] By setting the stage for an early confrontation over spending, House Republicans agreed to suspend the debt through mid-May.

In March, Congress also completed action on final 2013 appropriations bills, President Obama already having implemented the 2013 sequester at the reduced level agreed to in the fiscal cliff agreement. Deficit savings from the 2013 spending caps and sequesters, however, were erased by a $60 billion disaster relief bill Congress had approved in late January and by wartime defense appropriations that were exempt from spending limits. For House Republicans, federal spending remained unacceptably high, and they redoubled their efforts to cut short-term discretionary spending and long-term entitlements.

The budget resolution that the House adopted on March 21 called for balancing the budget by 2023 through major cutbacks in discretionary domestic appropriations and healthcare and public assistance entitlements. Repeal of the ACA's healthcare coverage provisions was an obvious Republican priority, but more substantial savings were to be achieved through Medicaid and Medicare spending controls. In addition, the House plan included changes in spending caps and sequestration formulas to shift funds from discretionary domestic programs to defense.

The budget resolution that the Democratic Senate adopted on March 22 was, not surprisingly, vastly different. Deficit reduction in the Senate plan was based on tax increases rather than spending cuts, and its discretionary spending total for 2014 was almost $100 billion above the figure adopted by the House.[39] In addition, the added funding for discretionary programs was primarily directed toward domestic programs rather than defense. The Senate's budget resolution was passed without any Republican votes and the House's budget resolution without any Democratic votes, yet another sign that the partisan differences over spending had not been eased by the 2011 agreement. Indeed, House Republicans were convinced that a more determined stance on government shutdowns and debt limit increases would force the Obama administration and Senate Democrats to make much greater concessions than they had in 2011.

In the House, the tight limits on discretionary spending stalled the appropriations process in committee and on the floor. None of the major domestic appropriations bills had passed the House by early September, and Senate Republicans had prevented the Senate from passing any of its 12 appropriations bills. The House passed several continuing resolutions that provided additional time for appropriations differences to be resolved but each contained funding and implementation restrictions on the ACA. These were rejected by the Senate and, of course, were completely unacceptable to the White House. The House refused to pass the "clean" continuing resolution that the Senate and President Obama demanded, and the 16-day government shutdown of 2013 began on October 1.

The debt ceiling issue also resurfaced at this point. The Treasury Department, which had been relying on "extraordinary measures" to support its borrowing for several months, notified Congress that its borrowing capacity would be completely exhausted "no later than October 17."[40] Senate Republican leaders, who were apprehensive about the political fallout from the House's shutdown strategy, were even more concerned about the repercussions from a debt limit standoff. When talks between congressional leaders of both parties and President Obama failed to produce an agreement, the Senate's Democratic and Republican leaders seized the initiative. On October 15, they agreed on a three-month continuing resolution with presequester funding levels and a debt limit suspension through February 7, 2014. The Senate passed the necessary legislation on October 16 by a vote of 81–18, and the House cleared the bill by 285–144. President Obama signed it into law the next day.

The House was also forced to retreat on the discretionary spending limits that had disrupted the appropriations process in the first place. The Bipartisan Budget Act of 2013 (BBA 2013) increased the discretionary spending caps for 2014 and 2015 and reduced the scheduled sequesters for both years. The spending cap adjustments for defense and nondefense programs, for example, totaled more than $60 billion in 2014–2015, and the sequestration reduction was roughly similar.[41] When BCA 2011 was passed, there were strong reservations about its feasibility. BBA 2013 was a clear acknowledgement that discretionary spending alone could not provide the amount of deficit reduction that House Republicans insisted was necessary.

With a more realistic fiscal framework in place, the House and the Senate passed a 2014 omnibus appropriations bill in January by comfortable margins in both chambers. This bipartisan comity also produced a drama-free resolution of another debt limit increase. On February 11, the House voted to suspend the debt limit through March 15, 2015, and the Senate cleared the suspension the following day. The appropriations process, however, was disrupted by intraparty disputes among House Republicans over individual spending bills and interparty differences in the Senate over the allocations for these bills. The House and Senate then adopted a continuing resolution well in advance of the October 1 deadline that funded government operations through early December and allowed Congress to recess for the midterm elections. The lame-duck session that followed approved an omnibus appropriations consolidated measure that covered 11 of the 12 regular appropriations bills for fiscal year 2015 but only stopgap funding (through February 27) for the Department of Homeland Security. The latter was intended to provide the Republican-controlled 114th Congress with an early opportunity to challenge President Obama's initiatives on immigration enforcement, but the broader measure followed through on the increases in the 2013 Bipartisan Budget Act.

The Bipartisan Agreement of 2015

With a 55–45 majority in the Senate and a 247-seat majority in the House, House and Senate Republican leaders confidently predicted a return to regular order that would produce timely action on appropriations bills and debt ceiling increases while advancing their fiscal agenda. A budget resolution agreement was reached in late April that included reconciliation instructions for repealing the ACA, long-term reductions in entitlement program spending, and short-term cuts in discretionary domestic spending. With President Obama's veto standing in the way, ACA repeal was nothing more than a campaign issue for 2016, so Republicans drew out the reconciliation process for months. The Senate formally passed its repeal measure in December 2015, but the House postponed its vote until January to highlight its election year significance. President Obama promptly vetoed the bill, and the House override veto fell far short of the required two-thirds majority, but Republicans were satisfied they had successfully exploited the issue.

The entitlement savings in the Republican balanced-budget plan for the 2020s were also detached from legislative proposals that had any chance of becoming law regardless of which party controlled the White House. Republicans were far from unified on Medicaid block grants, Medicare premium support reforms, or sweeping public assistance cutbacks, while congressional Democratic opposition was virtually unanimous. The Republican Congress's budget resolution was therefore relevant only insofar as its discretionary spending totals could be enforced, and even this proved to be problematic.

In the House, for example, Freedom Caucus Republicans were prepared to shut down the government again in order to implement the domestic spending cuts that had been promised in 2011 but which were subsequently bargained away. Republican members of the Appropriations Committee, however, were more concerned with spending ceilings that could accommodate funding for domestic programs with broad support within the party. Senate Republicans faced similar internal divisions and had to deal with a Democratic minority that had considerable leverage over the appropriations process. Senate Democrats had agreed during the early summer to filibuster any appropriations bill that contained sequestration-based spending cuts, and none of the spending measures for the upcoming fiscal year made it to the Senate floor before Congress's August recess.

The impasse over spending was, once again, paired with the need to raise the debt ceiling. The Treasury Department's notification to Congress in mid-October had requested legislative authorization by early November for additional borrowing.[42] House Republicans had previously insisted that any continuing resolution for fiscal year 2016 appropriations would have to include a defunding provision for the Planned Parenthood organization, and hard-line conservatives now threatened to block a debt limit increase that was not offset by spending cuts. They settled instead for the resignation of Speaker John Boehner, whose antispending commitment they considered suspect.

A clean continuing resolution—the Planned Parenthood defunding provision was dropped after Boehner's announcement—was approved on September 30. Over the next several weeks, House and Senate leaders worked with Obama administration representatives on a spending and debt agreement along the lines of the 2013 pact. Under BBA 2015 the discretionary spending levels for defense and nondefense programs were raised by equal amounts—$25 billion in 2016 and $15 billion in 2017.[43] These increases effectively canceled the sequestrations scheduled for 2016 and 2017, assuming that actual appropriations matched the limits in the agreement. Another debt limit suspension was approved, in this case an extension through March 15, 2017. Funding limits for war operations—Overseas Contingency Operations—were set at approximately $75 billion annually, although these limits were nonbinding. A number of corollary issues were also addressed, including Medicare Part B premium payments for low-income retirees, funding for the Social Security disability program, and ACA employer mandates.

In both the House and Senate, BBA 2015 was approved by large margins—266–167 and 64–35—but a majority of Republicans in both chambers voted against it. Democratic support, by comparison, was unanimous. With the higher spending ceilings in place, House and Senate appropriators reached agreement in mid-December on an omnibus spending bill that funded government operations for the remainder of fiscal year 2016. The omnibus bill, which included a number of tax preference extensions, was approved by the House (316–113) and the Senate (65–33).

Promises of a return to regular order in 2016 quickly evaporated as election year politics upended the appropriations process. President Obama's veto of the ACA reconciliation bill in January was followed by the refusal of the House and Senate Budget Committee chairmen to hold hearings on the president's budget that was submitted in February. The Budget Committees then failed to pass budget resolutions, as Republicans grappled with how to reconcile their ten-year balanced budget goal with the discretionary spending levels needed to accommodate defense and nondefense spending requirements.

Conservative Republicans in the House were intent on cutting the non-defense spending totals in the budget agreement Congress had approved the previous October, which undercut efforts by the new House Speaker, Paul Ryan, to begin early markups of appropriations bills under the agreement's framework. With House action delayed, the Senate process stalled as well. In late September, the Military Construction and Veterans Affairs fiscal year 2017 appropriations bill was passed and coupled to a ten-week continuing resolution for the remaining 11 bills. A post-election session then approved another continuing resolution through April 28, 2017. Both continuing resolutions incorporated the spending limits in the 2015 budget agreement.[44]

Governance and Deficit Politics

In an interview conducted by the *National Journal* in October 2010, Senator Mitch McConnell, the Republican Minority Leader at the time, clearly stated his party's goal in dealing with the Obama administration: "The single most important thing we want to achieve is for President Obama to be a one-term president."[45] If this were the only goal, McConnell and his fellow Republicans failed to achieve it. On the other hand, Republicans took control of the House in 2010 and of the Senate four years later. Then, in 2016, Republicans retained their hold on the House and the Senate, added the presidency, and regained unified party control for the first time in a decade.

By most conventional measures, Barack Obama's presidency had been successful. He was reelected, the nation recovered from the Great Recession, and he remained popular for most of his tenure. Economic growth during his second term, for example, averaged 2.3 percent annually, and the unemployment rate—which had reached 10 percent in 2009—had dropped to 4.7 percent when he left office.[46] At that point, his public approval rating stood at 59 percent, equal to Dwight D. Eisenhower's and just below that of Reagan and Clinton.[47]

Obama was unable, however, to check the deepening polarization in American national politics, and his public approval ratings reflected this. Among Democrats, his approval ratings were consistently high, averaging 83 percent from 2009–2017.[48] Among Republicans, the average rating over this period was 13 percent. Obama's 70 percent partisan approval gap was the highest for any president over the past several decades. His predecessor, George W. Bush, had previously held the record, with a 61 percent differential.

In Congress, polarization became more pronounced as well, and budget-related legislation was one of the main casualties. High-profile bills, such as the 2009 stimulus package and the 2010 ACA, attracted almost no

Republican votes. Even "must-pass" legislation, such as annual appropriations bills and periodic debt limit increases, no longer served as a constraint on obstructionist opposition tactics. Governance norms had weakened during the Clinton administration. They nearly disappeared under Obama, as Republicans threatened time after time to shut down the government and even flirted with government defaults. These tactics kept the Obama administration and congressional Democrats constantly on the defensive regarding taxes, spending, and debt. They also helped Republicans to regain control of Congress.

Republicans also succeeded in preserving the Bush tax cuts, while promoting balanced budgets and reduced debt. Post-recession spending levels under Obama were not unusually high. They averaged 20.6 percent, roughly in line with average spending since the 1970s. In addition, post-recession discretionary domestic spending under Obama was less than it had been under Bush. Retirement and healthcare entitlement spending, however, was much higher. In 2007, mandatory spending-GDP was 10.1 percent. In 2016, it was over 13 percent, with much of this increase accounted for by Social Security, Medicare, and Medicaid. The deficits at the end of Obama's presidency—2.8 percent of GDP in 2014, 2.4 percent in 2015, and 3.2 percent in 2016—were larger than those at a similar point under Bush, but the "high spending" driving these deficits was from the major entitlement programs.

On the revenue side of the budget, there was a sharp falloff in 2009–2010, when revenues were at 14.6 percent, the lowest level in 60 years. In 2015–2016, revenue-GDP averaged 17.8 percent, almost exactly the same as peak revenue levels during the Bush administration. Democrats did increase Medicare and other taxes to help to fund the ACA, but these increases were dwarfed by the 2012 tax cut. The Bush tax cuts in 2001 and 2003 had helped to create the structural deficit problem. A decade later, they helped to perpetuate it.

A serious and realistic approach to deficit reduction in the wake of the Great Recession required entitlement reforms and tax increases, not just discretionary spending cuts. Simpson-Bowles offered a useful starting point, but bipartisan compromises on entitlements and taxes could not be reached during the Obama presidency. As a result, deficit politics remained firmly entrenched when Republicans returned to power in 2017. Whether they would try to change course, and how Democrats would respond, would be a defining issue for the Trump presidency and an important determinant of the nation's fiscal future.

Notes

1 Minnesota's U.S. Senate election was not decided until summer, when Democrat Al Franken was declared the victor. In April, Arlen Specter, a Pennsylvania Republican serving his fifth term in the Senate, switched parties. When Franken was officially sworn in at the beginning of July, Democrats had a 60–40 margin.

2 In January 2009, the Congressional Budget Office projected a $1.2 trillion (8.3 percent of GDP) deficit for the current fiscal year, the largest deficit since World War II. It noted that the expected "enactment of an economic stimulus package would add to that deficit." Congressional Budget Office, *The Budget and Economic Outlook: Fiscal Years 2009 to 2019* (Washington, D.C.: Congressional Budget Office, 2009), 1.
3 *Congressional Quarterly Almanac, 2009* (Washington, D.C.: Congressional Quarterly, 2010), 7-3–7-4.
4 *Congressional Quarterly Almanac, 2009*, 7-5.
5 *Congressional Quarterly Almanac, 2009*, 7-5.
6 Congressional Budget Office, *Estimated Cost of the American Recovery and Reinvestment Act of 2009* (Washington, D.C.: Congressional Budget Office, February 13, 2009), Table 1; *Congressional Quarterly Almanac, 2009*, 7-7–7-9.
7 Susan Davis, "A Different Place," *National Journal* 42 (October 16, 2010), 8.
8 *Congressional Quarterly Almanac, 2008* (Washington, D.C.: Congressional Quarterly, 2009), 7-4.
9 *Congressional Quarterly Almanac, 2009*, 4-9.
10 *Congressional Quarterly Almanac, 2009*, 4-11.
11 Carl Hulse, "Regretting Past, Democrats Aim to Bypass G.O.P. on Stimulus Bill," *New York Times*, February 1, 2021, A18.
12 *Congressional Quarterly Almanac, 2009*, 13-9.
13 Congressional Budget Office, "Enacted Legislation, Item 1: Final Cost Estimate, March 20, 2010," *Selected CBO Publications Related to Health Care Legislation, 2009–2010* (Washington, D.C.: Congressional Budget Office, December 2010), 11.
14 Congressional Budget Office, "Enacted Legislation, Item 1: Final Cost Estimate, March 20, 2010," *Selected CBO Publications Related to Health Care Legislation, 2009–2010*, Table 4.
15 Bowles was a Democrat who had served as chief of staff for President Clinton. Simpson was a Republican who served three terms in the Senate before retiring in 1997.
16 *The Moment of Truth: Report of the National Commission on Fiscal Responsibility and Reform* (Washington, D.C.: The White House, December 2010), 12.
17 "Gallup Daily: Obama Job Approval," Gallup, Inc., https://news.gallup.com/poll/113980/Gallup-Daily-Obama-Job-Approval.aspx.
18 *Historical Tables, Budget of the United States Government, Fiscal Year 2021* (Washington, D.C.: Government Printing Office, 2020), Table 8.1, Table 8.6.
19 Deirdre Walsh and Dana Bash, "GOP's 'Pledge to America' Lays Out a Governing Agenda," CNN.com, September 23, 2010, www.cnn.com/2010/POLITICS/09/22/gop.pledge.to.america/index.html.
20 According to the ATR's list for the 112th Congress, 238 House members and 41 members of the Senate had signed the pledge. All but a handful were Republicans. "The Taxpayer Protection Pledge Signers, 112th Congressional List," Americans for Tax Reform, http://s3.amazonaws.com/atrfiles/files/files/091411-federalpledge signers.pdf.
21 *Congress and the Nation, 2009–2012* (Washington, D.C.: Congressional Quarterly, 2014), 902–903.
22 An "official" recommendation required 14 votes. The commission delayed its report for two days, until December 3, in an unsuccessful attempt to secure the necessary votes. "Official" in this case simply meant that the commission's recommendations could be formally reported to Congress.
23 *Congress and the Nation, 2009–2012*, 151–152.
24 *Congress and the Nation, 2009–2012*, 152.
25 *Congress and the Nation, 2009–2012*, 160.

26 D. Andrew Austin, *The Debt Limit Since 2011* (Washington, D.C.: Congressional Research Service, March 29, 2018), 7–8.
27 *Congress and the Nation, 2009–2012*, 159.
28 *Congress and the Nation, 2009–2012*, 164.
29 *The Budget Control Act: Frequently Asked Questions* (Washington, D.C.: Congressional Research Service, October 1, 2019), 1–2; Austin, *The Debt Limit Since 2011*, Summary.
30 Mark Labonte and Mindy R. Levit, *The Budget Control Act of 2011: Effects on Spending Levels and the Budget Deficit* (Washington, D.C.: Congressional Research Service, October 5, 2011), 1, 11.
31 Labonte and Levit, *The Budget Control Act of 2011*, 5.
32 Labonte and Levit, *The Budget Control Act of 2011*, 17.
33 *Congress and the Nation, 2009–2012*, 170.
34 *Congress and the Nation, 2009–2012*, 179–180.
35 *Congress and the Nation, 2009–2012*, 181.
36 Margot L. Crandall-Hollick, *An Overview of the Tax Provisions in the American Taxpayer Relief Act of 2012* (Washington, D.C.: Congressional Research Service, January 10, 2013), Summary.
37 "2012 Democratic Party Platform, September 3, 2012," The American Presidency Project, www.presidency.ucsb.edu/documents/2012-democratic-party-platform.
38 Austin, *The Debt Limit Since 2011*, 10–11.
39 *Congress and the Nation, 2013–2016* (Washington, D.C.: Congressional Quarterly, 2020), 73.
40 Austin, *The Debt Limit Since 2011*, 14.
41 *Congress and the Nation, 2013–2016*, 75.
42 Austin, *The Debt Limit Since 2011*, 22.
43 Grant A. Driessen, *Bipartisan Budget Act of 2015: Adjustments to the Budget Control Act of 2011* (Washington, D.C.: Congressional Research Service, November 6, 2015), 1–2.
44 *Congress and the Nation, 2013–2016*, 109.
45 Glenn Kessler, "When Did McConnell Say He Wanted to Make Obama a 'One-Term President'?" *Washington Post*, September 25, 2012, www.washingtonpost.com/blogs/fact-checker/post/when-did-mcconnell-say-he-wanted-to-make-obama-a-one-term-president/2012/09/24/79fd5cd8-0696-11e2-afff-d6c7f20a83bf_blog.html.
46 "FRED Graph Observations, Federal Reserve Economic Data," Federal Reserve Bank of St. Louis, https://fred.stlouisfed.org/series/A191RL1Q225SBEA, https://fred.stlouisfed.org/series/UNRATE.
47 "Final Presidential Job Approval Ratings," The American Presidency Project, www.presidency.ucsb.edu/statistics/data/final-presidential-job-approval-ratings.
48 *Congress and the Nation, 2013–2016*, xvii.

5 Raising the Deficit

The Trump Presidency

Donald J. Trump's presidency was tumultuous from beginning to end. It began with false claims about the size of his election victory in 2016 and ended with his refusal to accept electoral defeat four years later. Trump was impeached twice by the House of Representatives. In 2019, the House voted to charge Trump with abuse of power and obstruction of Congress. In January 2021, he was charged with "incitement of insurrection," after his supporters attacked the Capitol in an attempt to overturn the 2020 Electoral College results. In both cases, the Senate voted to acquit Trump, although a majority of senators supported his conviction in the second impeachment.[1]

As president, Trump flouted institutional norms governing rhetoric and conduct and broke with long-standing Republican party principles regarding free trade, immigration, and the international role of the United States. On social and domestic issues, however, Trump followed a more conventional course. His extraordinary hold on Republican voters translated into unwavering support from Republican legislators for Trump's domestic agenda. At the heart of that agenda were deregulation and tax cuts. In addition, the Trump administration was extremely successful in reshaping the federal judiciary to accommodate a complementary conservative view of federal power.

Trump also made certain that congressional Republicans did not allow concerns about spending and deficits to interfere with popular spending programs or "pro-growth" tax cuts. Trump and his fellow Republicans often warned of the dangers posed by rising deficits and debt but never made a serious attempt to reduce deficits, much less balance the budget. The result was a steady increase in deficits and debt from 2017 through 2019 and a dramatic spike in both when the coronavirus disease (COVID-19) pandemic nearly shut down the economy in the spring of 2020. The 2020 deficit was more than $3.1 trillion, and the 2021 deficit was also expected to exceed $3 trillion.

President Trump's pre-pandemic deficit record was especially striking given the sharp criticism that Republicans had leveled at the Obama administration's fiscal record. Trump's first budget, for example, pledged to "reverse the damaging trends from previous administrations … put our Nation's budget

DOI: 10.4324/9781003167266-5

back into balance and begin to reduce the national debt."[2] In 2018, Trump called for "spending restraint to ensure long-term fiscal health … [and] a critical step toward balance."[3] The following year was much of the same, with "a clear roadmap for the Congress to bring Federal spending and debt under control … [and] protect future generations from Washington's habitual deficit spending."[4] The budget policies that Trump actually promoted, and that congressional Republicans invariably supported, however, were completely at odds with these prescriptions. Spending levels increased under Trump, but revenue levels were cut, and deficits rose accordingly.

While deficits were routinely ignored by the Trump administration, the budget was used to advance the president's policy and political priorities. Budgetary resources were routinely used to reward or punish agencies, an established practice for administrations of both parties, but President Trump's efforts to discipline departments and agencies were unusually aggressive.[5] The politicization of budget policy execution by the Office of Management and Budget reflected the president's push for unchecked spending powers on issues that mattered to him—which some Trump officials characterized as "the president's authority to spend money at any time and in any manner that he determines appropriate."[6] President Trump used executive budget powers to control what departments and agencies could or could not do; enforcing spending discipline or reducing deficits was a peripheral concern.

The Republican Agenda, 2017–2018

At the beginning of the 115th Congress, Republicans had a solid 241–194 margin of control in the House but only a 52–48 majority in the Senate. Given the latter, Republican leaders decided to use the filibuster-proof budget reconciliation procedure for their most important legislative priorities—repeal of the Affordable Care Act (ACA) and enactment of a large, "pro-growth" tax cut. Congress would also have to deal with routine budget matters, such as final appropriations for 2017, pending appropriations for 2018, and the debt limit. Democrats would be able to influence how these fiscal issues were decided, but Republicans alone would control the outcome on ACA repeal and tax cuts. The key question was whether Republicans could summon the same unity on an entitlement "reform" as they did on tax cuts.

The End of Entitlement Reform

In January 2011, House Republicans had quickly approved a full-scale repeal of the healthcare law that Democrats had passed the previous year. The "Repealing the Job-Killing Health Care Law Act of 2011" was followed by several dozen bills limiting the funding and implementation of various provisions of the ACA over the next few years.[7] Since these measures were routinely blocked by Senate Democrats, Republicans could ignore their potential impact on healthcare access in the districts and states that they represented. The repeal bill passed by the Republican-controlled 114th Congress had a similar fail-safe, since it faced a certain veto by President Obama. Nevertheless, it revealed some cracks in Republican unity, with conservatives favoring a straightforward, full-scale repeal and moderates pressing to retain some of the expanded healthcare access that the ACA provided. These intraparty divisions would have to be resolved in 2017, and this time the party would be responsible for how "repeal and replace" actually worked.

The Legislative Impasse

Both the House and the Senate quickly approved a joint budget resolution in January 2017 that provided reconciliation instructions for an expedited ACA repeal. There were scattered complaints from Republicans that the budget resolution did not include a balanced-budget fiscal plan, but House and Senate leaders dismissed these concerns. The sole purpose of the budget resolution, in their view, was to trigger the reconciliation process.

Speaker Paul Ryan and the House leadership had drafted a repeal bill in advance, and it was referred to the Ways and Means and the Energy and Commerce Committees for what was expected to be perfunctory review and markup. On March 6, both committees concluded their markups and reported out their respective sections of what was labeled the American Health Care Act (AHCA). The House Budget Committee then took the committee texts, conducted its own markup, and went before the Rules Committee for a special rule that would allow the House to limit floor debate and amendments on the AHCA.

The streamlined process House leaders orchestrated then began to unravel. Freedom Caucus Republicans, most of whom represented extremely safe districts, were committed to a wholesale repeal of the coverage, taxes, and regulations in the ACA. From their perspective, the leadership bill did not go far enough in curbing federal interference with private healthcare markets. Moderate Republicans, by comparison, complained that the proposed cutbacks in Medicaid, health insurance subsidies, and health insurance mandates were too severe. Their complaints were buttressed by a Congressional Budget Office (CBO) assessment that the changes could increase the number of uninsured Americans by as many as 24 million over the next decade.[8] As hard-line conservatives pressed for even stronger restrictions to be added to the AHCA, other Republicans withdrew their support, and Speaker Ryan pulled the bill from the House floor on March 24.

At this point, it was unclear whether Republican leaders could get a revised bill through the House. And even if they managed to do so, the prospects for Senate action were much less favorable than they had appeared to be back in January. The same intraparty disputes over repeal versus replacement that had derailed the AHCA bill in the House would be magnified in a Senate where Republicans had a smaller and more fragile majority.

Further complicating matters was the lack of policy guidance from the White House. The administration had been taking administrative actions to undermine what the president derisively termed "Obamacare" but left to Congress the specifics of when and how to replace it. In February, President Trump stated, "I have to tell you, it's an unbelievably complex subject. Nobody knew that health care could be so complicated."[9] After the House found itself deadlocked in March, he confidently predicted that "Obamacare ... will explode," and "Democrats will come to us and say, 'Look, let's get together and get a great health care bill ... for the people of our country.'"[10]

Bipartisanship was not at all what congressional Republicans had in mind, and House leaders moved to renew their repeal effort after the March debacle. During April, the leadership bill was revised, primarily by easing federal regulation of private health insurance plans. An opt-out provision for states brought Freedom Caucus members back into the fold, and the House passed the AHCA by a vote of 217–213 on May 4. The House bill was, as expected, unanimously opposed by Democrats, but 20 Republicans also voted "no." Their main objection was the abrupt loss of coverage that millions of Americans would face from canceling the Medicaid expansion and reducing health insurance subsidies. In addition, the AHCA would convert the traditional Medicaid program into a block grant, further curtailing federally supported healthcare coverage in the 2020s and beyond, and its deregulatory provisions were likely to result in costlier and less available private insurance coverage.

In the Senate, Majority Leader Mitch McConnell placed the House-passed bill on the Senate calendar in early June but acknowledged that it was too restrictive to pass the Senate. He then streamlined the process for drafting a revised bill, bypassing committee hearings and markups and appointing a small working group instead. The latter completed its work in late June, and the leadership's initial bill was then released. The Better Care Reconciliation Act (BCRA) took the same general approach the House had taken—major reductions in Medicaid and health insurance subsidies; full repeal of individual and employer insurance mandates; and reduced taxes and fees enacted under the ACA (see Table 5.1).

The Medicaid cutbacks in the Senate bill, however, were smaller than those that the House had adopted, and they were phased in more slowly. The BCRA's immediate impact on healthcare coverage was slightly less severe as a result. By the mid-2020s, the Senate bill would increase the number of insured Americans by an estimated 22 million, a substantial number but again somewhat lower than the estimate for the AHCA.[11]

The BCRA "compromise" was still too severe for some Republicans, and McConnell never scheduled it for a vote. In late July, several alternatives were considered, but each was rejected. An amended version of the BCRA, which would allow insurers to offer nonsubsidized plans with limited coverage and low costs—an option favored by conservatives—was defeated on a 43–57

Table 5.1 Budget Deficit Effects of the Better Care Reconciliation Act (BCRA) and American Health Care Act (AHCA) (in billions of dollars)

		Increase or Decrease, 2017–2026	
	Major Components	*BCRA*	*House-Passed Version of the AHCA*
Medicaid	Reduction and termination of enhanced federal matching funds; per capita-based cap on Medicaid payments	–772	–834
Tax Credits and Selected Coverage Provisions	Reduced subsidies for nongroup health insurance	–408	–276
Funds to States and Insurers	Spending to reduce premiums and for other purposes	+107	+117
Penalty Payments	Reduced collections of penalty payments from employers and uninsured people	+210	+210
Non-coverage Provisions	Repeal or delay of taxes on high-income people, fees imposed on manufacturers, and excise taxes enacted under the ACA; modification of various tax preferences for medical care	+541	+664
Total		–321	–119

Source: Congressional Budget Office, *Cost Estimate: Better Care Reconciliation Act of 2017* (Washington, D.C.: Congressional Budget Office, June 26, 2017), 38.

vote. A "repeal without replacement" bill was voted down by 45–55. Finally, McConnell offered a so-called skinny repeal that targeted the ACA's individual and employer insurance mandates. His intent was to pass a narrow bill that would allow a House-Senate conference committee to negotiate the comprehensive bill that was needed. Whether the conference route would succeed was far from certain, but the Senate's 49–51 rejection of McConnell's "skinny repeal" foreclosed that option.

Three Senate Republicans—Susan Collins, Lisa Murkowski, and John McCain—joined all 48 Senate Democrats on this dramatic vote. Collins and Murkowski had been critical from the outset of the truncated process McConnell used to draft the BCRA, and they continued to voice their concerns about healthcare coverage and costs even as other Republicans fell into line. McCain's vote came at the last minute and as something of a surprise given his past criticism of the ACA. In explaining his about-face, McCain complained, as had Collins and Murkowski, that the Senate's failure to follow regular order—no committee hearings, markups, or reports—had produced a flawed bill. What was needed, in McCain's view, was a viable replacement for the ACA and that could only be achieved through an open and deliberative legislative process.

McCain raised the same objections several weeks later to a new bill that would have converted the ACA into a healthcare block grant to the states. Senators Lindsey Graham and William Cassidy had drafted the measure and secured President Trump's support for it. Given McCain's opposition, along with that of Collins and Murkowski, McConnell never brought Graham-Cassidy to the Senate floor. Despite his promise to revisit ACA repeal at some future date, McConnell never did. He turned his attention instead to tax cuts, over which Republicans truly were unified. The tax cut bill that Congress passed in December 2017 included a provision that canceled the ACA's individual mandate tax penalty, but Republicans still fell far short of fulfilling their promise to repeal the ACA.

Administration Attacks

After a bungled enrollment system for the ACA health insurance exchanges in the fall of 2013, the Obama administration put in place public outreach and technical support to insure widespread participation in the exchanges. It also took steps to stabilize funding for private insurers and encouraged states to adopt expanded Medicaid programs. Since the ACA's enactment was followed by a number of legal challenges, including a U.S. Supreme Court test of its constitutionality, the administration was actively involved in defending it in the courts as well. President Obama and the officials who were responsible for implementing the ACA were committed to its success and acted accordingly.

President Trump, however, had campaigned against the ACA, and his administration worked to undermine it. This included efforts to curb enrollments and disrupt the health insurance exchanges.[12] In January 2017, the administration cut back on funding for ACA-related advertising that promoted enrollment in the private insurance exchanges. It subsequently limited support for the "navigator" program that assisted individuals in purchasing insurance on these exchanges. Application periods for ACA enrollment were pared back and special enrollment periods for people with serious medical conditions were curbed. Federal officials, including President Trump, also issued public statements that warned potential enrollees of the high costs and uncertain future of the ACA's private insurance program.

The administration worked to discourage private insurance companies from participating in the health insurance exchange by cutting subsidies for high-risk coverage.[13] At the same time, it encouraged insurers to offer limited coverage, low-cost plans that did not meet ACA standards, and it followed the same approach with small employer association health plans.[14] These attempts to destabilize the exchanges were mirrored by Congress's termination of the individual insurance mandate penalty.

Medicaid was also targeted by Trump administration officials.[15] Funding waivers, for example, assisted states that were not participating in the Medicaid expansion program authorized by the ACA. In addition, the administration supported efforts by some states to add work requirements and beneficiary cost-sharing to their traditional Medicaid programs. As with its ACA health insurance initiatives, the Trump administration was hoping to reduce the number of people applying for and receiving subsidized healthcare coverage.

Given the plethora of executive orders, agency directives, and funding waivers the Trump administration employed in its attacks against the ACA, it often found itself in court. Medicaid work requirements, for example, were challenged in a number of federal court cases. The most important case, however, did not involve the administration defending itself against state and local officials but rather joining state officials who were seeking to overthrow the ACA in its entirety.

After Congress terminated the individual mandate penalty, a number of Republican attorneys general filed suit in a federal district court to have the mandate itself declared unconstitutional. They then argued that the mandate was such an integral part of the ACA's design that it could not be severed from other provisions, such as the healthcare exchanges and Medicaid expansion. If it was unconstitutional, the entire law would have to be invalidated. A federal district court agreed, as did an appellate court, and the U.S. Supreme Court accepted the case in 2020. The appeal was brought, in this instance, by Democratic state attorneys general who were defending the law's constitutionality. In February 2021, the Biden administration joined this appeal, which the U.S. Supreme Court subsequently upheld.

The Aftermath

In 2018, the legislative and administrative efforts to weaken the ACA achieved some success, as the rate of uninsured persons rose to its highest level since 2015.[16] But the ACA survived and then began to recover. First, the 2018 midterms gave Democrats control of the House, putting an end to legislative repeal efforts for the last two years of Trump's presidency. Second, in 2019 and 2020, the number of states with expanded Medicaid programs increased to 37.[17] In the fall of 2020, public approval of the ACA reached 55 percent, the highest level of support in its ten-year history.[18] The Biden administration's American Rescue Plan legislation enacted in March 2021 expanded eligibility and raised subsidies for the ACA's private insurance option. The administration also planned to strengthen and expand Medicaid. What looked like an endangered program in 2017 now appeared to be entrenched.

It is also difficult to imagine that entitlement "reform" will gain traction any time soon. The failure of a committed Republican Congress and supportive president to "repeal and replace" the ACA was not simply a matter of a one-vote loss in the Senate. Republicans were, in fact, divided over how to deal with the serious policy challenge that "repeal and replace" posed. In 2017, 31 states and the District of Columbia had expanded Medicaid coverage, increasing the number of insured persons by 11 million, and enrollment in subsidized private insurance plans had increased to more than seven million.[19] Employer-provided health insurance was now more widely available, people with preexisting conditions had much better insurance options and young adults (below the age of 26) enjoyed guaranteed coverage under their parents' policies. The percentage of the U.S. population without insurance coverage was approximately 14 percent before these coverages were implemented; in 2017, the rate of uninsured persons had dropped to just over 8 percent.[20] At stake, therefore, was healthcare coverage for some 20 million adults and children.

The importance of these major advances in healthcare coverage and access was made clear by influential interest groups that opposed the repeal effort—the American Hospital Association; America's Essential Hospitals; America's Health Insurance Plans (the largest private insurance trade association); and the National Association of Medicaid Directors.[21] The National Governors Association, which had successfully lobbied against Medicaid block grants since the 1980s, did not present a united front in 2017. As might be expected, Democratic governors strongly opposed repeal, while a majority of their Republican counterparts supported it. Of the 16 Republican governors whose states had adopted the ACA's Medicaid expansion, however, eight opposed the repeal effort.[22]

In addition, the public's views on repeal turned out to be quite negative. A number of national polls conducted in the spring and summer of 2017 reported substantial opposition—an average of 55 percent against repeal compared to 22 percent in favor.[23] Even among Republican identifiers, the repeal plans in the House and the Senate barely commanded majority support. For Republicans in competitive districts and states, these polling results were troubling, particularly given Democratic plans for a national campaign on healthcare access in the 2018 midterm elections.

It is also worth noting that conservative Republicans viewed ACA repeal as merely the first step in revamping healthcare entitlements. Medicaid block grants, for example, would allow the federal government to cut costs and, equally as important, transfer to the states much of the responsibility for deciding coverage and benefits. Medicare privatization would likewise control costs and transfer responsibilities, in this case to beneficiaries and private insurance companies. Both programs, however, are enormous—in 2017, approximately 60 million Americans were covered by the traditional (i.e., not expanded) Medicaid program, while another 54 million had one or more Medicare program coverages—and they were growing. If Republicans could not agree to retrench the seven-year-old ACA with its 20 million beneficiaries, they could hardly be expected to "reform" the vastly larger healthcare entitlements that had been in place for more than half a century.

The history of entitlement programs in the United States offers very few examples of successful retrenchments.[24] In the modern era, Republicans could not revoke the New Deal's Social Security and public assistance entitlements. They then failed to reverse the Great Society entitlement programs in the 1980s and 1990s, to "reform" Social Security in the early 2000s, or to repeal the Obama administration's ACA in the 2010s. Strong opposition from Democrats has blocked some of these efforts, but intraparty divisions created problems on others. In the case of tax cuts, however, Republican unity is much stronger, and this allowed the Trump administration to add another major tax cut to the long list of Republican-sponsored bills that began in 1981.

The Trump Tax Cut

After their embarrassing setback over the ACA, Republicans desperately needed to achieve their second legislative priority—a major tax cut. Their goal was expedited passage of corporate and individual tax cuts by the end of 2017. To insure a coordinated approach, a small group of congressional leaders and administration officials drafted a policy framework that was announced in late September. The budget resolution authorizing a reconciliation tax cut was then adopted in October, and the Ways and Means and the Finance Committees completed their work in November.

Party-line votes in the tax committees were followed by party-line votes on their tax bills by the House and the Senate. A House-Senate conference committee quickly ironed out differences between the House and Senate bills in mid-December, and the conference bill was approved several days later. On December 22, President Trump signed the Tax Cuts and Jobs Act of 2017 (TCJA), a package of corporate and individual tax cuts totaling approximately $1.5 trillion over a ten-year period.[25] He described it as "very much a bill for the middle class, and for jobs. Corporations are literally going wild for this."[26] He went on to chide Democrats for having opposed it.

The TCJA was the most comprehensive overhaul in tax policy since the Tax Reform Act of 1986.[27] Its changes in individual tax rates were smaller, but the combination of lower tax rates and reduced tax preferences was similar. The corporate tax provisions, however, were very different. In 1986, corporate taxes had been increased to offset the revenue losses from the individual tax cuts, but the 2017 tax law lowered both corporate and individual taxes. In addition, the corporate tax cuts in 2017 were permanent, while the individual tax cuts were temporary (2018–2025).

The 1986 and 2017 tax bills were enacted with the budget in deficit by substantial amounts—the fiscal year 1985 deficit was over $212 billion, while the fiscal year 2016 deficit was over $440 billion. The 1986 tax bill, which was strongly bipartisan, was designed to be deficit neutral. The 2017 tax cut was neither. It was passed solely with Republican votes, and its deficit impact was decidedly negative. Taking into account the TCJA's economic and budgetary effects, the CBO projected a net deficit increase of $1.9 trillion for fiscal years 2018–2028.[28]

While Trump officials, including Secretary of the Treasury Steven T. Mnuchin, often declared that the 2017 tax cut would pay for itself by generating so much growth that revenue levels would increase, few took this claim seriously. The 1981 tax cut, for example, had boosted growth but revenue losses were substantially greater than predicted. The 2001 and 2003 tax cuts had been a disappointment in terms of growth and revenues. In 2017, fiscal conservatives vowed to avoid a repeat, with House Republicans calling for a revenue-neutral tax bill. When this proved impossible, they decided to ignore the deficit effects.

The "Unified Plan"

The need for corporate tax reform did not suddenly arise in 2017. For years, tax policy experts in both parties had agreed that the 35 percent corporate tax rate—the highest among industrialized democracies—was discouraging business investment in the United States and also making it financially attractive for U.S. businesses to move their operations abroad.[29] A related problem was the tax treatment of profits earned in foreign countries. Subsidiaries of U.S. firms would be taxed in the country in which they operated but could usually invest after-tax profits outside the United States without paying an additional tax. Bringing the profits back to the United States, however, would result in a second tax of up to 35 percent (with a credit for the foreign tax already paid). In 2017, an estimated $2.6 trillion in overseas profits was being left abroad in U.S. foreign subsidiaries to escape this double taxation.[30]

Despite this bipartisan consensus, congressional Republicans decided that a broader and costlier tax cut would better serve their interests and were prepared to use reconciliation to overcome any Democratic opposition. Their starting point was a one-page outline of President Trump's tax program issued by the White House in late April. It featured greatly reduced tax rates for corporations and small businesses (15 percent) and lesser reductions for individuals (10, 25, and 35 percent). Other proposed changes would eliminate the estate tax, the individual and corporate alternative minimum tax (AMT), and related tax preferences. Corporations would also be encouraged to "repatriate" their foreign profits by a new territorial tax rule governing these profits.

House leaders, including Ways and Means chairman Kevin Brady, decided to postpone committee consideration until a more detailed framework for tax law changes was agreed to by the White House and Senate and House Republicans. This work was delegated to the so-called Big Six—Speaker Ryan and Chairman Brady, Majority Leader McConnell and Finance Committee Chairman Orrin Hatch, Treasury Secretary Mnuchin, and White House National Economic Council Director Gary Cohn. Their deliberations were closed to the public and stretched out over several months. Then, in late September, "The Unified Framework for Fixing Our Broken Tax Code" was unveiled.

The centerpiece of the Framework was lower tax rates—20 percent for corporations and 12, 25, and 35 percent rates for individuals. For small businesses—"pass throughs"—the maximum tax rate would be lowered to 25 percent, but small firms (and corporations) would also benefit from accelerated depreciation of capital investments and would no longer be subject to the AMT. One of the more controversial items in the Framework was the elimination of state and local tax (SALT) deductions for individual taxpayers, a change that would disproportionately affect high-tax states such as New York, New Jersey, and California. "Blue state" Democrats were predictably outraged, which was no great worry, but congressional Republicans from these states were another matter.

Republicans repeatedly emphasized that the doubling of the standard deduction (to $24,000 for a joint return) and increase in the child tax credit would more than compensate low- and middle-income taxpayers for the SALT change, while lower rates would raise their after-tax income. Nevertheless, the SALT issue contributed to public perceptions that the Republican tax plan was unfair and unbalanced, and Democratic critics sharply attacked "tax cuts for the wealthy." In response, President Trump delivered speeches in a number of states to defend the tax cut as "pro-growth, pro-worker and pro-American."[31] Trump also reached out to several Senate Democrats who would be running for reelection in 2018 in states he had carried the previous year in an attempt to recruit bipartisan support for his tax cut program.

A bipartisan tax bill, however, was a remote possibility, given that House and Senate Democratic leaders were working to keep intact the unified opposition strategy that had worked so well with the ACA repeal. In late August, for example, Minority Leader Charles E. Schumer set conditions for Democratic engagement that he expected Republicans to reject out of hand—no tax cut for the top 1 percent of taxpayers, no deficit increase, and no use of reconciliation to pass a tax bill.[32] These conditions were elaborated in a letter sent to Trump and Republican leaders that was signed by all but three Democrats. House Democratic leaders made it clear that they also were ready to mount a full-scale opposition effort.

The Budget Resolution

Both the House and the Senate had postponed votes on the final 2018 budget resolution until the Unified Framework was released. As the budget resolutions were being drafted, however, fiscal conservatives made their case for deficit reduction and a balanced budget. In the House, where the Freedom Caucus had outsize influence, there was strong sentiment for a budget resolution that would cut domestic spending and require a revenue-neutral tax bill. To achieve the latter, House Republicans were prepared to support a new tax—a border adjustment tax, or BAT, that would offset the revenue losses from corporate and individual tax cuts.

The rationale for the tax was the desire to promote domestic manufacturing and exports. Companies would no longer be able to deduct the cost of imported goods from their gross income but could deduct export earnings. The resulting differences in taxable profits would lead to a net increase in corporate tax revenues and at the same time discourage imports and encourage exports. Whether this would actually occur was arguable, as was the assertion that costs would ultimately be borne by foreign producers and consumers, but the business community's reaction to the BAT was so overwhelmingly negative that House leaders simply decided to drop it.[33]

The House's initial budget resolution, however, included $200 billion in mandatory program savings, as well as the revenue-neutral tax cut requirement. The Senate's version did not require mandatory program cuts and authorized a much larger $1.5 trillion tax cut without any revenue offsets. The Senate's sole deficit reduction provision was a $1 billion reconciliation instruction that served a very different purpose that Republicans had pursued for years—opening up the Arctic National Wildlife Refuge (ANWR) in Alaska to oil and gas exploration. The estimated $1 billion in royalty payments that the federal government would receive allowed Republicans to add the ANWR initiative to the tax bill.

On October 19, the Senate adopted its budget resolution by a 51–49 vote. The only "no" vote among Republicans was Rand Paul, who objected to the absence of spending cuts and a balanced-budget plan. Paul would, however, fall into line when the tax bill itself came to the Senate floor. Democrats, as expected, unanimously opposed the budget resolution. House leaders decided to forego a conference and simply adopt the Senate's budget resolution, but the vote was delayed for several days as the SALT issue and deficit-neutral requirement debates were replayed among Republicans. On October 26, the budget resolution was adopted by a narrow 216–212 margin, with 20 Republicans joining the united Democratic opposition.

The Tax Committees

With the budget resolution in place, the Ways and Means Committee began its deliberations on November 2. No hearings were held, and the committee's markup of the draft bill that Chairman Brady had prepared was perfunctory. At this point, Republicans were no longer concerned about revenue losses and deficits. Instead, they focused on specific tax benefits to make the bill more attractive to wavering Republicans. The SALT deduction repeal, for example, was modified to allow a $10,000 deduction for property taxes, and the pass-through business tax rates were lowered and extended to professional small businesses. In addition to technical revisions needed to keep within the $1.5 trillion limit, Ways and Means approved a new 39.6 percent marginal tax rate for high-income taxpayers and tighter restrictions on the home mortgage interest deduction. On November 9, Ways and Means reported out the tax bill on a 24–16 party-line vote. One week later, with President Trump weighing in on its behalf, the Ways and Means tax bill passed by a fairly comfortable 227–205 margin.

The Senate Finance Committee conducted an equally brief markup that was concluded on November 16. There were minor differences with the House bill on individual tax rates and the SALT deduction, but the most important departure was the decision to make the corporate tax cuts permanent and the individual ones temporary. The latter would terminate in 2025, keeping the tax cut's ten-year cost at $1.5 trillion. In addition, the increased revenues after 2025 would avoid Byrd Rule restrictions that would otherwise limit the corporate tax cuts to ten years. Since most Republicans (and Democrats) fully expected many if not all of the individual tax cuts to be extended in 2025, the true cost of the 2017 tax cut was actually disguised. As a final sweetener, the Finance Committee bill also repealed the ACA individual mandate penalty. During the committee's markup, all the amendments proposed by Democrats were rejected, including one that would have made the corporate tax cuts temporary and the individual tax cuts permanent. The final version of the Finance Committee bill was then reported out on a 14–12 party-line vote.

The Senate Budget Committee combined the Finance tax bill with the ANWR bill that had been assigned to the Energy and Natural Resources Committee. Among Senate Republicans, there were still scattered problems with narrow provisions, such as the tax treatment of pass-through businesses versus large corporations, and the individual mandate repeal proved problematic for some. Two Budget Committee Republicans also proposed the addition of a trigger provision that would cancel some tax cuts in future years if actual revenue losses exceeded projections. After assurances from Senate leaders that these issues would be addressed on the floor, the Budget Committee reported out the reconciliation tax bill on November 28 on a 12–11 vote.

Majority Leader McConnell was able to negotiate satisfactory modifications of the pass-through business rules and other tax benefit issues raised by individual senators. The trigger provision, however, fell victim to the Senate's Byrd Rule restrictions, and efforts to work out an alternative mechanism for raising future revenues were rejected outright by a large and vocal group of Republican conservatives. With the leadership's amendment package approved at the conclusion of the Senate's floor debate, the Senate passed its reconciliation tax bill on a 51–49 vote at 1:30 a.m. on December 2.

House and Senate Republican leaders then worked out the major differences between the tax bills prior to the conference committee deliberations that began on December 13. Minor changes were made in the corporate tax sections of the bill—a tax rate of 21 percent versus 20 percent, effective in 2018 rather than in 2019, and an adjustment of the provision governing the repatriation of corporation profits from foreign operations—but the full repeal of the corporate AMT was approved, and, most importantly, the corporate tax cuts would be permanent. On the individual side, the estate tax and AMT repeals that the House had approved were replaced with higher exemption levels; differences over tax rates, tax credits, and the mortgage interest deduction were resolved without great difficulty. The SALT deduction remained capped at $10,000, but was extended to cover state and local income taxes as well as property taxes.

As the conference came to a conclusion, the prospects for final passage appeared solid. The most important roadblock—concerns about the deficit—had just about disappeared in the House, and the senators who had argued for trigger provisions to prevent excessive deficits had acquiesced as well. More parochial considerations, such as protections for small businesses and certain types of investments, had been resolved as the tax bill moved through its several iterations. On December 19, the House passed the conference agreement on a 227–203 vote. The SALT deduction compromise did not go far enough to satisfy the dozen Republicans who voted no, but with hard-line fiscal conservatives back in the fold, their votes were not needed. In the Senate, last-minute challenges involving the Byrd Rule led to some minor changes—including the elimination of the TCJA title that Republicans had attached to the bill—but the revised conference agreement was then approved by a 51–48 vote (one Republican senator was absent).[34] The House quickly revoted by 224–201 to send the bill to the president. In both the House and the Senate, every Democrat had voted "no" on the budget resolution authorizing the reconciliation tax bill, and they unanimously opposed the bill itself. Nevertheless, congressional Republicans had managed to keep their tax cut majority intact. Five months after the ACA repeal debacle, Republicans had achieved a major legislative victory and, in the process, made it much more difficult to reduce deficits and control debt.

Taxes and Budget Policy

The changes in tax law under the TCJA were numerous—more than 110 significant revisions in individual income taxation, corporate and business taxation, and international commercial taxation.[35] The most important and costly changes, however, were those that lowered tax rates and revised tax preferences for individuals, corporations, and small businesses (see Table 5.2). The new tax rates for individuals had a ten-year estimated cost of $1.2 trillion, and the flat 21 percent tax rate for corporations was estimated at $1.35 trillion. The new pass-through business tax rules added nearly $415 billion in revenue losses. The biggest offsets, or revenue raisers, on the individual tax side were the repeal of personal exemptions ($1.2 trillion) and the SALT and mortgage interest deduction limits ($668 billion). Modifications of corporate tax preferences, such as interest and operating loss deductions, reduced the net cost of corporate rate cuts by nearly $700 billion. The net effect of the international tax system changes, such as the reduced tax on

Table 5.2 Major Provisions of the Tax Cuts and Jobs Act of 2017 (TCJA 2017)

Tax Provision	*Current Law (2017)*	*TCJA 2017*
Individual Provisions		
Individual tax rates	7 brackets: 10%, 15%, 25%, 28%, 33%, 35%, 39.6%.	7 brackets: 10%, 12%, 22%, 24%, 32%, 35%, 37%.
Personal exemptions and standard deduction	Personal exemption: $4,050. Standard deduction: $6,350 (single) and $12,700 (married).	Personal exemptions repealed. Standard deduction: $12,000 (single) and $24,000 (married) in 2018.
Child-related credits	Refundable child tax credit of $1,000. Phase out begins at $110,000 (married) and $75,000 (single).	$2,000 credit per child (up to $1,400 refundable). Phase-out thresholds increased to begin at $400,000 (married) and $200,000 (single). $500 nonrefundable credit for nonchild dependents.
Mortgage interest deduction	Mortgage interest deductible on up to $1 million loan, plus $100,000 for home equity loan.	Modified deductions include state and local taxes (SALT) limited to $10,000; mortgage interest limited to $750,000 on new loans.
SALT deduction	Deductible subject to limits on itemized deductions and alternative minimum tax (AMT).	Limited to $10,000.
Education incentives	Various credits and deductions for education-related expenses.	Provisions generally retained.
Individual AMT	Alternative minimum tax.	Increase exemption amount ($109,400, married and $70,300, single) and phase-out threshold ($1 million, married and $500,000, single).
Estate tax	Tax above exemption ($5.49 million, 2017).	Double exemption amount.
ACA individual mandate penalty	$695 per adult and $347.50 per child (maximum of $2,085 or 2.5% of income).	Repealed.
Business Provisions		
Corporate tax rate	Maximum rate of 35%.	Flat 21% rate in 2018.

Tax Provision	*Current Law (2017)*	*TCJA 2017*
Pass-through businesses tax rate	Taxed according to ordinary individual rates up to 39.6%.	Taxed according to ordinary individual rates. Taxpayers may deduct 20% of qualified pass-through income. Deduction limited to the greater of 50% of W-2 wages, or 25% of W-2 wages plus 2.5% multiplied by qualified property. Specified service business may not claim deduction. Deduction limitation and specified service business limitation do not apply if taxable income is less than $157,500 (single) or $315,000 (married).
Business interest	Deduction for net interest limited to 50% of adjusted taxable income for firms with debt-equity ratio above 1.5. Interest above limitation may be carried forward indefinitely.	Deduction for net interest limited to 30% of adjusted taxable income. Interest above limitation may be carried forward indefinitely. Businesses with average annual gross receipts over last three years of $25 million or less are exempted.
Depreciation	Most assets depreciated over time. Bonus depreciation for equipment through January 1, 2020. Immediate expensing up to $500,000.	Full and immediate expensing (100% bonus depreciation) for equipment through 2022; percentage reduced by 20% per year for four years starting 2023. Expansion of expensing to $1 million for small businesses.
Corporate AMT	20% in excess of $40,000.	Repealed.
International tax system	Worldwide-based with deferral of active income.	Territorial-based with taxation of income from intangibles and other anti-base erosion provisions.
Tax on repatriated earnings	Tax due when foreign-source income is repatriated to U.S. parent; exceptions for certain passive and branch income. Taxed at 35%. Foreign tax credits available.	One-time deemed repatriation: 15.5% on cash and cash equivalents, 8% otherwise, paid over 8 years. Foreign tax credits partially available.

Sources: Mark P. Keightley and Molly F. Sherlock, *Comparing Key Elements of H.R. 1 to 2017 Tax Law* (Washington, D.C.: Congressional Research Service, December 22, 2017); Ryan J. Rosso, *The Individual Mandate for Health Insurance Coverage: In Brief* (Washington, D.C.: Congressional Research Service, August 25, 2020), 1–3.

repatriated foreign profits, was a projected revenue increase of nearly $325 billion.[36]

Given the numerous and complicated changes in tax law, the economic effects of the TCJA were far from clear. According to Republicans, business investment and job creation would increase dramatically as the law took effect, and GDP growth would accelerate. In 2018 and 2019, however, these predictions turned out to be too optimistic. In 2018, for example, a Congressional Research Service report concluded that "the growth effects [from the TCJA] tend to show a relatively small (if any) first-year effect on the economy."[37] Business investment, both domestic and from abroad, increased only marginally, wage growth was not appreciably higher than pre-TCJA levels, and businesses used their tax savings primarily for stock repurchases rather than worker compensation.[38] In addition, job growth increased in 2018 and 2019 but was lower than it had been during President Obama's second term.[39]

The budgetary impact of the TCJA was also very different from that which congressional Republicans and administration officials had predicted. In 2016 and 2017, annual corporate tax revenues had averaged nearly $300 billion. In 2018, corporate tax revenue was $205 billion, and the total for 2019 was just over $230 billion. More important, the decline in overall revenue-GDP after the TCJA was implemented was sharp and immediate.

In January 2017, baseline estimates for revenue-GDP projected a slight increase to 18.1 percent in 2018 and stable levels thereafter (see Table 5.3). Instead, post-TCJA revenue-GDP fell to 16.4 percent in 2018 and failed to rebound over the next two years. Corporate tax receipts accounted for a disproportionate share of this decline and individual income taxes for virtually all of the remainder. Payroll taxes and excise and other taxes, which had not been part of the TCJA, remained very close to January 2017 baseline projections. Overall, however, the Trump tax cuts, like the Reagan and George W. Bush tax cuts, had a dramatic and negative impact on revenue levels.

It would still have been possible, albeit much more difficult, to keep deficits in check by cutting spending. Over the course of three decades, Republicans had argued that tax cuts and domestic spending cuts could not only reduce deficits but balance budgets, but this strategy had never succeeded. It had, in fact, never even come close, since the spending cuts necessary to make it work were too damaging for many Republicans to support. The inevitable results were large deficits after the Reagan and Bush tax cuts. Not surprisingly, this same outcome took place after the Trump tax cuts, as spending remained stubbornly high.

Spending and Debt

The Trump administration's first budget outlined a ten-year deficit reduction program leading to a balanced budget in 2027. Its component parts included

Table 5.3 Baseline Revenue Projections and Actual Revenue Levels, 2017–2021 (as a percentage of GDP)

	Fiscal Year				
	2017	2018	2019	2020	2021
Individual Income Taxes					
January 2017 Baseline	8.6	8.9	9.1	9.2	9.3
Actual	8.2	8.3	8.1	7.7	n/a
(+/–)	–0.4	–0.6	–1.0	–1.5	
Corporate Income Taxes					
January 2017 Baseline	1.7	1.7	1.7	1.8	1.7
Actual	1.5	1.0	1.1	1.0	n/a
(+/–)	–0.2	–0.7	–0.6	–0.8	
Social Insurance Taxes					
January 2017 Baseline	6.0	6.0	6.0	5.9	5.9
Actual	6.0	5.8	5.9	6.2	n/a
(+/–)	0.0	–0.2	–0.1	0.3	
Other					
January 2017 Baseline	1.5	1.5	1.4	1.3	1.3
Actual	1.4	1.4	1.3	1.4	n/a
(+/–)	–0.1	–0.1	–0.1	0.1	
Total Revenues					
January 2017 Baseline	17.8	18.1	18.1	18.1	18.1
Actual	17.2	16.4	16.3	16.3	n/a
(+/–)	–0.6	–1.7	–1.8	–1.8	

Sources: January baseline projections: Congressional Budget Office, *The Budget and Economic Outlook: 2017 to 2027* (Washington, D.C.: Congressional Budget Office, 2017), 10; actual revenue levels: *Historical Tables, Budget of the United States Government, Fiscal Year 2021* (Washington, D.C.: Government Printing Office, 2020), Table 2.3; Congressional Budget Office, *The 2021 Long-Term Budget Outlook* (Washington, D.C.: Congressional Budget Office, 2021), 9.

a comprehensive but deficit-neutral tax reform; large reductions in discretionary domestic and healthcare entitlement spending; and sustained increases in the defense budget.[40] It also incorporated extremely optimistic economic assumptions, notably "a permanently higher trend growth rate as a result of … tax reform, infrastructure investments, reductions in regulation, and a greatly improved fiscal outlook."[41]

The Trump budget program was, in sum, quite similar to that which the Reagan administration had called for in 1981. Reagan officials had conceded that "a strategy of reducing taxes in advance of spending cuts implies that it will take some time to achieve the desired level of deficits."[42] At the time, it was understood that cuts in entitlements as well as in discretionary domestic programs would be needed for that strategy to work. When the necessary entitlement retrenchments were rejected by Congress, the strategy failed, and Reagan's promises of balanced budgets and small government evaporated.

In Trump's case, bringing spending into line with revenues would be even more difficult. The discretionary spending cuts that Congress had mandated in 2011 were proving to be unworkable, and Trump was assuming that much more severe cuts exclusively aimed at domestic programs would somehow be feasible. The administration's proposed entitlement reforms exempted Social Security and Medicare, the two largest spending programs, and depended entirely on Medicaid cutbacks that would be extremely difficult to get through Congress. In 2017, the Republicans had demonstrated, once again, their inability to deliver entitlement retrenchments. Moreover, differences within the party were causing problems with more modest tasks, such as funding government operations and raising the debt limit in a timely fashion.

Fiscal Year 2017 Spending

It took three continuing resolutions, spanning seven months, before Congress completed action on fiscal year 2017 spending bills. In 2016, Congress had passed only one of the 12 appropriations bills for fiscal year 2017 by the October 1 deadline, and a continuing resolution for the others was approved through mid-December. President Obama then signed a second continuing resolution through April 28, 2017. Republicans were unable to reconcile their differences over several domestic spending bills by that deadline, and a third continuing resolution was necessary before Congress completed action on the Consolidated Appropriations Act of 2017 in early May. In addition to the spending increases authorized by the Bipartisan Budget Act of 2015 (BBA 2015), the 2017 spending bill included emergency appropriations for wartime spending (Overseas Contingency Operations) and disaster relief. Not included were the numerous nondefense spending cuts the Trump administration had proposed.[43] As a result, discretionary defense and nondefense outlays in 2017 increased by approximately $15 billion over prior-year spending.

The Debt Limit and Fiscal Year 2018 Spending

Despite the change to a Republican administration, Congress procrastinated on a debt limit increase. The 2015 debt limit suspension that Congress had enacted expired on March 15, 2017. Treasury Secretary Mnuchin asked Congress to raise the limit, while stating that the Treasury would utilize the usual "extraordinary measures" until this was done.[44]

Six months later, the Treasury's available borrowing authorities were nearly exhausted, but Congress still had not acted. In the meantime, business and financial leaders had repeatedly called upon Congress to act. As the president of the American Bankers Association explained, "We'd like this to be resolved quickly. The whole brinkmanship around the debt ceiling rattles the markets and is counterproductive."[45] Secretary Mnuchin agreed, cautioning Congress that "We need to be able to pay our debts," and President Trump sharply criticized House and Senate leaders for the "Debt Ceiling … mess."[46]

Congress was also running well behind schedule on appropriations bills for fiscal year 2018. In addition to the usual disagreements between the parties over defense and nondefense spending, House and Senate Republicans were at odds over proposed cuts in the major domestic appropriations bills. Spending for disaster relief created another complication, following the passage of enormously costly hurricanes in August and September. Congress then agreed to combine supplemental appropriations for disaster relief and a debt limit suspension with a continuing resolution that funded government operations through December 8. Two more continuing resolutions in December extended temporary funding through January 19, 2018.

During 2017, Republicans had delivered a massive tax cut, but ACA repeal was dead, Democrats had managed to protect their domestic spending priorities in the final 2017 omnibus spending package enacted in May, and Republicans were struggling to avoid a similar outcome in fiscal year 2018. The regular order that Republicans had promised was nowhere to be found. Instead, continuing resolutions and debt limit suspensions were the best that Congress could do. The 2017 deficit had climbed to $665 billion, at least $100 billion more than the baseline deficit when Trump took office. With tax cuts and rising spending, the 2018 deficit would be even higher.

The Bipartisan Budget Act of 2018

When the third continuing resolution for fiscal year 2018 expired on January 19, Democrats blocked an extension in a failed attempt to get concessions on immigration policy. The three-day government shutdown ended when both sides agreed to a continuing resolution that funded the government through February 8. Republican and Democratic Senate leaders then announced that agreement had been reached on the third bipartisan budget agreement in five years—the BBA 2018.

Like its 2013 and 2015 predecessors, the 2018 agreement eased the spending limits that Congress had enacted in 2011. In this case, however, the increases were considerably larger—nearly $300 billion for discretionary defense and nondefense spending over two years.[47] The defense increases totaled $165 billion, while the nondefense allowances were $63 billion for 2018 and $68 billion for 2019. The debt ceiling problem was resolved, with a suspension until March 2019. The 2018 agreement also contained tax cuts (an extension of expiring individual and business tax preferences) and new spending (funding for disaster relief and the Children's Health Insurance

Program). Incorporated into the agreement was another continuing resolution to allow Congress to complete the appropriations process.

With the introduction of the TCJA in December and the BBA in February, the Trump administration and Congress had widened the gap between revenues and spending. In March, the generous spending ceilings in the budget agreement led to quick approval by the House and the Senate of the 2,300-page 2018 Consolidated Appropriations Act in which every domestic spending bill was funded at higher levels than the president and House and Senate Republicans had initially proposed.[48] Nevertheless, a majority of Republicans in both chambers voted for it, and President Trump signed it. His only complaint was that Congress had refused to provide the necessary funding that he sought for the construction of a border wall between the United States and Mexico.

Fiscal 2019 and the Midterms

Given the two-year budget agreement, President Trump's 2019 budget was irrelevant, even assuming that its call for "spending restraint" as a "critical step toward balance" was meant to be taken seriously.[49] In any case, with midterm elections coming up in November, Republicans were anxious to avoid prolonged battles over spending bills. Five appropriations bills, including the ordinarily contentious Labor, Health and Human Services, and Education measure, were passed in late September, and a continuing resolution for the remaining seven was approved as well. The votes in both chambers were overwhelmingly bipartisan.

The midterm elections in November put an end to unified Republican control. Democrats picked up 41 House seats, giving them a 235–199 majority when the 116th Congress convened on January 3, 2019. Democrats made major gains as well in state gubernatorial and legislative elections, but Republicans were able to add two seats to their U.S. Senate majority. President Trump thus found himself with the same divided control challenge that President Obama had faced eight years earlier, but this time the budget brinkmanship would be caused by the president rather than the opposition House party.

The Deficit Issue Disappears

In the lame-duck session after the November midterms, Congress had to complete action on seven fiscal year 2019 appropriations bills. The continuing resolution approved in September expired on December 7, and a two-week extension was enacted without serious controversy. Several days later, however, President Trump met with the House and Senate Democratic leaders and demanded that funding for a border wall with Mexico be included in the next funding bill. Otherwise he promised "to shut down the government for border security… I will shut it down, I'm not going to blame you for it."[50]

The Border Wall Shutdown

After Democrats rejected Trump's demand, the president appeared to back down, signaling to Senate Republicans that he would sign a temporary funding bill without the border wall provisions. The Senate then proceeded to pass a "clean" continuing resolution on December 19. The next day, Trump reversed course, threatening to shut down the government unless Congress agreed to provide funding for the border wall. House Republicans dutifully complied, amending the Senate-passed continuing resolution to include the $5.7 billion appropriation Trump had demanded.

Senate Democrats, in turn, promised to filibuster the amended measure, at which point Republican leaders agreed to postpone further action until the border wall funding impasse was resolved. White House officials met with House and Senate leaders from both parties, but the negotiations failed to produce an acceptable compromise. On December 22, a partial government shutdown began. It lasted until January 25, 2019. Nine executive departments, a number of executive agencies, and 800,000 federal employees were affected by the longest shutdown in U.S. history.

On January 3, the 116th Congress convened, and the Democratic-controlled House elected Nancy Pelosi as Speaker. The following day, Pelosi, Senate Minority Leader Schumer, and congressional Republicans met with President Trump, but no agreement was reached on reopening the government. On January 9, another meeting was held. When Democrats again rejected Trump's demand, he ended the meeting, and no further talks between Trump and Democratic leaders took place.

Over the next two weeks, Senate Republicans refused to schedule votes on House-passed legislation to reopen the government. Finally, on January 24, Majority Leader Mitch McConnell brought two measures to the Senate floor—a "clean" continuing resolution that House Democrats had passed and an administration-backed alternative with border wall funding. While neither reached the required 60-vote threshold, six Republicans supported the Democratic plan, underscoring the growing frustration with the president's shutdown strategy. Later that day, it was announced that Trump would accept a three-week funding extension if Congress agreed to address border security. With this assurance, the House and Senate promptly approved the necessary legislation. Trump signed it, and the government shutdown ended on January 25.

Both the House and the Senate then completed action on the seven outstanding bills for fiscal year 2019, including the Department of Homeland Security (DHS) measure that contained the designated border security provisions. The Consolidated Appropriations Act of 2019 incorporated the non-DHS funding levels that congressional appropriators had agreed to prior to the shutdown. The DHS section of the bill contained the compromise on border security—less than $1.4 billion for "55 miles of new border barriers in high-priority sectors" and additional funding for detention facilities.[51] The

House and Senate approved the measure on February 14, and President Trump signed it the following day. He then declared a national emergency, which allowed him to use previously appropriated Department of Defense funds and other "reprogrammed" appropriations for border wall construction.[52] The House of Representatives filed suit in federal court to block the transfers, but Trump was allowed to proceed with a diversion of funds that contravened Congress's "power of the purse."

The Bipartisan Budget Act of 2019

With the shutdown having ended and fiscal year 2019 appropriations finally settled, congressional appropriators were anxious to avoid similar disruptions in the next appropriations cycle. Senate Appropriations Committee chairman Richard Shelby announced plans to accelerate hearings and to "try to get the bills to the floor as soon as we can."[53] House Democrats were also prepared to package appropriations bills in so-called mini-buses to facilitate House and Senate action. The potential roadblocks were polarizing issues such as border wall funding and abortion policy and the lack of agreement between the House and Senate on discretionary spending totals for the 2020 appropriations totals.

The latter problem was solved with another two-year agreement on defense and nondefense spending. Drafted primarily by Speaker Pelosi and Treasury Secretary Mnuchin, the BBA 2019 obliterated what little was left of the 2011 BCA's spending limits. House Democrats had spent the past eight years on defense, protecting discretionary domestic programs against cutbacks. They had been reasonably effective in doing so, aided in part by Senate Republicans who did not share the anti-spending beliefs of their more strident House counterparts. In 2019, they finally managed to go on offense and expand funding for their domestic agenda.

As a result, the BBA 2019 spending increases were the largest to date—a combined $322 billion in defense and nondefense funding above the discretionary spending caps for fiscal years 2020 and 2021.[54] Exempted from the caps were wartime supplementals (Overseas Contingency Operations), disaster relief and other emergency spending, and even the costs of the 2020 census ($2.5 billion). In addition, the budget agreement suspended the debt limit for two years, through August 1, 2021, allowing both parties to avoid what had become increasingly pointless debates about deficits and debt.

President Trump called upon "House Republicans [to] support the TWO YEAR BUDGET AGREEMENT which greatly helps our Military and our Vets."[55] The House easily passed it on a 284–149 vote, but a majority of Republicans (65–132) voted "no." As one fiscal conservative complained, "There's no incentive within Congress to keep the debt down … They believe they can keep spending forever."[56] Still, Republican dissenters were casting a free vote since Democratic support was nearly unanimous.

In the Senate, where Republicans would be responsible for the outcome, the Senate leadership relentlessly lobbied for what Majority Leader

McConnell emphasized was "the agreement the administration has negotiated … the deal President Trump is waiting [for] and eager to sign into law."[57] One Republican warned that Trump would be "taking names" of those who voted against the bill.[58] On the final Senate vote, 29 of the 52 Senate Republicans were part of the 67–28 majority. On August 2, President Trump signed into law a spending agreement that everyone understood would lead to higher deficits and growing debt.

The Appropriations Breakdown

When Congress returned from its August recess, early hopes for an expedited appropriations process and bipartisan comity did not last. By early September, the House had passed ten of the 12 appropriations bills for fiscal year 2020, but the combined domestic spending levels in the House bills were nearly $20 billion above the budget agreement limits, and the defense bill was $5 billion below the agreed-upon cap.[59] The House had also added provisions on border wall funding, gun violence prevention research, family planning assistance, and other partisan agenda items that Senate Republicans, and the Trump administration, would not readily accept. In addition, House Democrats were moving ahead with an impeachment inquiry that raised partisan tensions even higher. About the only thing all sides could agree upon was avoiding another government shutdown, and a seven-week continuing resolution easily passed both chambers well before the October 1 deadline.

In the Senate, Republicans and Democrats had clashed over the discretionary spending allocations for the 12 appropriations bills, and partisan disagreements intensified as these bills were considered by the Appropriations Committee. Border wall funding in the Department of Homeland Security bill was a flashpoint, as were other immigration policy provisions. The Labor-HHS-Education bill funding level was too low for Democrats, who also objected to new funding for military construction projects whose initial appropriations had been reprogrammed by Trump to build the border wall. According to Senate Republicans, Democrats were now insisting on "poison pill" policy riders that the bipartisan budget agreement had prohibited. Democrats countered that "Republicans may well be abandoning a bipartisan appropriations process."[60]

On October 31, the Senate passed a package of four appropriations bills, but none of these was controversial, as the 84–9 vote indicated.[61] On the pivotal bills, especially the DHS and Labor-HHS-Education appropriations measures, partisan differences were delaying floor consideration, and significant funding level and policy disagreements with House-passed bills would have to be resolved when the Senate was finally able to act. The first continuing resolution for fiscal year 2020 ran through November 21. As that date approached, none of the regular appropriations bills had passed either the House or the Senate, and a second continuing resolution was enacted to fund government operations through December 20.

On December 16, House and Senate appropriators reached agreement on two packages of spending bills—the Consolidated Appropriations Act of 2020 that contained the Defense and DHS appropriations bill, along with three others, and the Further Consolidated Appropriations Act of 2020 that contained the remaining seven appropriations measures.

Given the realities of divided government, there were victories for both sides. Democrats prevailed on border wall funding, but no restrictions on reprogramming or transfers were included. The defense and nondefense budget increases generally followed the bipartisan budget agreement. The prohibition on gun violence prevention research was eased, but the funding provided was minuscule ($12.5 million). These and other compromises were enough to insure bipartisan majorities in the House and the Senate for the Consolidated Appropriations Act. Blocs of liberal Democrats and conservative Republicans in the House voted against the bill, but the overall margin was 280–138. The Senate vote was even more one-sided, with only seven Democrats and four Republicans voting "no." The second appropriations package had such broad support that no roll call vote was held.

One of the bipartisan attractions of the Further Consolidated Appropriations Act was that it included an estimated $425 billion in individual and business tax cuts.[62] Republicans secured repeal of the ACA's medical device excise tax and health insurance provider fee with a combined revenue cost of more than $175 billion; Democrats were able to repeal the excise tax on high-cost employer-provided health insurance—the so-called Cadillac tax that labor unions had criticized—reducing ten-year revenues by more than $195 billion. The remaining revenue reductions were primarily extensions of expiring tax preferences favored by Democrats (work opportunity tax credits, employer credits for paid family and medical leave), Republicans (expanded retirement savings, empowerment zone tax credits), or both (disaster tax relief). With these year-end measures, the projected deficit for 2020 was more than $1 trillion. Current policy deficits for the 2020s were considerably larger, totaling more than $13 trillion.[63]

Trump vs. Obama: Deficits

As the fourth year of the Trump presidency began, his deficit and debt record was very different from the budget-balancing fiscal discipline that he and congressional Republicans had promised at the outset. In fact, the deficit problem that Trump had inherited had become markedly worse under his stewardship. In January 2017, baseline budget projections could reasonably be interpreted as an extension of Obama-era tax and spending policies. Since the economy at that point was relatively strong and wartime or other emergency spending fairly limited, the deficit projections reflected a structural imbalance between spending and revenues. As shown in Table 5.4, these structural deficits were expected to remain below 3 percent for several years but to rise above 4 percent by 2022. For fiscal years 2018–2022, average debt-

GDP was estimated at 3.3 percent. This was the deficit problem, more or less, that Trump inherited.

The 2017 baseline projection when Obama left office turned out to be fairly close to actual spending for the year, but revenues were slightly lower, and the deficit was higher. In 2018, however, the drop in revenue levels was dramatic as the TCJA 2017 took effect. Outlay-GDP changed very little, and deficit-GDP was well above the baseline projection. With increased spending in 2019, deficit-GDP increased to 4.6 percent. In January 2020, the Trump budget baseline for 2020–2022 was essentially unchanged from 2019.

The structural deficit increased under Trump, primarily because of the 2017 tax cut but also because Republicans were unable to cut spending levels. When Republicans controlled Congress during Trump's first two years in office, they could have used reconciliation to reduce spending and deficits but failed to do so. In 2019, Republicans and Democrats agreed to increase discretionary spending, mandatory spending programs continued to grow, and deficits rose accordingly. Much the same was expected in 2020, but the COVID-19 pandemic relief efforts that began in the spring raised deficits and debt to dramatically higher levels.

Table 5.4 The Obama Budget Baseline and Trump Administration Budget Policy (as a percentage of GDP)

	January 2017 Baseline Projections					
	2017	2018	2019	2020	2021	2022
Spending	20.7	20.5	21.0	21.3	21.7	22.3
Revenues	17.8	18.1	18.1	18.1	18.1	18.1
Deficit	–2.9	–2.4	–2.9	–3.2	–3.6	–4.2
Publicly Held Debt	77.5	77.4	77.9	78.8	79.9	81.3
	Trump Budgets and 2020 Baseline Projections					
	Actual			Baseline		
	2017	2018	2019	2020	2021	2022
Spending	20.6	20.2	21.0	21.0	20.9	21.4
Revenues	17.2	16.4	16.3	16.4	16.6	16.7
Deficit	–3.5	–3.8	–4.6	–4.6	–4.3	–4.7
Publicly Held Debt	76.0	77.4	79.2	80.8	82.0	83.9

Sources: Congressional Budget Office, *The Budget and Economic Outlook: 2017 to 2027* (Washington, D.C.: Congressional Budget Office, 2017), 10; Congressional Budget Office, *The Budget and Economic Outlook: 2020 to 2030* (Washington, D.C.: Congressional Budget Office, 2020), 7; *Historical Tables, Budget of the United States Government, Fiscal Year 2021* (Washington, D.C.: Government Printing Office, 2020), Tables 1.2, 7.1.

Pandemic Relief and Emergency Deficits

As President Trump's fourth year in office began, baseline deficits for 2020 and 2021 were projected to reach $1 trillion annually—the highest levels of his presidency and the largest since the Great Recession.[64] Several months later, relief bills in response to the COVID-19 pandemic more than tripled the 2020 deficit. The 2021 deficit also rose above $3 trillion with stimulus bills that President Trump signed in December and President Joseph Biden sponsored the following March.

The COVID-19 Bills

In January 2020, health officials in China reported a new virus that was affecting its citizens. Two months later, as the number of cases of infection and deaths from the disease skyrocketed around the world, the World Health Organization officially declared the novel coronavirus (COVID-19) outbreak a global pandemic. The United States was especially hard hit, with reported cases in March increasing to more than 20,000 daily, and the death toll quickly began to mount.[65] Lockdowns and the imposition of other public health restrictions then

Table 5.5 The Budgetary Effects of Laws Enacted in Response to the 2020 Coronavirus Pandemic, March and April 2020 (in billions of dollars)

	Estimated Effects on the Budget, 2020–2030			
	Coronavirus Preparedness and Response Supplemental Appropriations Act, 2020	Families First Coronavirus Response Act	Coronavirus Aid, Relief, and Economic Security (CARES) Act	Paycheck Protection Program and Health Care Enhancement Act
	P.L. 116–123	P.L. 116–127	P.L. 116–136	P.L. 116–139
	March 6, 2020	March 18, 2020	March 27, 2020	April 24, 2020
Increase in Discretionary Outlays	8	2	326	162
Increase in Mandatory Spending	*	95	988	321
Decrease in Revenues	0	94	408	0
Increase in the Deficit	+8	+192	+1,721	+483

Source: *Congressional Budget Office, The Budgetary Effects of Laws Enacted in Response to the 2020 Coronavirus Pandemic, March and April 2020* (Washington, D.C.: Congressional Budget Office, June 2020), 1.

Note: * Between zero and $500 million.

brought the economy nearly to a halt. Between February and April, the unemployment rate rose from 3.5 percent to 14.8 percent, as the number of unemployed persons rose to more than 23 million.[66] The annualized decline in GDP during the second quarter of 2020 was more than 31 percent, the highest quarterly drop in real GDP of the post-World War II era.[67]

As was the case during the Great Recession a decade earlier, the Federal Reserve lowered interest rates and created emergency lending facilities to help to stabilize the economy. The Trump administration and Congress also provided public health funding and direct assistance to households and businesses in several pandemic relief bills enacted during March and April. As shown in Table 5.5, their estimated deficit cost was more than $2.4 trillion over a ten-year period, with approximately $1.9 trillion in additional spending and the remainder in reduced revenues. Most of this new spending and virtually all of the tax relief was scheduled to take effect in 2020.[68]

As these costs mounted, there were scattered complaints from congressional Republicans about fiscal excess. The Trump administration and most members of the House and Senate, however, agreed that the scale of the nation's public health and economic crisis—to say nothing of the upcoming election—dwarfed any concerns about deficits and debt. Action on a fifth relief bill did stall during the summer and early fall, as did the regular appropriations process, but both were then combined in a $2.3 trillion measure that passed in late December. In this case, several dozen House Republicans voted "no," as did a handful of Senate Republicans, but the bipartisan vote margins were again overwhelming.

Phase 1

The first of the 2020 COVID-19 bills was an $8.3 billion supplemental appropriation for public health agencies in support of medical care and research.[69] In late February, the Trump administration had requested $2.5 billion in new funding, but House and Senate appropriators quickly negotiated a much larger package that contained vaccine research and development, public health initiatives, and healthcare preparedness, as well as support for international efforts to combat the pandemic. The House bill was introduced on March 4 and passed by a 415–2 vote the same day. The Senate cleared the bill on March 5, with only one dissenting vote (a Republican who objected to the lack of spending offsets in other programs), and President Trump signed it on March 6.

Phase 2

Less than two weeks later, the House and the Senate passed a $192 billion emergency spending and tax relief bill.[70] In this case, Democratic House Speaker Nancy Pelosi and Treasury Secretary Steven Mnuchin took the lead in drafting the legislative framework. Its major provisions included additional funding for unemployment benefits and food and medical assistance and for tax credits to support emergency sick leave and emergency medical leave that employers were required to provide. The House passed the bill by a vote of 363–40 on March 14, with all the "no" votes on the Republican side. President Trump's strong endorsement convinced Senate Republican leaders to drop their initial objections to the measure, and the Senate approved it by a 90–8 vote on March 18. The president signed it into law that same day.

Phase 3

The third, and most costly, relief measure was the Coronavirus Aid, Relief, and Economic Security Act (CARES Act) that passed the Senate on March 25 by a vote of 96–0. Two days later, the House approved it by voice vote, and President Trump proceeded to sign it into law. Senate Republicans, acting in concert with Trump administration officials, had drafted the first version of what was called "Phase 3" coronavirus relief. Direct cash payments to individuals, which Trump had proposed, were included as were financial assistance and loans to major industries and small businesses.

Majority Leader Mitch McConnell attempted to bring this narrow Republican-drafted bill to the Senate floor on March 22, but Democrats were able to block it. Over the next several days, leaders from both parties successfully negotiated a substantially larger $2.2 trillion package that featured $1,200 refundable tax credits for eligible adults (and $500 for dependent children); expanded food and rental assistance for individuals; extended unemployment benefits; financial assistance—in the form of grants or loans—to small businesses (the Paycheck Protection Program—PPP) and major industries, such as airlines and airplane manufacturers; aid to state and local governments; and additional funding for hospitals, healthcare providers, and medical care and research.[71] The CARES Act also included numerous forms of tax relief for individuals and businesses, such as modified rules governing retirement fund withdrawals, charitable contributions, business income and net operating losses, and business interest payments.

Phase 4

The PPP included in the CARES Act provided low-interest loans for small businesses. If used for employee salaries and other eligible expenses, these loans were forgivable—i.e., they were converted to grants. Funded at approximately $340 billion, primarily through Small Business Administration-sponsored bank loans, the heavy demand for these loans quickly exhausted this initial authorization. The fourth COVID-19 relief bill provided an additional $321 billion to the PPP, along with more than $60 billion for the economic disaster relief program. Healthcare also received additional funding, with $75 billion to reimburse healthcare providers for pandemic-related expenses and revenue losses and $25 billion for COVID-19 testing.[72] The Senate approved this legislation by voice vote on April 21. The House vote, on April 23, was 388–5.

The Impasse

Bipartisanship quickly came to a halt with the Heroes Act, a $3 trillion relief bill that House Democratic leaders characterized as an essential next step in pandemic relief.[73] The primary focus of the Democratic bill was increased financial assistance to households and substantial new aid to state and local governments. For eligible families, cash payments of up to $6,000 would be provided, along with additional funding for food and housing assistance and extended unemployment benefits. Grants to state and local governments totaled $1 trillion, with few restrictions on how these funds could be utilized. Substantial new funding was also provided to supplement the pay of essential workers and underwrite student loan forgiveness. Tax relief provisions included employee retention tax credits and temporary repeal of the $10,000 SALT deduction limit that Republicans had included in the 2017 TCJA. On May 15, the leadership bill was narrowly approved by the House on a 208–199 vote. Only one Republican voted for the Heroes Act, and 14 Democratic moderates voted against it.

Senate Republicans, like their House counterparts, criticized the Heroes Act as a Democratic wish list and were especially critical of the state and local financial assistance. They also insisted that any additional relief legislation had to include liability shields for employers whose customers or employees contracted COVID-19. With President Trump promising to veto anything remotely resembling the Democratic bill, Senate Republican leaders could safely ignore it.

Appropriations Bills

Bipartisanship was missing as well on regular appropriations bills for fiscal year 2021. The House managed to pass most of its spending bills by the summer, but the Senate Appropriations Committee suspended its markups when Democratic members insisted on adding policy riders regarding law enforcement and racial justice issues. By late September, none of the Senate spending bills had been reported out of committee, and a ten-week continuing resolution was agreed to on October 1. At this point, Senate Republicans announced that another round of economic stimulus would also be acted upon after the election. A major sticking point on this legislation would be cost, with Senate Republicans endorsing only a fraction of the amount that House Democrats had authorized in May, and the Trump administration somewhere in between.

Democrats managed to retain control of the House in the November elections but failed to make the big gains they had anticipated. Instead, their majority was reduced to 222–213. With two Georgia Senate races undecided pending runoff elections in early January, Republicans had a 50–48 advantage, but President Trump's defeat meant that the runoff races could give Democrats effective control in the upcoming Congress.

Against this backdrop, the lame-duck congressional session approved a $1.4 trillion consolidated appropriations bill for fiscal year 2021, combined with a $900 billion stimulus package. It required several weeks of negotiations between House and Senate party leaders, and four temporary continuing resolutions, to resolve differences over the stimulus bill's unemployment benefit supplements and direct cash assistance to individuals and families. A third major component, additional funding for PPP loans, had broad support in both parties, as did fiscal assistance to public schools and universities and to healthcare providers for COVID-19 vaccines and testing. The final bill did not include either the state and local financial aid that House and Senate Democrats had called for or the employer liability protections that Republicans wanted, but the compromise was supported by large bipartisan majorities in both chambers. After threatening to veto the measure over appropriations provisions that he mistakenly thought were part of the stimulus package and then calling upon Congress to raise cash assistance payments from $600 to $2,000, Trump finally signed the bill on December 27.

The House then passed separate legislation to authorize the $2,000 cash payments Trump had endorsed, but Majority Leader McConnell refused to allow the Senate to vote on the House-passed bill. Instead, he combined the stimulus checks provision with unrelated legislation enabling a voter fraud study commission and reviving legal protections for internet service providers. Democrats opposed these measures, and the 116th Congress came to an end without further action.

With Democratic victories in the two Georgia runoff elections on January 5, the Senate was divided 50–50 for the 117th Congress. After the inauguration of President Biden and Vice President Kamala Harris on January 20, however, Democrats had the tiebreaking vote they needed to control the Senate. Their first legislative priority would be the additional stimulus funding they had been unable to secure the previous year.

The Trump Debt Legacy

As a presidential candidate in 2016, Donald Trump explained that he would retire the national debt "over a period of eight years" through policies that spurred economic growth and international trade benefits for the United States.[74] Two years later, he predicted that accelerated growth from the 2017 tax cut would make possible "paying off that debt like it's water." Shortly thereafter, he boasted that revenues from his tariff program would pay "down large amounts of the $21 trillion in debt that has been accumulated, much by the Obama Administration."

None of this was remotely possible, nor was it necessarily meant to be taken seriously. Nevertheless, Trump's final, pre-pandemic budget warned that "Unsustainable Federal deficits and debt are a serious threat to America's prosperity."[75] In fact, the large and growing debt was deemed a "crisis" that if not addressed in a timely fashion would lead to "lower economic growth" and "a much lower standard of living" for America's families.[76] According to the administration, the problem was Congress's failure to control spending. The president had proposed "more spending reductions than any other Administration in history," but these had been ignored. Fortunately, the $4.4 trillion in savings in the 2021 budget would give Congress another opportunity to lower the deficit and bring the budget into balance. Unfortunately, the timetable for doing so was a rather distant 15 years.

Trump was not the only president in the era of deficit politics whose fiscal record did not reflect his rhetoric about unsustainable debt. The deficit at the end of Ronald Reagan's tenure was much larger than the deficit he inherited, and the same has been true for each of his successors except Bill Clinton and Barack Obama. Similarly, debt-GDP had increased under Reagan and did so again under both Bushes, Obama, and, of course, Trump.

The pre-pandemic Trump deficits, however, were growing even though the economy was relatively strong. Each of his predecessors going back to Reagan had taken office when the economy was in or close to recession, and George W. Bush had the added expense of a new war. Rising structural deficits under Trump were an anomaly given the healthy economy and benign security environment he inherited.

What also distinguished the Trump presidency was the absence of any credible attempt to curb deficits and debt as they moved inexorably higher. The Reagan tax cut of 1981, for example, was followed by deficit reduction tax increases in 1982 and 1984, sustained cuts in discretionary domestic spending, and a bipartisan, if unworkable, balanced-budget enforcement mechanism in his second term. George H. W. Bush and Bill Clinton signed the largest comprehensive deficit reduction agreements of the modern era. Barack Obama tried to implement a similar plan in 2011 but failed to secure Republican support for the required tax increases.

The Trump administration did none of these things, nor did congressional Republicans encourage the president to do so. Rather, they all embraced the electorally driven fiscal strategy of the George W. Bush administration. Tax cuts were the key legislative priority. Politically costly spending cuts, however, could safely be avoided, since deficits did not matter. Neither Bush or Trump wavered in their insistence that budgets could be balanced through pro-growth tax policies and lower spending even though the promised revenue windfalls never occurred and the spending restraint was never applied.

Meanwhile, congressional Republicans readily abandoned their balanced-budget principles when Republican presidents were in charge. The confrontational tactics they employed during the Clinton and Obama presidencies, such as shutdowns and debt limit brinkmanship, were ostensibly directed toward strengthening fiscal discipline, and their accompanying denunciations of deficit and debt sometimes verged on the apocalyptic. This fervor, however, dissipated with Bush and disappeared completely with Trump. A central theme in Republican platforms over the past several decades had been the party's core belief in balanced budgets and low debt. The 2016 platform, for example, deplored the "huge increase in the national debt demanded by … the current [Obama] Administration" and pledged the "repayment of the trillions we now owe."[77] Four years later, with the public debt having increased by nearly 50 percent, the Republican national convention unhesitatingly renominated Donald Trump and did not bother to adopt a new platform. The convention instead readopted the 2016 platform in its entirety, along with a prefatory statement of fealty to Trump: "The Republican Party has and will continue to enthusiastically support the president's America-first agenda."[78]

Notes

1 The Senate found Trump not guilty on the 2019 impeachment charges by votes of 52–48 and 53–47. One Republican (Mitt Romney, the party's 2012 presidential nominee) voted with Senate Democrats to convict Trump on the abuse of power article. In 2021, seven Republicans and all 50 Senate Democrats voted to convict Trump on the incitement of insurrection article.
2 *Budget of the United States Government, Fiscal Year 2018: A New Foundation for American Greatness* (Washington, D.C.: Government Printing Office, 2017), 6.
3 *Budget of the United States Government, Fiscal Year 2019* (Washington, D.C.: Government Printing Office, 2018), 5.
4 *Budget of the United States Government, Fiscal Year 2020* (Washington, D.C.: Government Printing Office, 2019), 1.
5 See Eloise Pasachoff, "The President's Budget Powers in the Trump Era," in *Executive Policymaking: The Role of the OMB in the Presidency*, eds. Meena Bose and Andrew Rudalevige (Washington, D.C.: Brookings Institution Press, 2020).
6 Quoted in Pasachoff, "The President's Budget Powers in the Trump Era," 70.
7 Annie L. Mach and Janet Kinzer, *Legislative Actions to Modify the Affordable Care Act in the 111th–115th Congresses* (Washington, D.C.: Congressional Research Service, June 27, 2018).
8 Congressional Budget Office, *Cost Estimate: American Health Care Act* (Washington, D.C.: Congressional Budget Office, March 13, 2017), 2.
9 Robert Pear and Kate Kelly, "Trump Concedes Health Law Overhaul is 'Unbelievably Complex,'" *New York Times*, February 27, 2017, www.nytimes.com/2017/02/27/us/politics/trump-concedes-health-law-overhaul-is-unbelievably-complex.html.
10 Robert Pear, Thomas Kaplan, and Maggie Haberman, "In Major Defeat for Trump, Push to Repeal Health Law Fails," *New York Times*, March 24, 2017, www.nytimes.com/2017/03/24/us/politics/health-care-affordable-care-act.html.
11 Congressional Budget Office, *Cost Estimate: Better Care Reconciliation Act of 2017* (Washington, D.C.: Congressional Budget Office, June 26, 2017), 16–17.
12 See Frank J. Thompson, Kenneth K. Wong, and Barry G. Rabe, *Trump, the Administrative Presidency, and Federalism* (Washington, D.C.: Brookings Institution Press, 2020), 51–53.
13 Thompson, Wong, and Rabe, *Trump, the Administrative Presidency, and Federalism*, 53–56.
14 Thompson, Wong, and Rabe, *Trump, the Administrative Presidency, and Federalism*, 56–59.
15 Thompson, Wong, and Rabe, *Trump, the Administrative Presidency, and Federalism*, 65–70.

16 Edward R. Berchick, Jessica C. Barnett, and Rachel D. Upton, *Health Insurance Coverage in the United States: 2018* (*Current Population Reports, P-60–267(RV)*) (Washington, D.C.: Government Printing Office, 2019), 17.
17 This includes the District of Columbia. Missouri and Oklahoma have expansions planned for July 1, 2021, which would bring the total to 39. "Status of State Medicaid Expansion Decisions: Interactive Map," Kaiser Family Foundation, March 24, 2021, www.kff.org/medicaid/issue-brief/status-of-state-medicaid-expansion-decisions-interactive-map/.
18 "5 Charts About Public Opinion on the Affordable Care Act and the Supreme Court," Kaiser Family Foundation, December 18, 2020, www.kff.org/health-reform/poll-finding/5-charts-about-public-opinion-on-the-affordable-care-act-and-the-supreme-court/.
19 Andrew S. Kelly, "Finding Stability and Sustainability in the Trump Era: Medicare and the Affordable Care Act in Historical Perspective," in *American Political Development and the Trump Presidency*, eds. Zachary Callen and Philip Rocco (Philadelphia: University of Pennsylvania Press, 2020), 139.
20 Berchick, Barnett, and Upton, *Health Insurance Coverage in the United States: 2018*, 17.
21 Kelly, "Finding Stability and Sustainability in the Trump Era," 140–143.
22 Frank J. Thompson, Michael K. Gusmano, and Shugo Shinohara, "Trump and the Affordable Care Act: Congressional Repeal Efforts, Executive Federalism, and Program Durability," *Publius: The Journal of Federalism* 48, no. 3 (2018): 404–406.
23 Emily Guskin and Scott Clement, "Republicans' Obamacare Repeal Was Never Really That Popular," *Washington Post*, July 28, 2017, www.washingtonpost.com/news/the-fix/wp/2017/07/28/republicans-obamacare-repeal-was-never-really-that-popular/.
24 John F. Cogan, *The High Cost of Good Intentions: A History of U.S. Federal Entitlement Programs* (Stanford, CA: Stanford University Press, 2017).
25 U.S. Congress, Joint Committee on Taxation, *Estimated Budget Effects of the Conference Agreement for H.R. 1, the "Tax Cuts and Jobs Act"* (JCX-67–17) (Washington, D.C.: Government Printing Office, December 18, 2017), 8.
26 Louise Radnofsky, "Trump Signs Sweeping Tax Overhaul Into Law," *Wall Street Journal*, December 22, 2017, www.wsj.com/articles/trump-signs-sweeping-tax-overhaul-into-law-1513959753.
27 George K. Yin and Lawrence A. Zelenak, "The Past, Present, and Future of the Tax Legislative Process," *Law and Contemporary Problems* 81, no. 2 (2018): 1.
28 Congressional Budget Office, *The Budget and Economic Outlook: 2018 to 2028* (Washington, D.C.: Congressional Budget Office, 2018), 106.
29 Martin Feldstein, "The Tax Reform Legislation of 2017," *Journal of Policy Modeling* 40, no. 3 (2018): 503.
30 Feldstein, "The Tax Reform Legislation of 2017," 503.
31 "GOP Enacts Sweeping Tax Overhaul, Handing Trump Big Legislative Victory," *CQ Almanac 2017*, 73rd ed. (Washington, D.C.: CQ-Roll Call, Inc., 2018), http://library.cqpress.com/cqalmanac/cqal17-1942-108535-2911952.
32 "GOP Enacts Sweeping Tax Overhaul, Handing Trump Big Legislative Victory," http://library.cqpress.com/cqalmanac/cqal17-1942-108535-2911952.
33 Feldstein, "The Tax Reform Legislation of 2017," 507.
34 The actual title of P.L. 115–97 is "To Provide for Reconciliation Pursuant to Titles II and V of the Concurrent Resolution on the Budget for Fiscal Year 2018." While unofficial, the Tax Cuts and Jobs Act is the title that is currently used.
35 U.S. Congress, Joint Committee on Taxation, *Estimated Budget Effects of the Conference Agreement for H.R. 1, the "Tax Cuts and Jobs Act,"* 1–10.
36 U.S. Congress, Joint Committee on Taxation, *Estimated Budget Effects of the Conference Agreement for H.R. 1, the "Tax Cuts and Jobs Act,"* 1–10.

37 Jane G. Gravelle and Donald J. Marples, *The Economic Effects of the 2017 Tax Revision: Preliminary Observations* (Washington, D.C.: Congressional Research Service, June 7, 2019), 1.
38 Gravelle and Marples, *The Economic Effects of the 2017 Tax Revision*, 5–9.
39 Chuck Jones, "Trump Has Created 1.5 Million Fewer Jobs Than Obama," *Forbes*, September 20, 2019, www.forbes.com/sites/chuckjones/2019/09/20/trump-has-created-15-million-fewer-jobs-than-obama/?sh=1822cf5d27ce.
40 Grant A. Driessen, *The Federal Budget: Overview and Issues for FY2018 and Beyond* (Washington, D.C.: Congressional Research Service, June 30, 2017), 15–17.
41 Driessen, *The Federal Budget*, 17.
42 James Tobin and Murray Weidenbaum, eds., *Two Revolutions in Economic Policy: The First Economic Reports of Presidents Kennedy and Reagan* (Cambridge: Massachusetts Institute of Technology Press, 1988), 420.
43 "Congress Passes Fiscal 2017 Omnibus That Sidesteps Government Shutdown," *CQ Almanac 2017*, 73rd ed. (Washington, D.C.: CQ-Roll Call, Inc., 2018), http://library.cqpress.com/cqalmanac/cqal17-1942-108521-2911472.
44 "U.S. Debt Limit Is Again Suspended," *CQ Almanac 2017*, 73rd ed. (Washington, D.C.: CQ-Roll Call, Inc., 2018), http://library.cqpress.com/cqalmanac/cqal17-1942-108523-2911612.
45 "U.S. Debt Limit Is Again Suspended," http://library.cqpress.com/cqalmanac/cqal17-1942-108523-2911612.
46 "U.S. Debt Limit Is Again Suspended," http://library.cqpress.com/cqalmanac/cqal17-1942-108523-2911612.
47 *The Budget Control Act: Frequently Asked Questions* (Washington, D.C.: Congressional Research Service, October 1, 2019), 5.
48 Randy Leonard, "CQ Data Bank: How the Omnibus Toplines Stack Up," *CQ Magazine*, April 9, 2018, 34, https://library.cqpress.com/cqmagazine/file.php?path=/files/wr20180409-11databank-cht.pdf.
49 *Budget of the United States Government, Fiscal Year 2019*, 5.
50 Jordan Fabian, "Trump Reverses, Says Dems to Blame for Shutdown," *The Hill*, December 21, 2018, https://thehill.com/homenews/administration/422457-trump-reverses-says-dems-to-blame-for-shutdown.
51 "The Consolidated Appropriations Act 2019," Senate Republican Policy Committee, February 14, 2019, www.rpc.senate.gov/legislative-notices/the-consolidated-appropriations-act-2019.
52 George M. Guess and James D. Savage, *Comparative Public Budgeting*, 2nd ed. (Cambridge: Cambridge University Press, 2021), 63–64.
53 "Dollars and Sense: Same Strategy, Same Results in Appropriations Process?" *CQ Magazine,* February 25, 2019, http://library.cqpress.com/cqmagazine/weeklyreport116-000005467955.
54 Grant A. Driessen and Megan S. Lynch, *The Bipartisan Budget Act of 2019: Changes to the BCA and Debt Limit* (Washington, D.C.: Congressional Research Service, August 5, 2019), 2–3.
55 Emily Cochrane, "Divided House Passes 2-Year Budget Deal to Raise Spending," *New York Times*, July 25, 2019, www.nytimes.com/2019/07/25/us/politics/budget-spending-deal.html.
56 Cochrane, "Divided House Passes 2-Year Budget Deal to Raise Spending," www.nytimes.com/2019/07/25/us/politics/budget-spending-deal.html.
57 Burgess Everett and John Bresnahan, "Senate Passes Massive 2-Year Budget Deal," *Politico*, August 1, 2019, www.politico.com/story/2019/08/01/budget-deal-senate-vote-1444084.
58 Everett and Bresnahan, "Senate Passes Massive 2-Year Budget Deal," www.politico.com/story/2019/08/01/budget-deal-senate-vote-1444084.

59 "Fall Preview: Appropriations Overview," *CQ Magazine*, September 9, 2019, http://library.cqpress.com/cqmagazine/weeklyreport116-000005717029.
60 "2020 Appropriations: A Standoff on Spending," *CQ Magazine*, October 28, 2019, http://library.cqpress.com/cqmagazine/weeklyreport116-000005755062.
61 "Appropriations Status Table: FY2020, Regular Appropriations," Congressional Research Service, https://crsreports.congress.gov/AppropriationsStatusTable.
62 U.S. Congress, Joint Committee on Taxation, *Estimated Budget Effects Of The Revenue Provisions Contained In The House Amendment To The Senate Amendment To H.R. 1865, The Further Consolidated Appropriations Act, 2020* (JCX-54–19 R) (Washington, D.C.: Government Printing Office, December 17, 2019), 1–8.
63 Congressional Budget Office, *The Budget and Economic Outlook: 2020 to 2030* (Washington, D.C.: Congressional Budget Office, 2020), 7.
64 Congressional Budget Office, *The Budget and Economic Outlook: 2020 to 2030*, 7.
65 "New Cases by Day," Centers for Disease Control and Prevention, Previous U.S. COVID-19 Case Data, www.cdc.gov/coronavirus/2019-ncov/cases-updates/previouscases.html.
66 "Civilian unemployment rate, seasonally adjusted," February–April 2020, Bureau of Labor Statistics, www.bls.gov/charts/employment-situation/civilian-unemployment-rate.htm, and "Civilian unemployment, seasonally adjusted," April 2020, Bureau of Labor Statistics, www.bls.gov/charts/employment-situation/civilian-unemployment.htm.
67 Lida R. Weinstock, *COVID-19 and the U.S. Economy* (Washington, D.C.: Congressional Research Service, November 16, 2020), summary.
68 William L. Painter, *Tallying Federal Funding for COVID-19: In Brief* (Washington, D.C.: Congressional Research Service, July 13, 2020), 6.
69 Painter, *Tallying Federal Funding for COVID-19: In Brief*, 5.
70 Painter, *Tallying Federal Funding for COVID-19: In Brief*, 1–2.
71 Congressional Budget Office, *The Budgetary Effects of Laws Enacted in Response to the 2020 Coronavirus Pandemic, March and April 2020* (Washington, D.C.: Congressional Budget Office, June 2020), 2–13.
72 Congressional Budget Office, *The Budgetary Effects of Laws Enacted in Response to the 2020 Coronavirus Pandemic, March and April 2020*, 2, 3, 6.
73 Erica Werner, "House Democrats Pass $3 Trillion Coronavirus Relief Bill Despite Trump's Veto Threat," *Washington Post*, May 15, 2020, www.washingtonpost.com/us-policy/2020/05/15/democrats-pelosi-congress-coronavirus-3-trillion-trump/.
74 Allan Sloan and Cezary Podkul, "Trump's Most Enduring Legacy Could Be the Historic Rise in the National Debt," *Washington Post*, January 14, 2021, www.washingtonpost.com/business/2021/01/14/trump-legacy-national-debt-increasee/.
75 *Budget of the United States Government, Fiscal Year 2021* (Washington, D.C.: Government Printing Office, 2020), 6.
76 *Budget of the United States Government, Fiscal Year 2021*, 7.
77 "2016 Republican Party Platform, July 18, 2016," The American Presidency Project, www.presidency.ucsb.edu/documents/2016-republican-party-platform.
78 Reid J. Epstein, "The G.O.P. Delivers Its 2020 Platform. It's From 2016," *New York Times*, August 25, 2020, www.nytimes.com/2020/08/25/us/politics/republicans-platform.html.

6 The Future of Deficit Politics—And Why It Matters

Long-term budget projections are uncertain, given the many unknown factors—notably economic crises, pandemics, and wars—that can dramatically affect future spending and revenues. What is certain, however, is that policymakers in the 2020s are facing an unusually challenging deficit and debt problem. When the Biden administration took office in January 2021, current policy deficits over the next decade were more than $12 trillion, and public debt-GDP was at its highest level since World War II.[1] The long-term outlook was even more daunting, with deficits and debt rising at accelerating rates.[2]

These scenarios are connected. Policy adjustments that reduce or stabilize deficits in the 2020s would narrow the fiscal gap in the years that follow. Conversely, adding to these near-term deficits will make matters considerably worse. The Congressional Budget Office (CBO) explains, "Addressing high and rising debt sooner rather than later means that smaller policy changes would be required to achieve long-term objectives. The benefits … include a smaller accumulated debt and therefore less risk to long-term economic growth and stability."[3]

Regardless, deficit reduction is not on Congress's legislative agenda, nor is it likely to be introduced anytime soon. The Biden administration's fiscal program, examined in detail later in this chapter, has focused instead on temporary stimulus spending and a permanent expansion of discretionary domestic programs and entitlements. The first installment of the Biden program—the American Rescue Plan Act of 2021 (ARPA)—was passed in March 2021. It provided $1.9 trillion in economic stimulus spending and tax credits with minor revenue offsets.

President Biden's other initiatives—the American Jobs Plan and the American Families Plan—have a potential cost of more than $4 trillion. These proposals include corporate and high-income tax increases that would, if enacted, cover only a portion of their costs. As a result, the president's budget would boost deficits and debt well above baseline levels over the next decade. Each of the last three Democratic presidents has come into office with a large structural deficit in place—and a weak economy that amplified the deficit. President Clinton managed to eliminate both structural and

DOI: 10.4324/9781003167266-6

cyclical deficits. President Obama succeeded in erasing the cyclical deficit and at least tried to stabilize the structural deficit. At the time of writing, it appears that President Biden will follow a different course. The starting point for assessing the future of deficit politics is therefore the core structural deficit now in place and its spending and revenue components.

The Fiscal Context for the 2020s

As shown in Figure 6.1, the gap between spending and revenues will narrow as the economy recovers from the outbreak of the coronavirus disease (COVID-19) pandemic in early 2020. After massive back-to-back deficits in 2020 and 2021, the deficit is expected to return to pre-pandemic levels over the next few years. Under current policy, spending levels would then begin to rise, but revenues would not keep pace. For the 2022–2031 period, projected deficits average 4.4 percent of GDP—much higher than the average over the past several decades. In addition, the deficit gap widens over time. Baseline deficits for the 2030s, for example, average nearly 8 percent, and estimates for the 2040s are even greater.[4]

These projections are based on positive assumptions about economic growth, employment, inflation, and interest rates.[5] In other words, they exclude potential cyclical (or emergency) deficits. They also assume that current policy remains in effect, which is in keeping with their intended

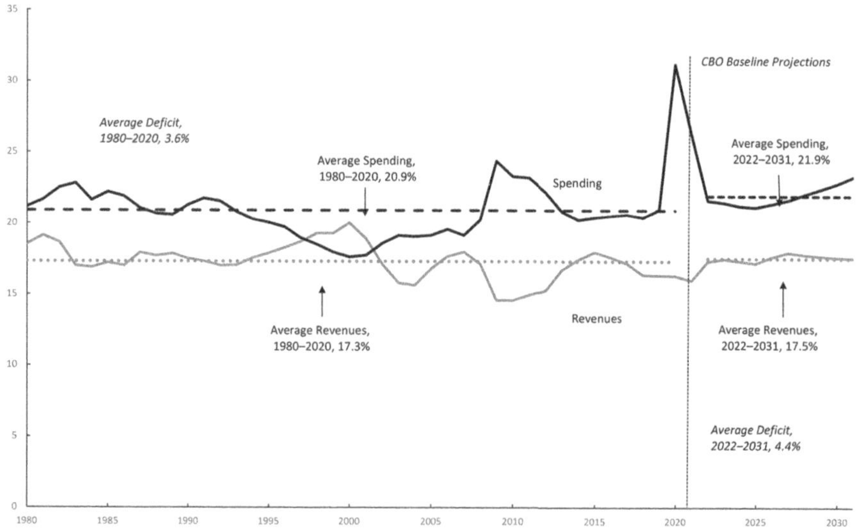

Figure 6.1 Spending and Revenues in the Deficit Politics Era, 1980–2031 (as a percentage of GDP)

Sources: Congressional Budget Office, *Additional Information About the Budget Outlook: 2021 to 2031* (Washington, D.C.: Congressional Budget Office, 2021), 5; "Data Underlying Figures and Tables," www.cbo.gov/publication/56996.

purpose—serving as "a benchmark that policymakers can use to assess the potential effects of future policy decisions."[6] Two of these current policy baseline assumptions, however, are especially problematic: (1) the reductions in discretionary spending-GDP; and (2) the scheduled expiration of all individual tax cuts from the 2017 tax act. Congress is unlikely to allow either to occur, which would result in even larger deficits.

Federal Spending: An Upward Trajectory

In 1980, federal spending reached 21.2 percent of GDP, its highest level since World War II, and climbed still higher over the next several years. Two decades later, spending-GDP had dropped to 17.7 percent, its lowest level since the Great Society. This reduction came at the expense of discretionary spending programs—with nondefense cutbacks in the 1980s and a post-Cold War defense retrenchment in the 1990s (see Table 6.1). Equally as important, the growth in mandatory spending-GDP of the late 1960s and 1970s came to a halt in the decades that followed.

Several policy adjustments helped to stabilize mandatory spending levels. Retirement benefits were trimmed as part of the 1983 Social Security program reforms; the 1972 General Revenue Sharing program was repealed in 1986; cost controls on Medicare payments to healthcare providers were introduced in 1983 and were periodically strengthened thereafter. A new healthcare entitlement, the Medicare Catastrophic Care Act, was enacted in 1988 but repealed the next year. In 1996, Aid to Families with Dependent Children, which had its roots in the New Deal, was converted into a less expensive block grant. Medicaid eligibility was liberalized on several occasions and a Children's Health Insurance entitlement was enacted in 1997, but the budgetary impact of these and other public assistance expansions was limited. What would have been a costly new entitlement—the Clinton

Table 6.1 The Composition of Federal Spending in the Deficit Politics Era (as a percentage of GDP)

	Discretionary				
Fiscal Year	*Defense*	*Nondefense*	*Mandatory Programmatic*	*Net Interest*	*Total*
1980	4.8	5.1	9.4	1.9	21.2
1990	5.1	3.4	9.6	3.1	21.2
2000	2.9	3.2	9.4	2.2	17.7
2015	3.2	3.3	12.7	1.2	20.4
2019	3.2	3.1	12.9	1.8	21.0

Source: *Historical Tables, Budget of the United States Government, Fiscal Year 2021* (Washington, D.C.: Government Printing Office, 2020), Table 8.4.

administration's Health Security Act—failed to pass a Democratic-controlled Congress in 1994.

By 2000, the United States had a much larger welfare state than it had prior to the Great Society. Well over one-half of the federal budget was devoted to retirement and healthcare entitlements and other public assistance programs, but with mandatory spending-GDP held at a more or less fixed level after the Great Society expansion, its costs were offset by reductions in discretionary spending. Post-1980 fiscal constraints on entitlements and other domestic programs, the Cold War "peace dividend," and tax increases produced the balanced budgets of the late 1990s.

From 2000 to the present day, spending-GDP has increased, and its future trajectory is higher still. This expansion started under the George W. Bush administration, with increases in spending-GDP for discretionary programs and entitlements that raised total spending above 20 percent in 2008. After the spending surge during the Great Recession, spending levels dropped to the 20–21 percent range during President Obama's second term and remained there for the first three years of the Trump presidency.

The current policy spending baseline is quite a bit higher (see Table 6.2). By the late 2020s, spending-GDP is projected to reach 22 percent, and to continue to rise thereafter—averaging more than 25 percent during the 2030s and nearly 30 percent during the 2040s.[7] These baseline estimates are conservative, since they assume a decline in discretionary spending—to less than 6 percent over the next decade and even lower thereafter—which is highly unlikely. A decade ago, for example, Congress attempted to scale back discretionary spending through spending caps and sequesters but was soon forced to retreat. Pre-pandemic discretionary spending-GDP never fell below 6 percent, and this is arguably the minimum that will be acceptable in the years ahead. It could well be higher, since Democrats plan to expand domestic programs, and Republicans can be expected to protect the defense budget. Mandatory programs are growing so rapidly that total spending-GDP will increase regardless of whether discretionary savings are realized, but deficits will be larger if they are not.

It is also worth noting that, under current policy, the vast majority of entitlement programs would remain relatively small. Public assistance entitlements—means-tested programs such as food and nutrition assistance, refundable tax credits, unemployment compensation, and Supplemental Security Income—have accounted for 1–2 percent of GDP since the 1970s.[8] In 2019, spending for these programs and other minor entitlements, such as federal civil and military retirement, veterans' benefits, and agriculture subsidies, was 2.7 percent.[9] The extended baseline—excluding pandemic relief that is being phased out—drops to approximately 2.2 percent in 2031 and 1.9 percent in 2051.

By comparison, Social Security and the major healthcare entitlements (Medicare, Medicaid, Children's Health Insurance, and the Affordable Care Act's health insurance subsidies) have grown steadily since the early 2000s

Table 6.2 Baseline Spending Projections, 2020–2031 (as a percentage of GDP)

	Actual, 2020	*2021*	*2022*	*2023*	*2024*	*2025*	*2026*	*2027*	*2028*	*2029*	*2030*	*2031*
Outlays												
Mandatory	21.8	17.3	13.7	13.7	13.5	13.8	14.0	14.1	14.7	14.3	14.8	15.1
Discretionary	7.8	7.6	7.0	6.6	6.3	6.2	6.0	6.0	5.9	5.8	5.7	5.7
Net Interest	1.6	1.4	1.2	1.2	1.1	1.2	1.3	1.5	1.7	2.0	2.2	2.4
Total	31.2	26.3	21.9	21.5	20.9	21.1	21.4	21.6	22.4	22.1	22.8	23.2

Source: Congressional Budget Office, *Additional Information About the Budget Outlook: 2021 to 2031* (Washington, D.C.: Congressional Budget Office, 2021), 2.

and will continue to grow in the decades ahead (see Table 6.3). Social Security will remain the federal government's single largest spending program for quite some time, but the healthcare programs collectively are more costly and almost certainly will account for a much larger share of the budget going forward. The post-2000 growth in spending-GDP for Social Security has been, in large part, the result of demographic factors (i.e., population aging). Its projected future increase—to 6.0 percent in 2030 and to 6.3 percent in 2050—is due to population aging as well.[10] The moderate growth in Social Security, at least in comparison to the healthcare entitlements, reflects the continued impact of the reforms enacted in 1983. Benefit adjustments reduced Social Security spending-GDP in the late 1980s and 1990s, and retirement age increases in the 2000s (from 65 to 66) and those scheduled for the 2020s (from 66 to 67) have curbed the rate of increase since that time. There is currently a trust fund imbalance between Social Security benefit payments and taxes that Congress will need to correct fairly soon, but the policy options are, like those in 1983, straightforward.

The healthcare entitlements present a more difficult problem. First, Congress has enacted new programs—the Medicare Modernization Act of 2003 and the Affordable Care Act of 2010 (ACA)—with substantial costs. In 2019, for example, spending for the 2003 prescription drug benefit (Medicare Part D) was nearly $100 billion, roughly 12 percent of total Medicare spending.[11] Beneficiary premiums and other payments cover less than 30 percent of Part D costs, with the remainder funded by general revenues. With Medicaid, most of the enrollment increase since 2014 has been for "expansion adults"—those made eligible for Medicaid coverage by the ACA.[12] The most recent estimate is that the expansion adult category represents 17 percent of total Medicaid enrollment and 12 percent of total spending.[13] In addition, health insurance subsidies under the ACA now cost approximately $55 billion.[14]

Table 6.3 The Growth of Social Security and Federal Health Programs, 1990–2050 (as a percentage of GDP)

Fiscal Year	*Social Security*	*Major Health Programs*
1990	4.2	2.3
2000	4.0	3.1
2010	4.7	4.9
2020	5.3	6.1
2030	6.0	6.9
2040	6.3	8.2
2050	6.3	9.2

Sources: 2000: calculated by the author from *Historical Tables, Budget of the United States Government, Fiscal Year 2021* (Washington, D.C.: Government Printing Office, 2020), Tables 1.2, 8.5; all other entries: Congressional Budget Office, *The 2020 Long-Term Budget Outlook* (Washington, D.C.: Congressional Budget Office, 2020), 28; "Data Underlying Figures," www.cbo.gov/publication/56516.

Second, efforts to limit the growth of healthcare spending through cost controls and regulation have had mixed results, particularly for Medicare. Congress sets reimbursement rates for healthcare providers but must take into account the availability and quality of healthcare services. It is also difficult to regulate the volume or types of services that beneficiaries receive. Since the 1980s, there have been numerous changes in reimbursement formulas, covered benefits, and healthcare delivery services, but a workable balance between access and costs remains elusive.[15]

The steep rise in healthcare spending-GDP over the past two decades—from 3.1 percent in 2000 to 6.1 percent in 2020—was caused by larger beneficiary populations for the Medicare and Medicaid programs and increases in per beneficiary costs. Excess cost growth, a measure of how the rate of increase in healthcare spending per beneficiary exceeds the GDP growth rate, has had a major impact on Medicare and Medicaid spending in the past and is expected to have an even greater impact in the future. Roughly two-thirds of the projected increase in healthcare spending-GDP, from 6.1 percent in 2020 to 9.2 percent in 2050, is accounted for by excess cost growth, with the remainder due to population aging.[16] If excess cost growth turns out to be more of a problem than officials anticipate, healthcare spending-GDP would rise even faster.

In sum, mandatory spending levels are expected to increase steadily for an extended period because of demographic changes affecting Social Security and the major healthcare entitlements and cost factors associated with Medicare and Medicaid benefits. Interest costs will also affect future spending. Over the past 50 years, net interest costs have ranged from 1.2 percent to 3.2 percent of GDP, with an average of 2.0 percent.[17] Despite a nearly fourfold increase in the public debt since 2000, interest costs are currently very low (1.6 percent of GDP in 2020).[18] Net interest-GDP will remain stable if interest rates remain low; higher rates would raise interest costs and, in turn, total spending.

The Revenue Shortfall

Under current policy, the projected increase in revenue levels during the 2020s is relatively small (see Table 6.4). Almost all of the increase is in the individual income tax category, where rising real income and the scheduled expiration of the 2017 individual income tax cuts—its lower marginal rates, higher standard deductions, and small business pass-through provisions—would raise revenue-GDP significantly. If the president and Congress decide instead to extend the 2017 tax law for the vast majority of taxpayers—as they did with the expiring Bush tax cuts in 2013—revenue-GDP would grow much more slowly. Increases in real income, which move a larger share of individual income into higher tax brackets, would still boost revenue levels, but these effects would be fairly small for the ten-year projection period.[19]

Today's individual income tax policy—and its revenue-raising potential—reflects the lasting effects of the Bush tax cuts. The revenue cost of the 1981

Table 6.4 Baseline Revenue Projections, 2020–2031 (as a percentage of GDP)

	Actual, 2020	*2021*	*2022*	*2023*	*2024*	*2025*	*2026*	*2027*	*2028*	*2029*	*2030*	*2031*
Revenues												
Individual income taxes	7.7	7.7	8.8	8.7	8.5	8.5	9.1	9.5	9.4	9.4	9.4	9.4
Payroll taxes	6.2	6.0	5.9	6.0	6.0	5.9	5.9	5.9	5.9	5.8	5.8	5.8
Corporate income taxes	1.0	0.7	1.1	1.3	1.3	1.4	1.3	1.3	1.2	1.2	1.2	1.2
Other	1.4	1.4	1.5	1.5	1.5	1.4	1.3	1.3	1.2	1.2	1.1	1.1
Total	16.3	16.0	17.3	17.5	17.3	17.2	17.6	17.9	17.8	17.7	17.6	17.5

Source: Congressional Budget Office, *Additional Information About the Budget Outlook: 2021 to 2031* (Washington, D.C.: Congressional Budget Office, 2021), 2.

Reagan tax cuts, for example, was lowered by the deficit reduction tax increases in 1982 and 1984 and entirely erased by the much larger ones in the early 1990s. By 2000, revenue-GDP had climbed to 20 percent, which was above pre-Reagan levels. With the Bush tax cuts, revenues have never fully rebounded. Pre-Great Recession revenue levels during the Bush presidency averaged approximately 17 percent of GDP, and post-recession revenues under Obama were only slightly higher. After the Trump administration's tax cut, revenue-GDP fell to 16.4 percent in 2018 and to 16.3 percent in 2019. The post-2000 decline in revenue levels has not been limited to individual income taxes. Social insurance taxes (or payroll taxes) and "other taxes" (primarily excises) are all below the levels of the late 1990s as a share of GDP, and, under current policy, will continue to fall over the next decade (see Table 6.5). Longer-term projections are similar to those for the 2020s.

In the case of the corporate income tax, the 2017 tax law lowered revenue-GDP to recession-like levels. The previous major tax cut—the Economic Recovery Tax Act of 1981—had a similar short-term impact, but the tax increases that followed produced higher revenue-GDP levels from the mid-1980s through the mid-2000s. In 2006 and 2007, for example, corporate tax-GDP was 2.6 percent, its highest level since the late 1970s. Revenues plunged during the Great Recession, falling to 1.0 percent in 2009, but moved upward as the economy recovered. With the Trump tax cuts, corporate tax-GDP has dropped again and will remain at historically low levels unless corporate taxes are raised.

The decline in social insurance taxes-GDP is more complicated. Social Security and Medicare taxes were increased in the 1980s and 1990s, and their combined share of GDP climbed to approximately 6.5 percent over that period. It has since fallen to approximately 6 percent, and the current policy

Table 6.5 Revenues, by Category, 1980–2030 (as a percentage of GDP)

Fiscal Year	*Individual Income Taxes*	*Corporate Income Taxes*	*Social Insurance Taxes*	*Other*[a]	*Total*
1980	8.7	2.3	5.7	1.8	18.5
1990	7.9	1.6	6.4	1.6	17.5
2000	9.9	2.0	6.5	1.6	20.0
2010	6.1	1.3	5.8	1.5	14.6
2020	7.7	1.0	6.2	1.4	16.3
2030 (est.)	9.4	1.2	5.8	1.1	17.6

Sources: *Historical Tables, Budget of the United States Government, Fiscal Year 2021* (Washington, D.C.: Government Printing Office, 2020), Table 2.3; Congressional Budget Office, *Additional Information About the Budget Outlook: 2021 to 2031* (Washington, D.C.: Congressional Budget Office), 2.

Note: [a] Includes excise taxes, estate and gift taxes, customs duties and fees, Federal Reserve deposits, etc.

baselines for the 2020s and future years are slightly lower. Pending shortfalls in the Social Security trust funds (early to mid-2030s) and Medicare Hospital Insurance trust fund (mid-2020s) will require legislative changes in taxes and/or benefits. To the extent that Congress relies on tax increases to restore trust fund solvency, total revenue-GDP would increase as well. The remaining revenue source, excises and other federal taxes, is expected to drop slightly in the 2020s. In this case, Congress has failed to adjust excise tax rates to maintain a stable revenue share, while cutting estate and gift taxes (most recently in 2017) and repealing the tax on health insurance that providers levied in 2010. While these are minor revenue sources, it is worth noting that estate and gift taxes generated nearly $30 billion in revenues in 2000 but just over one-half of that amount in 2019.

Partisan debates over tax policy are typically about fairness (vertical equity, horizontal equity, individual equity) versus economic efficiency (economic growth). By most measures, the federal tax system is progressive. The share of federal taxes paid by upper-income taxpayers has increased over the past four decades, particularly for the top 1 percent of taxpayers, and has outpaced their income growth.[20] Average federal tax rates over this period have declined sharply for the lowest income quintile, moderately for the three middle income quintiles, but have remained fairly stable for the top quintile.[21] Whether this is sufficiently progressive or fair is another matter. It is indisputable, however, that the United States is a low-tax country and has been for some time. Its ratio of taxes-to-GDP is well below that of the major industrialized democracies (e.g., the G7) and it ranks sixth lowest out of the 37 countries in the Organisation for Economic Co-operation and Development (OECD).[22] With the 2017 tax act, corporate tax revenue as a share of GDP is approximately one-third of the G7 and OECD averages.[23]

Whether lower taxes and lower tax rates, at least within the post-1980 parameters for the United States, have significantly enhanced long-term economic growth is questionable. The available evidence is, at best, ambiguous in terms of labor force participation, savings rates, and investment.[24] Moreover, after the last major tax increase in 1993, real GDP growth over the next decade averaged 3.68 percent. It had averaged 2.31 percent from 1987–1992 (the post-Tax Reform Act of 1986 period); from 2003–2007, after the Bush tax cuts, it was 2.79 percent.[25]

The basic goal of the tax system, however, is revenue raising. As Alexander Hamilton wrote in Federalist 30, "Money is, with propriety, considered as the vital principle of the body politic; as that which sustains its life and motion and enables it to perform its most essential functions."[26] In practice, this entrusts elected officials with the responsibility for levying taxes to pay for government programs that society has decided it needs and to do so without unacceptable deficits or debt.[27] As noted earlier in this chapter, the United States had a welfare state budget in 2000 that was fully funded by taxes. It now has a larger and fast-growing welfare state budget without the revenues to support it.

Structural deficits—an excess of spending over revenues when the economy is healthy and when wars or other emergencies are not a causal factor—have defined fiscal policy for much of the past four decades. Structural deficits in recent years, however, have been unusually large, and those projected for the 2020s are larger still. Changes in current spending and tax policies will no doubt take place in the years ahead, but the salient question is whether they reduce the deficit problem or merely add to it. The Biden administration's fiscal program, and how it fares in Congress, will therefore help to define the future of deficit politics.

The Biden Fiscal Agenda

During the 2020 Democratic presidential primaries and caucuses, former Vice President Joe Biden refused to endorse a number of expensive and expansive programs that his "progressive" opponents were promoting—Medicare for All, the Green New Deal, Universal Child Care, and Student Debt Forgiveness. Once he secured the nomination, however, Biden released a series of proposals that would significantly increase federal spending for education, healthcare, environmental protection, and other domestic initiatives. He endorsed higher taxes, especially for corporations and upper-income households, but pledged to protect those earning less than $400,000 from any tax increases, virtually guaranteeing that deficits would increase. The Biden campaign did not provide specific forecasts, but one nonpartisan group—the Penn Wharton Budget research project—predicted that Biden's program would add $2 trillion in deficits over ten years.[28] That estimate was much too low. Once candidate Biden became President Biden, his first legislative priority was a $1.9 trillion deficit-financed "rescue plan," and the spending proposals that followed were even more costly.

The Biden program is testing whether congressional Democrats across the ideological spectrum are ready to support "a new social and economic contract"[29] that goes well beyond what the party has promised in the past. They will also be required to jettison any immediate concerns about deficits and debt. In effect, Democrats will need to adopt the unconflicted mind-set on domestic spending that Republicans bring to tax cuts and be equally as willing to use reconciliation to advance a partisan fiscal agenda.

The American Rescue Plan Act of 2021

The first test of Democratic unity was a costlier version of the pandemic spending bill that House Democrats had passed in the summer of 2020 and that Senate Republicans then blocked. Fiscal relief for state and local governments remained a Democratic priority as did additional cash assistance for individuals and households, but the Biden administration's $1.9 trillion economic recovery package went considerably further.[30] The administration and Democratic congressional leaders agreed at the outset that reconciliation would be needed to bypass Republican opposition in the Senate, and a budget resolution was quickly adopted in early February 2021 for that purpose.

A Streamlined Process

As the House Budget Committee explained, "The 2021 budget resolution is not a comprehensive fiscal blueprint for the next 10 years. It is designed solely to provide the option of using reconciliation to deliver critical relief and achieve the goals of the American Rescue Plan."[31] The House passed its reconciliation instructions on a party-line vote of 218–212 on February 3. Under Senate rules, up to 30 hours of debate is permitted on a budget resolution, and numerous floor amendments were adopted over three days of Senate consideration in early February. All of this was superseded by the leadership's substitute bill adopted on a 51–50 vote on February 5, as Vice President Harris cast the tiebreaking vote. Minor differences with the House were resolved that same day, as the House approved the Senate's version by a vote of 219–209.

The reconciliation instructions in the 2021 budget resolution involved 12 House and 11 Senate committees, but Democratic leaders maintained tight control over their deliberations and markups. They were anxious to avoid a replay of the party's missteps on the stimulus and healthcare bills a decade earlier, and this meant expedited action on the entire $1.9 trillion package. Once it became clear that Republicans would only agree to a drastically scaled-back measure, Democrats moved ahead unilaterally. They worked to maintain party unity on key committee and floor votes and to minimize House-Senate differences that could delay or even derail the reconciliation bill.

House committees reported out their respective sections of the reconciliation package during the first three weeks in February, and the House approved the combined bill by a vote of 219–212 on February 27. As expected, every Republican voted "no," but only two Democrats defected. With a 50–50 Senate, even one Democratic defection would be fatal, and Majority Leader Charles Schumer orchestrated a series of compromises that kept his majority intact. Democratic Senator Joseph Manchin III had been an especially vocal critic of the amount and duration of added unemployment benefits in the House bill and what he considered the excessively high income phase-outs for certain tax credits and other benefits. The Senate bill was revised in line with Manchin's and other moderates' objections and did not include a controversial $15 per hour federal minimum wage provision that had been added to the House-passed reconciliation bill. The Senate parliamentarian ruled that minimum wage legislation was outside the scope of reconciliation protection, but Senator Bernie Sanders and other liberal Democrats nevertheless proposed a $15 minimum wage amendment that was rejected on a 42–58 vote. When the amendment failed, Sanders simply vowed to pursue the issue at a later time, and he, along with his fellow liberals, remained on board. The reconciliation bill then passed the Senate on a party-line vote on March 6, and the House agreed to the Senate version several days later. President Biden signed the ARPA into law on March 11.

Coverage, Benefits, Programs[32]

The spending and revenue provisions in the ARPA fell into several broad categories: (1) direct financial assistance to individuals and households; (2) in-kind benefits for individuals and households; (3) aid to state and local governments; (4) financial assistance for businesses and economic development; and (5) traditional public health measures directly or indirectly related to COVID-19. Much of this assistance was in the form of additional funding and broader eligibility for existing programs, including those established under previous pandemic relief bills. Several new programs were also created, including the Restaurant Revitalization Fund, the Coronavirus Capital Projects Fund, and emergency housing programs.

The largest assistance category—approximately $775 billion—was direct financial assistance to individuals and households. Cash rebates, tax credits, and unemployment compensation benefits accounted for the bulk of this spending. The maximum cash rebate of $1,400 would be paid to individuals and qualified dependents in income-eligible households (adjusted gross income below $75,000 for individuals and $150,000 for joint filers). The various tax credits—child tax credits, dependent care credits, and earned income tax credits—were subject to income phase-outs but were fully refundable for eligible households. The renewed authorization for federal support of state unemployment compensation programs extended the number of weeks during which individuals would remain eligible and provided a $300 federal supplement to payments made by states. For income-eligible households, up to $10,200 in unemployment benefits was nontaxable as well.

Approximately $260 billion in additional federal funding was made available for in-kind benefit programs. Over $10 billion was provided for increased benefits under the Supplemental Nutrition Assistance Program and extended EBT benefits (emergency food benefits to families whose children had lost access to school-provided free or reduced-price meals). More than $40 billion was added to housing programs, including rental vouchers, homeowners' assistance, and homeless programs. Expanded healthcare coverage included increased funding for Medicaid and private health insurance subsidies under the ACA; unemployed workers received direct cash subsidies for health insurance coverage previously provided by their employers. Federal assistance was extended to child and elderly care services, utility payments, and other emergency needs. Much of this was temporary, but Democrats made it clear that a permanent social safety net expansion would soon be addressed.

The ARPA authorized more than $360 billion in grants to state, local, and other governments with few restrictions. The federal funds could be used for government operations and services, assistance to individuals and businesses, and a variety of infrastructure projects. An additional $28 billion was provided for public transportation systems, whose revenues had plummeted during the pandemic. Elementary and secondary schools, a major expense for state and local governments, received more than $120 billion in new federal funding for staff, equipment, health protocols, and technology improvements. Public colleges and universities were eligible for $40 billion in higher education funding, most of which was allocated to student financial aid.

Businesses had received major federal support under the 2020 pandemic relief programs. One of the largest of these was the Paycheck Protection Program (PPP), which began in March 2020 and had then been renewed. The ARPA provided only $5 billion for the PPP and other ongoing programs, but it did establish a new $28 billion restaurant stabilization program. In addition, nearly $27 billion was provided for airlines and air transportation, $24 billion in small business disaster loans and credit was authorized, and over $10 billion was allocated to support farmers, ranchers, and rural development. Employer credits for paid sick leave, paid family leave, and employee retention totaled $10 billion, and more than $80 billion was authorized to support multiemployer pension plans threatened with insolvency.

Public health funding in the ARPA included vaccine production and distribution; testing, contact tracing, and mitigation activities; research; health workforce support; community health centers; mental health and substance abuse services; and emergency medical supplies. Total funding for these and related activities was nearly $150 billion. An additional $16 billion was authorized for veterans' healthcare services, much of which was related to COVID-19 treatment, training, and supplies.

Passing a bill of this magnitude without Republican votes demonstrated impressive discipline on the Democratic side. It also signaled that, at least for the short term, Democrats were willing to ignore deficits and debt. Republicans criticized the ARPA as wasteful and unnecessary, but their attacks were muted, a marked contrast to the strident denunciations of the Obama stimulus program a decade earlier. The high level of public support for the ARPA, which numerous polls affirmed as it worked its way through Congress, no doubt explained much of this reticence. There was a sense as well that the deficit issue had lost much of its salience after several trillion dollars of bipartisan deficit-financed stimulus in 2020.

Nevertheless, the ARPA was not a straightforward stimulus bill, since it would provide substantial relief well after the pandemic's worst effects had been left behind. This was especially true given the accelerated vaccine distribution program that the Biden administration implemented in January. Biden promised that 100 million Americans would be vaccinated in the first 100 days of his presidency; that goal was reached in less than two months, at which point the president doubled it. In the early spring of 2021, the administration stepped up its distribution plan once again, and states began to lift coronavirus restrictions on businesses. Most areas of the country were expected to reopen fully by summer at the latest.

Under the ARPA, however, federal unemployment support continued through the first week of September 2021, employee retention credits remained in effect through December, and state and local fiscal recovery funds would be available through 2024. The child tax credits in the ARPA amounted to a guaranteed family income program for the whole of 2021. The child and dependent care tax credits, with higher maximums and full refundability, provided an additional income supplement for 2021.[33]

The Rebuild America Program

With the American Rescue Plan in place, the Biden administration unveiled its economic and social reform agenda. Two long-term plans were announced in the spring—a $2.7 trillion infrastructure plan and a $1.8 trillion family support program. An increase of more than $100 billion in discretionary domestic spending was requested for the fiscal year 2022 budget, with additional spending scheduled thereafter. Taken together, these proposals rivaled the domestic spending initiatives of the Great Society era.

The fiscal and political conditions that had facilitated the Great Society expansion, however, had changed. The welfare state was no longer in its infancy but was now the largest and fastest-growing part of the federal budget. Deficit and debt levels were many, many times higher, and financing costly domestic programs with defense budget cuts was no longer an option. Tax increases had been difficult when Democratic control of Congress was uncontested; the parties of the 2020s, by comparison, were closely balanced and sharply polarized. Given the breadth and costs of the Biden program, the prospects for bipartisan budget legislation were limited at best.

The American Jobs Plan

Infrastructure programs have traditionally attracted broad support in Congress, but long-term funding commitments have been rare in recent decades. A five-year infrastructure bill of more than $300 billion in 2015 was the longest reauthorization since the mid-2000s, and the Trump administration's highly touted $1.0 trillion multiyear plan never progressed very far, despite general agreement that the nation's physical infrastructure needs were urgent. President Biden's plan came at an opportune time, but its scope and financing were problematic for many Republicans.

The American Jobs Plan included straightforward physical infrastructure investments—bridges, highways, air and rail transportation, electrical grids, and utilities—with an estimated ten-year cost of more than $700 billion.[34] Another $200 billion would support traditional research and development—the National Science Foundation, advanced semiconductor manufacturing, research laboratories, and supply chain modernization. These components have bipartisan appeal, and the administration began negotiations in the spring of 2021 with key Republicans on a possible carve-out that would include funding and financing for agreed-upon programs.

Investments in clean energy, housing, and healthcare, by contrast, were expected to draw little or no Republican support, which left congressional Democrats solely responsible for enacting them. The amounts, moreover, were substantial—$400 billion in clean energy tax credits, $400 billion in expanded long-term home and community-based healthcare services, $236 billion for housing and schools—and the administration proposed to cover these costs through tax increases and additional borrowing. The tax increases would affect corporations, with a scheduled increase in the corporate tax rate from 21 percent to 28 percent and the reduction or elimination of tax preferences, particularly for multinational corporations. Over a ten-year period, the American Jobs Plan tax program would increase revenues by $1.75 trillion, covering approximately two-thirds of its $2.65 trillion cost. The administration predicted that infrastructure investments would eventually boost economic growth and revenues so that long-term net costs would be close to zero. However, deficits for the 2020s would be at least $900 billion higher if Democrats managed to enact the entire American Jobs Plan package.

The American Families Plan[35]

The Biden administration's plan for improving the economic well-being of low- and moderate-income households includes new family leave and education entitlements, direct cash assistance, and expanded healthcare coverage. A national family and medical leave program, with an estimated ten-year cost of $225 billion, would guarantee partial wage replacement for parental, family, and sick leave. The American Families Plan would also fund at least four additional years of free education—two years of universal preschool ($200 billion) and two years of community college ($109 billion). Additional support for low-income college students would include more generous Pell Grants ($85 billion), funding for college retention and degree completion programs ($62 billion), and direct assistance to colleges and universities that serve minority students ($46 billion).

Since the refundable tax credits in the American Rescue Plan were temporary, the American Families Plan would extend the expanded child tax credit through 2025 and make permanent its child and dependent care tax credit, child tax credit, and earned income tax credit income-eligibility provisions. The combined cost would be $600 billion over a ten-year period. A permanent expansion of the ACA's private insurance subsidies, federal payments to families to defray the cost of child care, and more generous food and nutrition programs would add $470 billion in spending and tax credits.

The proposed revenue offsets for the American Families Plan include higher tax rates (39.6 percent on ordinary income, capital gains, and dividends) and scaled-back tax preferences for high-income households. In addition, taxes on large inheritances would be increased through new rules governing appreciated assets. The ten-year revenue estimate for these tax law changes is approximately $1.5 trillion, $300 billion less than estimated spending for the American Families Plan.

Legislative Strategy and Timetable

Democrats assumed from the beginning that the American Families Plan would require reconciliation protection in order to pass the Senate, and even then the hurdles would be steep. The American Jobs Plan, however, included physical infrastructure spending for which the Biden administration hoped to secure enough Republican votes to follow the normal legislative process. In both cases, the main obstacles were cost and financing.

In the late spring of 2021, agreement was reached on a $1.2 trillion Bipartisan Infrastructure Framework.[36] As expected, most of the funding would be devoted to physical infrastructure investments—roads, bridges, railroads and public transit, water and power projects, etc. The administration's broadband initiative was included, as were its environmental remediation and electric vehicle transportation programs, but the healthcare, housing, and other "human infrastructure" investments in the American Jobs Plan were not. Missing as well were the corporate income tax rate hikes in the original plan. In an interesting twist, Republicans offered to raise the excise tax on gasoline, but President Biden would not agree to any tax increases that affected low- and middle-income households. The financing compromise consisted instead of enhanced collection of individual income taxes and other existing taxes, reductions in new spending by repurposing unused funds from the 2020 and 2021 emergency relief bills, and additional borrowing to cover the remainder.

With this framework in place, House and Senate committees drafted a $1.2 trillion infrastructure bill that Congress approved in the fall. In addition, Democrats began to negotiate a reconciliation package incorporating the human infrastructure investments from the original American Jobs Plan, new entitlements in the American Families Plan, and corporate and individual income tax increases from both. The size of this package would be determined solely by Democrats, but the difference between what some progressives were demanding and moderates seemed willing to support amounted to trillions of dollars. The only certainty was that deficit financing would be needed for much of the new spending Democrats managed to approve.

The Discretionary Spending Program

Finally, the Biden administration has called for reinvesting in the "core functions of Government" through targeted increases in domestic appropriations.[37] For 2022, the administration has requested a nearly 16 percent increase in discretionary nondefense funding compared to base, or nonemergency, appropriations for 2021.[38] Especially large increases have been proposed for education, public health, housing, and climate change-related environmental initiatives. By comparison, the proposed increase in the defense budget is 1.6 percent.

The fiscal year 2022 budget is the first installment of what the administration hopes will be a long-term shift in discretionary spending priorities. For fiscal years 2022–2031, defense spending-GDP would average 2.9 percent under the administration's plan, while the average for nondefense programs would be 3.4 percent.[39] The CBO's baseline spending projection for nondefense programs over this period totals $8.7 trillion.[40] The Biden budget's proposed spending totals $9.4 trillion.[41]

Deficits and Debt

The Biden administration has been unusually forthright about the additional borrowing its fiscal program will require. The American Rescue Plan, for example, raised the 2021 deficit by $1.1 trillion.[42] The administration's fiscal year 2022 budget proposals, including the American Jobs Plan and American Families Plan, would require substantial borrowing over the next decade. When President Biden took office, baseline deficit-GDP estimates for 2022–2031 were approximately 4.4 percent, with public debt-GDP levels moving upward at a modest rate (see Table 6.6). With the Biden budget, deficits average 5.2 percent of GDP, public debt grows more rapidly, and debt-GDP climbs to 117 percent in 2031. No administration in the deficit politics era has proposed borrowing remotely close to this scale. Even more striking, some Democrats in Congress would enthusiastically support even larger deficits to secure their domestic agenda.

The administration has defended its program as "fiscally responsible," promising a $2 trillion reduction in baseline deficits in the 2030s.[43] Since current deficit projections for that period are extremely high, any reduction would be helpful, but the Biden budget's "second decade" effects would be marginal. Large structural deficits would continue indefinitely, and elevated public debt levels would persist as well. Given the unreliability of five-year or ten-year budget forecasts, second-decade estimates cannot be taken too seriously, but the important point is that deficit politics will remain firmly in place even if they turn out to be accurate.

Deficit Financing and the Welfare State

In making the case for tax cuts, Republicans downplay concerns about deficits and debt. The Biden administration and congressional Democrats have adopted a similar strategy for their domestic spending program. Supportive economic experts had previously argued that since "[t]he economics of deficits have changed … [i]t's time for Washington to put away its debt obsession

Table 6.6 Deficits and Debt: Baseline Estimates and Biden Administration Budget Estimates, 2022–2031 (as a percentage of GDP)

											Averages	
	2022	*2023*	*2024*	*2025*	*2026*	*2027*	*2028*	*2029*	*2030*	*2031*	*2022–2026*	*2022–2031*
Deficits												
CBO Baseline	–4.6	–4.0	–3.6	–4.0	–3.7	–3.7	–4.6	–4.4	–5.2	–5.7	–4.0	–4.4
Biden FY 2022 Budget	–7.8	–5.6	–5.3	–5.5	–5.1	–4.6	–4.8	–4.2	–4.6	–4.7	–5.9	–5.2
Debt												
CBO Baseline	102.0	102.0	101.4	101.2	100.9	101.0	102.2	103.2	105.0	107.2	n/a	n/a
Biden FY 2022 Budget	111.8	112.7	113.8	115.2	116.1	116.4	116.8	116.6	116.8	117.0	n/a	n/a

Sources: Congressional Budget Office, *The Budget and Economic Outlook: 2021 to 2031* (Washington, D.C.: Congressional Budget, 2021), 2; *Budget of the United States Government, Fiscal Year 2022* (Washington, D.C.: Government Printing Office, 2021), 41, 62.

and focus on bigger things."[44] Skeptics might counter that neither party has suffered from a debt obsession for most of the past two decades, which is precisely why the structural deficit problem has become so serious.

George W. Bush, for example, never let deficits stand in the way of tax cuts, new entitlements, or even war, and he was abetted by congressional Republicans at every stage. The Great Recession at the end of his presidency then amplified the deficit costs of what clearly were politically expedient policy choices. Barack Obama's ACA, by comparison, was deficit neutral, and he called for a "grand bargain" to reduce structural deficits soon thereafter. Republicans had at this point rediscovered the dangers of deficits and debt but nonetheless rejected the tax increases without which a grand bargain was impossible. They insisted instead on deficit reduction spending cuts that turned out to be illusory, and neither party has since paid much attention to deficits or debt.

On the contrary, Democrats and Republicans agreed to make most of the Bush tax cuts permanent in 2013; negotiated discretionary defense and non-defense spending increases in 2013, 2015, 2018, and 2019; and passed several trillion dollars in pandemic relief in 2020. Republicans proceeded on their own with a $1.5 trillion tax cut in 2017, and Democrats followed suit with a $1.9 trillion spending bill in March 2021. As a result, we now have the highest peacetime debt levels in the nation's history and the near-certain prospect of even higher ones in the years ahead.

Deficits and the Economy

In 2019, public debt was $16.8 trillion, or nearly 80 percent of GDP.[45] More than $6 trillion in deficits over the past two years has raised that total to $23 trillion, or 103 percent of GDP.[46] Over the past several years, foreign holdings of U.S. debt has averaged approximately 40 percent, the majority of which is owned by foreign central banks and other official institutions.[47] The largest shares of U.S. debt at the end of 2020 were held by Japan (18 percent of foreign holdings) and China (15 percent).

Despite this large debt, current interest costs are quite low—$345 billion in 2020 and an estimated $331 billion in 2021.[48] The CBO expects a moderate increase in interest rates over the next decade, with the rate on ten-year Treasury notes averaging approximately 3.2 percent in the late 2020s.[49] This would raise interest costs to more than $800 billion, or just over 10 percent of total spending, in 2030. Higher rates would, of course, increase interest costs and cause federal debt to increase more rapidly, and the CBO has warned that "growth in interest costs and debt reinforce one another: Rising interest costs boost deficits and debt, and rising debt pushes up interest costs."[50]

Economists disagree about the consequences of this fiscal trajectory. The conventional view, echoed in the reports of government agencies, is that chronic deficits and rising debt pose economic and fiscal risks—higher interest rates, inflation pressures, and, over time, lower growth and reduced prosperity.[51] For government, potential budgetary shocks from unexpectedly high interest rates and reduced fiscal capacity in responding to future crises are cited as well.

For quite some time, however, interest rates have remained very low, inflation has not been a problem, and global capital markets have financed federal debt without serious disruptions. Given these circumstances, some economists have concluded that government should take advantage of low interest rates to finance worthwhile spending in areas of national need. In their view, policymakers can safely ignore deficits for the time being, without entirely abandoning fiscal constraints. Chief among those constraints are debt levels: under normal circumstances, these economists advise policymakers to make certain that "new spending and tax cuts do not add to the debt."[52] Unfortunately, this is a caution the Trump administration ignored, and the Biden administration seems to be intent on doing so as well.

Adherents of modern monetary theory (MMT) go much further. They dismiss deficit concerns and insist that government should spend whatever is necessary to "balance the economy so that prosperity is broadly shared and not concentrated in fewer and fewer hands."[53] Inflation must be carefully managed, but otherwise deficits are always good for the economy and debt is essentially irrelevant. The MMT school has only a small following in the economics profession, but it has attracted leading progressives who want to expand the welfare state without worrying about costs.

Of course, MMT's prescription for controlling inflation—higher taxes—is what progressives are trying to avoid and what policymakers more generally are reluctant to do. In addition, MMT would rely on these same policymakers to manage any debt crisis that might occur. Since the government controls its own currency, the president and Congress would simply demand that more money be printed to "make all payments as they come due."[54] For MMT critics, this would undermine a stable currency and make it even more difficult to control inflation. More broadly, MMT would free government from straightforward fiscal constraints and then expect it to manage inflation, growth, and employment with a degree of prescience and skill that is unrealistic to the point of being naïve.

In assessing future fiscal policy choices, economic uncertainties should be taken into account. It is helpful to recall, for example, that the U.S. economy has been buffeted by a Great Recession and a pandemic in the short space of 15 years. Neither was anticipated, and both turned out to be much more costly than expected. Given this all-too-recent experience, policymakers should be cautious when assuming that future economic conditions will be benign. Moreover, despite low interest rates and low inflation, economic growth over the past two decades has been disappointing. It has lagged behind rates for the preceding several decades, and future growth projections are lower as well.[55] The Bush and Trump tax cuts delivered little in the way of accelerated growth and never came close to being self-financing. However worthwhile President Biden's human investment spending might be, different outcomes are unlikely.

It is generally accepted that deficit spending is an indispensable tool of government. It is used to fight wars, end economic downturns, and meet emergency needs. It can profitably fund capital investments that yield tangible economic benefits. More problematic is the routine reliance on deficit financing for government's normal operations and permanent programs, particularly when deficits are sufficiently large to raise debt levels indefinitely. The economic and fiscal risks this poses may seem remote but are nonetheless real. Equally as troubling, however, is their political cost. If a basic principle of democratic governance is the prudent management of government finances, deficit politics is more than an economic liability.

Deficits and Governance

The budget policy challenge for the United States is straightforward—we do not have the revenue system to support a large and ever more costly welfare state. With the new entitlements that President Biden and congressional Democrats hope to enact, the mismatch will be even greater, since higher taxes on the wealthy and on corporations will not be nearly enough to solve the revenue problem. Most major democracies have recognized that universal entitlements for the elderly and the poor require broad-based taxation, including the great majority of the population that comprises the middle class. The Unites States, however, has moved further and further away from this type of revenue system, and there are no signs this is about to change.

President Biden's tax program, for example, would raise substantial revenues through targeted increases on wealthy taxpayers. Restoring the pre-2017 39.6 percent marginal tax rate for high-income households, nearly doubling their capital gains and dividend tax rates, and taxing pass-through income more heavily would lift individual income tax-GDP above even Clinton-era levels.[56] For corporations, the proposed changes—higher tax rates, and limited tax preferences for deductions, credits, and deferrals as well as for foreign profits of multinational corporations—would boost corporate income tax-GDP to more than 2.0 percent over the next decade, nearly double its post-2017 tax law level.[57] If Congress were to approve these or similar changes, total revenue-GDP would be close to 20 percent by the late 2020s.

Spending-GDP under the Biden budget plan, however, would be nearly 25 percent, primarily due to the cost of existing and new entitlements. Over the next decade, the Biden budget simply extends the current policy costs for Social Security and Medicare—which translates into combined spending of more than $26 trillion over the next decade.[58] For Medicaid, the Biden budget includes coverage and benefit increases that would raise baseline spending by approximately $400 billion over a ten-year period. The cost of new entitlements, however, would be much, much higher—$12.9 trillion as opposed to the $8.9 trillion under current policy—boosting total mandatory spending to well over 16 percent.

An expanded welfare state, discretionary spending commitments, and interest costs will therefore require much higher revenue levels than those under consideration if debt levels are to be stabilized. Unfortunately, President Biden's pledge to limit tax increases to the very small percentage of taxpayers above the $400,000 threshold makes this close to impossible. Since demographics alone will raise welfare state spending to an even greater share of the economy in the 2030s and 2040s, revenue shortfalls will be even harder to bridge.

Rather than addressing these fiscal realities, political leaders in both parties pursue electoral strategies that make matters worse. Republicans brook no dissent from their low-tax orthodoxy, insist that deficits are strictly a spending problem, and yet assure voters that popular entitlements are not at risk. Democrats offer a more generous welfare state but promise to shield 98 percent of the taxpaying population from having to pay for it.

In Federalist 30, Alexander Hamilton explained that the federal government's taxing power was designed "to procure a regular and adequate supply of revenue, as far as the resources of the community will permit."[59] The United States is an extremely wealthy nation with unusually low tax burdens. If the public wants a comprehensive welfare state, a capable military, and the myriad public goods that the modern state provides, the "resources of the community" are more than ample to finance these needs with only modestly higher taxes.

When political leaders disguise the true costs of government by continually relying on deficits, voters need not decide how big a government they are willing to pay for. Since taxes are, after all, their most potent check on what the government can do, circumventing that check undermines political accountability. Quite apart from its potentially adverse economic effects, deficit politics discourages responsible fiscal leadership that enlightens voters and serves the public interest.

In rejecting the balanced budget/low debt fiscal norms that guided budget policy for much of U.S. history, deficit politics allows political leaders and parties to pursue politically popular but diametrically opposite goals. We have, as a result, Democratic spending policy, Republican tax policy, and a bipartisan tolerance for the deficits and debt that accrue. With the country so closely divided at this time and likely to remain so for the foreseeable future, neither party can afford to take the electoral risks that deficit reduction and debt stabilization entail, and it will likely take an economic or political crisis to force the bipartisan compromises that all but the willfully ignorant in both parties know are inevitable.

This is unfortunate, since phasing in timely and calibrated fiscal adjustments today could insure that debt levels are at least stabilized in the decades ahead. Crisis-driven responses would almost certainly be more costly and disruptive and their long-term results less certain. It would also be preferable to begin the difficult work of reconnecting taxes and spending sooner rather than later, so that future budget decision-making avoids the deficit politics illusions that brought us to our current precarious state.

One must acknowledge, however, that the disruptive Trump presidency and the continuing aftershocks for American democracy have relegated deficits and debt to a political closet of sorts. In the U.S. Congress today, basic governance is no longer routine. The budget process is in shambles, debt limit threats are always looming, and regular order on budget legislation is a relic of the past. For members of the House and the Senate, taxes and spending are a zero-sum game, and long-term thinking means the next midterm elections. The early days of party polarization seem almost quaint in the current political environment, which is why fiscally competent government may be among the least of our worries.

Notes

1 Congressional Budget Office, *The Budget and Economic Outlook: 2021 to 2031* (Washington, D.C.: Congressional Budget Office, 2021), 2; Congressional Budget Office, *The 2021 Long-Term Budget Outlook* (Washington, D.C.: Congressional Budget Office, 2021), 6.
2 Congressional Budget Office, *The 2021 Long-Term Budget Outlook*, 7.
3 Congressional Budget Office, *The 2021 Long-Term Budget Outlook*, 11.
4 Congressional Budget Office, *The 2021 Long-Term Budget Outlook*, 7.
5 Congressional Budget Office, *The Budget and Economic Outlook: 2021 to 2031*, 12.
6 Congressional Budget Office, *The Budget and Economic Outlook: 2021 to 2031*, 1.
7 Congressional Budget Office, *The 2021 Long-Term Budget Outlook*, 7.
8 *Historical Tables, Budget of the United States Government, Fiscal Year 2021* (Washington, D.C.: Government Printing Office, 2020), Table 8.4.
9 Congressional Budget Office, *The 2021 Long-Term Budget Outlook*, 19.
10 Congressional Budget Office, *The 2020 Long-Term Budget Outlook* (Washington, D.C.: Congressional Budget Office, 2020), 28, 32.
11 Patricia A. Davis, Cliff Binder, Jim Hahn, Suzanne M. Kirchhoff, Paulette C. Morgan, Marco A. Villagrana, and Phoenix Voorhies, *Medicare Primer* (Washington, D.C.: Congressional Research Service, May 21, 2020), 1, 31.
12 Alison Mitchell, *Medicaid Primer* (Washington, D.C.: Congressional Research Service, November 30, 2020), 1.
13 Mitchell, *Medicaid Primer*, 2.
14 Congressional Budget Office, *The Budget and Economic Outlook: 2021 to 2031*, 4.
15 Davis et al., *Medicare Primer*, 3–6.
16 Congressional Budget Office, *The 2020 Long-Term Budget Outlook*, 32.
17 Congressional Budget Office, *The 2020 Long-Term Budget Outlook*, 34.
18 Congressional Budget Office, *Additional Information About the Budget Outlook: 2021 to 2031* (Washington, D.C.: Congressional Budget Office, 2021), 2.
19 Congressional Budget Office, *The 2020 Long-Term Budget Outlook*, 36.
20 This includes all federal taxes. Congressional Budget Office, *The Distribution of Household Income, 2017* (Washington, D.C.: Congressional Budget Office, 2020), 23.
21 Congressional Budget Office, *The Distribution of Household Income, 2017*, 18.
22 Organisation for Economic Co-operation and Development, Centre for Tax Policy and Administration, "Revenue Statistics 2020 – the United States," www.oecd.org/tax/revenue-statistics-united-states.pdf.

23 The Urban-Brookings Tax Policy Center, The Tax Policy Center's Briefing Book, "How Do US Corporate Income Tax Rates and Revenues Compare with Other Countries'?," www.taxpolicycenter.org/briefing-book/how-do-us-corporate-income-tax-rates-and-revenues-compare-other-countries.
24 Jane G. Gravelle and Donald J. Marples, *Tax Rates and Economic Growth* (Washington, D.C.: Congressional Research Service, January 2, 2014), 2–4.
25 Gravelle and Marples, *Tax Rates and Economic Growth*, 5.
26 Alexander Hamilton, James Madison, and John Jay, *The Federalist Papers* (New York: New American Library, 1961), 188.
27 C. Eugene Steuerle, *Contemporary U.S. Tax Policy*, 2nd ed. (Washington, D.C.: Urban Institute Press, 2008), 15.
28 "Study: Biden Budget Policies Would Grow Deficits by $2 Trillion," *CQ Magazine*, September 21, 2020, https://library.cqpress.com/cqmagazine/weeklyreport116-000006005784.
29 "The 2020 Democratic Platform, August 18, 2020," The Democratic National Committee, https://democrats.org/where-we-stand/party-platform.
30 The outlines of the Biden proposal and its $1.9 trillion cost had been announced prior to his inauguration. Jane G. Gravelle and Donald J. Marples, *Fiscal Policy and Recovery from the COVID-19 Recession* (Washington, D.C.: Congressional Research Service, February 1, 2021), 4.
31 Megan S. Lynch and James V. Saturno, *S.Con.Res. 5: The Budget Resolution for FY2021* (Washington, D.C.: Congressional Research Service, February 8, 2021), 1.
32 Outlay estimates below are from Congressional Budget Office, "Detailed Tables," *Cost Estimate: Estimated Budgetary Effects of H.R. 1319, American Rescue Plan Act of 2021*, www.cbo.gov/publication/57056.
33 Margot L. Crandall-Hollick, *The Child Tax Credit: Temporary Expansion for 2021 Under the American Rescue Plan Act of 2021 (ARPA; P.L. 117–2)* (Washington, D.C.: Congressional Research Service, May 3, 2021), 1–2.
34 Based on estimates for specific provisions. See Committee for a Responsible Federal Budget, "What's in President Biden's American Jobs Plan?," April 2, 2021, www.crfb.org/blogs/whats-president-bidens-american-jobs-plan.
35 Cost estimates for the provisions described below are included in The White House, "Fact Sheet: The American Families Plan," April 28, 2021, www.whitehouse.gov/briefing-room/statements-releases/2021/04/28/fact-sheet-the-american-families-plan/.
36 This is the estimated spending total over an eight-year period. The White House, "Fact Sheet: President Biden Announces Support for the Bipartisan Infrastructure Framework," June 24, 2021, www.whitehouse.gov/briefing-room/statements-releases/2021/06/24/fact-sheet-president-biden-announces-support-for-the-bipartisan-infrastructure-framework/.
37 *Budget of the United States Government, Fiscal Year 2022* (Washington, D.C.: Government Printing Office, 2021), 13.
38 *Budget of the United States Government, Fiscal Year 2022*, 57.
39 *Budget of the United States Government, Fiscal Year 2022*, 41.
40 Congressional Budget Office, *The Budget and Economic Outlook: 2021 to 2031*, 6.
41 *Budget of the United States Government, Fiscal Year 2022*, 40.
42 Congressional Budget Office, *An Update to the Budget and Economic Outlook: 2021 to 2031* (Washington, D.C.: Congressional Budget Office, 2021), 1.
43 *Budget of the United States Government, Fiscal Year 2022*, 26, 27.
44 Jason Furman and Lawrence H. Summers, "Who's Afraid of Budget Deficits? How Washington Should End Its Debt Obsession," *Foreign Affairs* 98, no. 2 (2019): 94.
45 Congressional Budget Office, *The Budget and Economic Outlook: 2020 to 2030* (Washington, D.C.: Congressional Budget Office, 2020), 7.

46 Congressional Budget Office, *An Update to the Budget and Economic Outlook: 2021 to 2031*, 2.
47 *Analytical Perspectives, Budget of the United States Government, Fiscal Year 2022* (Washington, D.C.: Government Printing Office, 2021), 36–38.
48 Congressional Budget Office, *An Update to the Budget and Economic Outlook: 2021 to 2031*, 2.
49 Congressional Budget Office, *An Update to the Budget and Economic Outlook: 2021 to 2031*, 4.
50 Congressional Budget Office, *The 2021 Long-Term Budget Outlook*, 24.
51 Congressional Budget Office, *The 2021 Long-Term Budget Outlook*, 10–13.
52 Furman and Summers, "Who's Afraid of Budget Deficits," 83.
53 Stephanie Kelton, *The Deficit Myth* (New York: Public Affairs, 2021), 2.
54 William Mitchell, L. Randall Wray, and Martin Watts, *Macroeconomics* (London: Red Globe Press, 2019), 13.
55 Congressional Budget Office, *The 2021 Long-Term Budget Outlook*, 16.
56 *Budget of the United States Government, Fiscal Year 2022*, 41.
57 *Budget of the United States Government, Fiscal Year 2022*, 41.
58 *Budget of the United States Government, Fiscal Year 2022*, 39–41.
59 Hamilton et al., *The Federalist Papers*, 188.

Bibliography

Adams, Henry. *The Life of Albert Gallatin*. New York: Peter Smith, 1943.

Amenta, Edwin. *Bold Relief: Institutional Politics and the Origins of Modern American Social Policy*. Princeton, N.J.: Princeton University Press, 1998.

Annual Report to the Congress, Fiscal Year 1987. Washington, D.C.: Department of Defense, 1986.

Austin, D. Andrew. *The Debt Limit Since 2011*. Washington, D.C.: Congressional Research Service, March 29, 2018.

Austin, Erik W. *Political Facts of the United States Since 1789*. New York: Columbia University Press, 1986.

Bank, Steven A., Kirk J. Stark, and Joseph J. Thorndike. *War and Taxes*. Washington, D.C.: Urban Institute Press, 2008.

Berchick, Edward R., Jessica C. Barnett, and Rachel D. Upton. *Health Insurance Coverage in the United States: 2018 (Current Population Reports, P-60–267(RV))*. Washington, D.C.: Government Printing Office, 2019.

Berkowitz, Edward D., and Kim McQuaid. *Creating the Welfare State: The Political Economy of Twentieth-Century Reform*. Rev. ed. Lawrence: University Press of Kansas, 1992.

Bolles, Albert S. *The Financial History of the United States from 1789–1860*. 2nd ed. New York: D. Appleton and Company, 1885.

Brown, E. Cary. "Episodes in the Public Debt History of the United States." In *Public Debt Management: Theory and History*, edited by Rudiger Dornbusch and Mario Draghi. Cambridge: Cambridge University Press, 1990, 229–254.

Buchanan, James M., and Richard E. Wagner. *Democracy in Deficit*. New York: Academic Press, 1977.

Burkhead, Jesse. *Government Budgeting*. New York: John Wiley and Sons, 1956.

Central Intelligence Agency. *A Dollar Comparison of Soviet and U.S. Defense Activities, 1965–1975*. Washington, D.C.: CIA, 1976.

Cogan, John F. *The High Cost of Good Intentions: A History of U.S. Federal Entitlement Programs*. Stanford, CA: Stanford University Press, 2017.

Cooke, Jacob E., ed. *The Reports of Alexander Hamilton*. New York: Harper & Row, 1964.

Crandall-Hollick, Margot L. *An Overview of the Tax Provisions in the American Taxpayer Relief Act of 2012*. Washington, D.C.: Congressional Research Service, January 10, 2013.

Crandall-Hollick, Margot L. *The Child Tax Credit: Temporary Expansion for 2021 Under the American Rescue Plan Act of 2021 (ARPA; P.L. 117–2)*. Washington, D.C.: Congressional Research Service, May 3, 2021.

Davis, Patricia A., Cliff Binder, Jim Hahn, Suzanne M. Kirchhoff, Paulette C. Morgan, Marco A. Villagrana, and Phoenix Voorhies. *Medicare Primer.* Washington, D.C.: Congressional Research Service, May 21, 2020.

Davis, Susan. "A Different Place." *National Journal* 42: October 16, 2010.

Department of Defense. *Soviet Military Power: An Assessment of the Threat, 1988.* Washington, D.C.: Government Printing Office, 1988.

Department of Defense Annual Report, Fiscal Year 1980. Washington, D.C.: Government Printing Office, 1979.

Dewey, Davis Rich. *Financial History of the United States.* 6th ed. New York: Longmans, Green and Co., 1918.

Driessen, Grant A. *Bipartisan Budget Act of 2015: Adjustments to the Budget Control Act of 2011*. Washington, D.C.: Congressional Research Service, November 6, 2015.

Driessen, Grant A. *The Federal Budget: Overview and Issues for FY2018 and Beyond.* Washington, D.C.: Congressional Research Service, June 30, 2017.

Driessen, Grant A., and Megan S. Lynch. *The Bipartisan Budget Act of 2019: Changes to the BCA and Debt Limit*. Washington, D.C.: Congressional Research Service, August 5, 2019.

Earmarks in Appropriations Acts: FY1994, FY1996, FY1998, FY2000, FY2002, FY2004, FY2005. Washington, D.C.: Congressional Research Service, January 26, 2006.

Feldstein, Martin. "The Tax Reform Legislation of 2017." *Journal of Policy Modeling* 40, no. 3 (2018): 503–508, https://doi.org/10.1016/j.jpolmod.2018.02.010.

Fenno, Richard F., Jr. *The Power of the Purse: Appropriations Politics in Congress.* Boston: Little, Brown and Company, 1966.

Ferguson, E. James. *The Power of the Purse: A History of American Public Finance, 1776–1790*. Chapel Hill: University of North Carolina Press, 1961.

Fiscal Year 1982 Budget Revisions. Washington, D.C.: Government Printing Office, 1981.

Fisher, Louis. *Presidential Spending Power.* Princeton, N.J.: Princeton University Press, 1975.

Fisher, Louis. *Congressional Abdication on War and Spending*. College Station: Texas A&M University Press, 2000.

Foreign Relations of the United States, 1952–1954. Vol. 2: *National Security Affairs.* Washington, D.C.: Government Printing Office, 1984.

Forsythe, Dall W. *Taxation and Political Change in the Young Nation, 1781–1833.* New York: Columbia University Press, 1977.

Franklin, Daniel P. *Making Ends Meet: Congressional Budgeting in the Age of Deficits.* Washington, D.C.: Congressional Quarterly, 1993.

Furman, Jason, and Lawrence H. Summers. "Who's Afraid of Budget Deficits? How Washington Should End Its Debt Obsession." *Foreign Affairs* 98, no. 2 (2019): 82–94.

Gale, William G., and Andrew A. Samwick. "Effects of Income Tax Changes on Economic Growth." Washington, D.C.: Tax Policy Center and Brookings Institution, 2016.

Gilbert, Charles. *American Financing of World War I.* Westport, CT: Greenwood, 1970.

Gordon, John Steele. *Hamilton's Blessing*. New York: Wallace and Company, 1997.

Gravelle, Jane G., and Donald J. Marples. *Tax Rates and Economic Growth*. Washington, D.C.: Congressional Research Service, January 2, 2014.

Gravelle, Jane G., and Donald J. Marples. *The Economic Effects of the 2017 Tax Revision: Preliminary Observations*. Washington, D.C.: Congressional Research Service, June 7, 2019.

Gravelle, Jane G., and Donald J. Marples, *Fiscal Policy and Recovery from the COVID-19 Recession*. Washington, D.C.: Congressional Research Service, February 1, 2021.

Guess, George M., and James D. Savage. *Comparative Public Budgeting*. 2nd ed. Cambridge: Cambridge University Press, 2021.

Guide to U.S. Elections. 2nd ed. Washington, D.C.: Congressional Quarterly, 1985.

Hamilton, Alexander. "Report Relative to a Provision for the Support of Public Credit of the United States." In Vol. 6 of *The Papers of Alexander Hamilton*, edited by Harold C. Syrett. New York: Columbia University Press, 1962, 65–110.

Hamilton, Alexander, James Madison, and John Jay. *The Federalist Papers*. New York: New American Library, 1961.

Heniff, Bill, Jr., Elizabeth Rybicki, and Shannon M. Mahan. *The Budget Control Act of 2011*. Washington, D.C.: Congressional Research Service, August 19, 2011.

Historical Statistics of the United States, Colonial Times to 1970, Part 2. Washington, D.C.: Bureau of the Census, 1975.

Historical Statistics of the United States, Earliest Times to the Present: Millennial Edition, Vol. 5. Cambridge: Cambridge University Press, 2006.

Historical Tables, Budget of the United States Government, Fiscal Year 1992. Washington, D.C.: Government Printing Office, 1991.

Historical Tables, Budget of the United States Government, Fiscal Year 2021. Washington, D.C.: Government Printing Office, 2020.

Ippolito, Dennis S. *Congressional Spending*. Ithaca, N.Y.: Cornell University Press, 1981.

Ippolito, Dennis S. *Uncertain Legacies: Federal Budget Policy from Roosevelt through Reagan*. Charlottesville: University Press of Virginia, 1990.

Ippolito, Dennis S. *Deficits, Debt, and the New Politics of Tax Policy*. New York: Cambridge University Press, 2012.

Ippolito, Dennis S. *Why Budgets Matter: Budget Policy and American Politics*. Rev. ed. University Park: Pennsylvania State University Press, 2015.

Jillson, Calvin, and Rick K. Wilson. *Congressional Dynamics: Structure, Coordination, and Choice in the First American Congress, 1774–1789*. Stanford, CA: Stanford University Press, 1994.

Johnson, Lyndon B. *Public Papers of the Presidents of the United States: Lyndon B. Johnson, 1965, Book I*. Washington, D.C.: Government Printing Office, 1966.

Johnson, Lyndon B. *Public Papers of the Presidents of the United States: Lyndon B. Johnson, 1967, Books I–II*. Washington, D.C.: Government Printing Office, 1968.

Keech, William R. *Economic Politics*. New York: Cambridge University Press, 1995.

Keightley, Mark P., and Molly F. Sherlock. *Comparing Key Elements of H.R. 1 to 2017 Tax Law*. Washington, D.C.: Congressional Research Service, December 22, 2017.

Kelly, Andrew S. "Finding Stability and Sustainability in the Trump Era: Medicare and the Affordable Care Act in Historical Perspective." In *American Political*

Development and the Trump Presidency, edited by Zachary Callen and Philip Rocco. Philadelphia: University of Pennsylvania Press, 2020, 130–150.

Kelton, Stephanie. *The Deficit Myth*. New York: Public Affairs, 2021.

Kennedy, John F. *Public Papers of the Presidents of the United States: John F. Kennedy, 1961*. Washington, D.C.: Government Printing Office, 1962.

Kimmel, Lewis H. *Federal Budget Policy and Fiscal Policy, 1789–1958*. Washington, D.C.: Brookings Institution, 1959.

LaBonte, Mark, and Andrew Hanna. *The Impact of Major Legislation on Deficits, 2001–2008*. Washington, D.C.: Congressional Research Service, March 23, 2010.

Labonte, Mark, and Mindy R. Levit. *The Budget Control Act of 2011: Effects on Spending Levels and the Budget Deficit*. Washington, D.C.: Congressional Research Service, October 5, 2011.

Lynch, Megan S., and James V. Saturno. *S.Con.Res. 5: The Budget Resolution for FY2021*. Washington, D.C.: Congressional Research Service, February 8, 2021.

Mach, Annie L., and Janet Kinzer. *Legislative Actions to Modify the Affordable Care Act in the 111th–115th Congresses*. Washington, D.C.: Congressional Research Service, June 27, 2018.

Mitchell, Alison. *Medicaid Primer*. Washington, D.C.: Congressional Research Service, November 30, 2020.

Mitchell, William, L. Randall Wray, and Martin Watts. *Macroeconomics*. London: Red Globe Press, 2019.

Morgan, Iwan W. *Eisenhower Versus "The Spenders": The Eisenhower Administration, the Democrats and the Budget, 1953–1960*. New York: St. Martin's Press, 1990.

Morgan, Iwan W. *The Age of Deficits: Presidents and Unbalanced Budgets from Jimmy Carter to George W. Bush*. Lawrence: University Press of Kansas, 2009.

Murphy, Henry C. *The National Debt in War and Transition*. New York: McGraw-Hill, 1950.

Nixon, Richard. *Public Papers of the Presidents of the United States: Richard Nixon, 1973*. Washington, D.C.: Government Printing Office, 1975.

Nixon, Richard. *Public Papers of the Presidents of the United States: Richard Nixon, 1974*. Washington, D.C.: Government Printing Office, 1975.

Noyes, Alexander Dana. *Forty Years of American Finance: A Short Financial History of the Government and People of the United States Since the Civil War, 1865–1907*. New York: G. P. Putnam's Sons, 1898.

Office of Management and Budget. *Major Savings and Reforms in the President's 2007 Budget*. Washington, D.C.: Government Printing Office, 2006.

Painter, William L. *Tallying Federal Funding for COVID-19: In Brief*. Washington, D. C.: Congressional Research Service, July 13, 2020.

Pasachoff, Eloise. "The President's Budget Powers in the Trump Era." In *Executive Policymaking: The Role of the OMB in the Presidency*, edited by Meena Bose and Andrew Rudalevige. Washington, D.C.: Brookings Institution Press, 2020, 69–98.

Patterson, Robert T. *Federal Debt-Management Policies, 1865–1879*. Durham, N.C.: Duke University Press, 1954.

Pechman, Joseph A. *Federal Tax Policy*. 5th ed. Washington, D.C.: Brookings Institution, 1987.

Public Papers of the President: George W. Bush, 2004, Book 1. Washington, D.C.: Government Printing Office, 2007.

Public Papers of the President: Ronald Reagan, 1981. Washington, D.C.: Government Printing Office, 1982.

Ratchford, B. U. *American State Debts.* Durham, N.C.: Duke University Press, 1941.

Rosso, Ryan J. *The Individual Mandate for Health Insurance Coverage: In Brief.* Washington, D.C.: Congressional Research Service, August 25, 2020.

Savage, James D. *Balanced Budgets and American Politics.* Ithaca, N.Y.: Cornell University Press, 1988.

Savage, James D. "Budgetary Collective Action Problems: Convergence and Compliance Under the Maastricht Treaty on European Union." *Public Administration Review* 61 (January/February 2001): 43–53.

Skocpol, Theda. *Protecting Soldiers and Mothers: The Political Origins of Social Policy in the United States.* Cambridge, MA: Harvard University Press, 1992.

Smithies, Arthur. *The Budgetary Process in the United States.* New York: McGraw Hill, 1955.

Smoke, Richard. "The Evolution of American Defense Policy." In *American Defense Policy*, 5th ed., edited by J. F. Reichart and S.B. Sturm. Baltimore, MD: Johns Hopkins University Press, 1982, 94–135.

Stein, Herbert. *The Fiscal Revolution in America.* Chicago: University of Chicago Press, 1969.

Stein, Herbert. *Presidential Economics.* New York: Simon and Schuster, 1984.

Steuerle, C. Eugene. *The Tax Decade.* Washington, D.C.: Urban Institute Press, 1992.

Steuerle, C. Eugene. *Contemporary U.S. Tax Policy.* 2nd ed. Washington, D.C.: Urban Institute Press, 2008.

Story, Joseph. *Commentaries on the Constitution of the United States.* Cambridge, MA: Brown, Shattuck and Co., 1833.

Tanzi, Vito, and Ludger Schuknecht. *Public Spending in the 20th Century: A Global Perspective.* Cambridge: Cambridge University Press, 2000.

Tempalski, Jerry. *Revenue Effects of Major Tax Bills.* Washington, D.C.: Department of the Treasury, 2013.

The Budget Control Act: Frequently Asked Questions. Washington, D.C.: Congressional Research Service, October 1, 2019.

The Disaster Relief Fund: Overview and Issues. Washington, D.C.: Congressional Research Service, November 13, 2020.

The Moment of Truth: Report of the National Commission on Fiscal Responsibility and Reform. Washington, D.C.: The White House, December 2010.

Thompson, Frank J., Michael K. Gusmano, and Shugo Shinohara. "Trump and the Affordable Care Act: Congressional Repeal Efforts, Executive Federalism, and Program Durability." *Publius: The Journal of Federalism* 48, no. 3 (2018): 396–424, https://doi.org/10.1093/publius/pjy007.

Thompson, Frank J., Kenneth K. Wong, and Barry G. Rabe. *Trump, the Administrative Presidency, and Federalism.* Washington, D.C.: Brookings Institution Press, 2020.

Tobin, James, and Murray Weidenbaum, eds. *Two Revolutions in Economic Policy: The First Economic Reports of Presidents Kennedy and Reagan.* Cambridge: Massachusetts Institute of Technology Press, 1988.

U.S. Congress. Joint Committee on Taxation. *General Explanation of the Economic Recovery Tax Act of 1981.* Washington, D.C.: Government Printing Office, 1981.

U.S. Congress. Joint Committee on Taxation. *Estimated Budget Effects of the Conference Agreement for H.R. 1, the "Tax Cuts and Jobs Act"* (JCX-67–17). Washington, D.C.: Government Printing Office, December 18, 2017.

U.S. Congress. Joint Committee on Taxation. *Estimated Budget Effects Of The Revenue Provisions Contained In The House Amendment To The Senate Amendment To H.R. 1865, The Further Consolidated Appropriations Act, 2020* (JCX-54–19 R). Washington, D.C.: Government Printing Office, December 17, 2019.

U.S. Senate. Committee on Armed Services. *United States/Soviet Military Balance: A Frame of Reference for Congress.* Washington, D.C.: Government Printing Office, 1976.

Weaver, R. Kent. *Automatic Government: The Politics of Indexation.* Washington, D.C.: Brookings Institution, 1988.

Webber, Carolyn, and Aaron Wildavsky. *A History of Taxation and Expenditure in the Western World.* New York: Simon and Schuster, 1986.

Weinstock, Lida R. *COVID-19 and the U.S. Economy.* Washington, D.C.: Congressional Research Service, November 16, 2020.

Wildavsky, Aaron. *The New Politics of the Budgetary Process.* Glenview, IL: Scott, Foresman, 1988.

Wildavsky, Aaron, and Naomi Caiden. *The New Politics of the Budgetary Process.* 3rd ed. New York: Longman, 1997.

Witte, John F. *The Politics and Development of the Federal Income Tax.* Madison: University of Wisconsin Press, 1985.

Yin, George K., and Lawrence A. Zelenak. "The Past, Present, and Future of the Tax Legislative Process." *Law and Contemporary Problems* 81, no. 2 (2018): 1–6.

Zelizer, Julian E. *Taxing America: Wilbur D. Mills, Congress, and the State, 1945–1975*. New York: Cambridge University Press, 1998.

Index

Page numbers in *italics* and **bold** indicate Figures and Tables, respectively.

Affordable Care Act *see* Patient Protection and Affordable Care Act of 2010
Afghanistan war 110
Agricultural Adjustment Act of 1933 15
agricultural sector 15
Aid to Families with Dependent Children (AFDC) 42, 187
alternative minimum tax (AMT) 94, **95**, 106–107, 131, 139–140
American Families Plan 185, 200–201
American Health Care Act (AHCA) 151, **153**
American Jobs Creation Act of 2004 100
American Jobs Plan 199–200, 201
American Recovery and Reinvestment Act of 2009 (ARRA 2009) 118–121, **120**
American Rescue Plan Act of 2021 (ARPA) 185, 194, 195–199, 200
American Taxpayer Relief Act of 2012 139–140
Archer, Bill 82
Arctic National Wildlife Refuge (ANWR) 160

Balanced Budget Act of 1997 79, 81
Balanced Budget and Emergency Deficit Reduction Act of 1985 (GRHI) 48–49
balanced-budget conservatism 9–14
balanced-budget rule 2, 6, 10, 23, 29
balanced budgets: budget policy and 10–12; budget reform and 10; Civil War debt retirement 7–8; deficits and 8–9; Democratic version of 14–26; domestic spending policies 15; Hoover's commitment to 13; Jeffersonian 2–6; Jefferson's views of 1; Mellon's commitment to 10–11; Republican version of 6–14; surplus budgeting 82–83; tax policies 15–16
baseline revenue projections, 2017–2021 **166**; 2020–2031 **192**
baseline spending projections, 2020–2031 **187**, 188
Baucus, Max 122, 124
Bernanke, Ben S. 121, 139
Better Care Reconciliation Act (BCRA) 152–154, **153**
Biden, Joseph (as vice president) 135, 137
Biden budget plan: American Families Plan 200–201; American Jobs Plan 199–200; American Rescue Plan Act of 2021 (ARPA) 195–199; American Rescue Plan legislation 155; defense budgets 199; deficits and debt **203**; discretionary spending programs 201–202; economic and social reform agenda 199; fiscal agenda 194; Rebuild America program 199–201; requiring substantial borrowing 202; spending-GDP under 206–207
Bipartisan Agreement of 2015 143–145
Bipartisan Budget Act of 2013 141–143
Bipartisan Budget Act of 2015 167
Bipartisan Budget Act of 2018 168–169
Bipartisan Budget Act of 2019 171–172
Blue Dog Coalition 123
Boehner, John A. 122, 134–135, 144
border adjustment tax (BAT) 159–160
border wall funding 170–173
Bowles, Erskine 129
Brady, Kevin 158, 160
Brown, Scott P. 125

Budget and Accounting Act of 1921 10
Budget Control Act of 2011 137–138
budget reform 10–12, 23, 28
Bureau of the Budget 10, 11–12
Bush, George H.W. presidency: defense budgets 63; defense spending 67; deficit reduction agreement 39, 61–62, **62**, 180; deficit reduction goals 63; deficit reduction plans 64; foreign and domestic policy records 68; nondefense spending 68; on raising taxes 61; reelection run 68; social welfare programs 102–103; strategic arms reduction treaty (START I) 131; tax increase compromises 65–66
Bush, George W.: "compassionate conservative" vision 88–89, 104; reelection win 104–105
Bush, George W. presidency: budget program 88–90, **89**; debt reduction **89**; debt reduction pledge 89–90; defense budgets 88–89; defense spending 101–102; deficit reduction plans 108–109; deficits during 90; discretionary domestic spending 102, 105, 107, 109–112; disregard for deficits 100; domestic spending policies 101–102; economic expansion 113; economic stimulus package 96; EGTRRA 2001 91–96; emergency war supplementals 110–111; entitlement reforms 109; growth and jobs package 96–98; income tax rates 91; Medicare "modernization" plan 103–104; nondefense spending 90, 98, 102; prescription drug coverage and 103–104; pro-growth tax cuts 113; reelection campaign 98; reviving domestic retrenchment 107–108; signature campaign issue 88; Social Security plan 103, 108; social welfare entitlements 102–103; social welfare programs 108–109; spending-GDP ratios 104, 108; TARP support 121; tax cuts 90–92, 98, 113–114, 117, 128–130, 139–140, 146, 165, 191–194, 204; tax preferences 99; tax program 88, 129–130; tax relief **89**

Cadillac tax 173
capital gains taxes 80, 97–98, 105–106
Carter, Jimmy 29–32
Carter presidency 39; defense budgets 29, 31; defense spending 29; domestic discretionary spending 56; tax preferences 31–32; welfare reform 29–31
Cassidy, William 154
Cheney, Dick 92, 97, 100, 109
Children's Health Insurance Program (CHIP) 126 *see also* State Children's Health Insurance Program (SCHIP)
child tax credits 80, 91, **95**
Civil War 2, 7–8
Clinton, Bill: reelection win 78; run for president 68
Clinton presidency: appropriations battles 75–76; budget program 70–74; defense spending 101; deficit reduction agreement 39, 180; deficit reduction efforts 70–71, 78–83, **84**; economic policy speech 69; eliminating deficits 185–186; entitlement protections 84; government shutdown 75; impeachment inquiry 82; nondefense spending 70; OBRA 1993 69; reconciliation failure 76–78; spending-GDP ratios 78; stimulus proposal 69–70; surplus budget agenda 81–83; tax preferences 71, 77, 82; welfare reform 74, 77–78, 81
Cohn, Gary 158
Cold War 2, 14, 20–22, 55, 68, 188 *see also* post-Cold War
Collins, Susan 119, 120, 129, 153
Congressional Budget and Impoundment Control Act of 1974 28, 70
Congressional Budget Office (CBO): addressing high/rising debt 185; American Health Care Act (AHCA) 151; American Recovery and Reinvestment Act of 2009 119; Biden budget 202; Bush, George H.W. budget 68; Clinton budget 78–79, 81; future interest rates 204; Gramm-Rudman-Hollings II and 62–63; Obama budget 134; Patient Protection and Affordable Act of 2010 126; Reagan budget 64; Ryan budget plan 135–136; Tax Cuts and Jobs Act of 2017 (TCJA) 157–158
Conrad, Kent 123
conservatism 1–2

Consolidated Appropriations Act of 2017 167
Consolidated Appropriations Act of 2018 169
Consolidated Appropriations Act of 2019 170–171
Consolidated Appropriations Act of 2020 172–173
Consolidated Appropriations Act of 2021 179
Contract with America 73, 74, 130
Coronavirus Aid, Relief, and Economic Security Act (CARES Act) 177–178
coronavirus disease (COVID-19) pandemic 149, 175–178, **175**, 186, 197–199
corporate dividends 15–16, **99**, 105–106
corporate excess profits tax 11, 17, 18, 21
corporate income taxation 11, 15–17, **43**, 100, 132, 157, **163**, 193
corporate income tax rates 201

Daschle, Tom 93
debt-GDP ratios 9, 12, **12**, 20–22, 89, 105, 113, 131–132, 180, 185, 202
defense budgets: Biden budget 199; Bush, George H.W. budget 63; Bush, George W. budget 88–89, 101; Carter budget 29, 31; Cold War 2; Eisenhower budget 21–22; Ford budget 28–29; growing disparities between Soviet and U.S. 29; Johnson budget 23–24; Korean War 24; Nixon budget 26; Obama budget 138–139; Reagan budget 40, 46, 53–55, 62; Roosevelt budget 18; Truman budget 20–21; Trump budget 165–166, 173; Vietnam War 26; welfare shift from 22–23
defense spending: 1940–1990 *54*; Bush, George H.W. budget 67; Bush, George W. budget 101–102; Carter budget 29; Clinton budget 101; closing gap with Soviets 34; Eisenhower budget 21; Ford budget 28–29; inflation-adjusted, by fiscal year *54*; Johnson budget 24; Kennedy budget 23; Nixon budget 26–27; during peacetime 32; Reagan budget 46, 48, 53–56; Roosevelt budget 18; *see also* nondefense spending
defense spending-GDP ratios 101, 110, 202
deficit finance: economy and 204–206; governance and 206–208; Jefferson's rejection of 1–2; routine use of 29; welfare state and 202–208
deficit reduction: as bipartisan priority 131–132; components of **84**
Deficit Reduction Act of 1984 46
Deficit Reduction Omnibus Reconciliation Act of 2005 108–109
Deficits Politics Era: composition of federal spending **187**; spending and revenues in *186*
defined contribution pension accounts 92
Department of Defense 53
Department of Homeland Security (DHS) 170
Department of the Treasury: Bureau of the Budget 10; establishment of 3; funding wartime operations 7; Hamilton as secretary of 3–4
Dependent Pensions Act of 1890 8
Disability Insurance trust fund 56–57
discretionary domestic spending: Biden fiscal agenda 201–202; Bush, George W. presidency 102, 105, 107, 111–112; Obama presidency 129, 132, 143, 146; Trump presidency 180, 199
discretionary spending, by fiscal year **57**
dividends *see* corporate dividends
Dole, Robert J. 73
domestic retrenchment 18–21, 40–42, 53, 81, 107, 114, 130, 135
"don't ask, don't tell" repeal 131

earned income tax credit 60, 72–73, 91
economic contraction 13
Economic Growth and Tax Relief Reconciliation Act of 2001 (EGTRRA 2001) 89–90, 91–96, **95**
economic recovery program 27–28
Economic Recovery Tax Act of 1981 (ERTA 1981) 40–42, **43**, **52**, 53, 193
economic stimulus package 107, 147n2
education tax incentives 80, **95**
Eisenhower, Dwight 21–22
Eisenhower presidency: defense budgets 21–22; defense spending 21
Emergency Revenue Act of 1914 10
energy tax 71
estate and gift tax 11, 42, **43**, 80–81, 92–96, **95**, 105–106, 128, 130–131, 140, **163**, 194
excess profits tax *see* corporate excess profits tax
excise tax *see* federal excise tax

extraordinary expenses **6**
Extraterritorial Income Exclusion subsidy 100

Family Assistance Plan 27
Family Support Act of 1988 59
federal borrowing authority 3
federal excise tax 4, 16, 24, 194
federal government, modernization of 9
Federalist 30 194, 207
Federalists 1, 5, 36n25
federal minimum wage 196
federal public works projects 7–8, 15 *see also* American Jobs Plan
Federal Reserve: anti-inflation policies 45–46; Bernanke, Ben S. 121, 139; controlling inflation 17; establishment of 9; Greenspan, Alan 93; stabilizing the economy 176
federal revenues: excise taxes and 16; source of 2, 9; during World War II **17**
First Bank of the United States 4
First Federal Congress 1
Ford, Gerald 26, 28–29
Fordney-McCumber Tariff Act of 1922 11
Ford presidency: defense budgets 28–29; defense spending 28–29; earned income tax credit 60; spending-GDP ratios 28; tax preferences 28
Franken, Al 146n1
Freedom Caucus Republicans 138, 143–144, 151, 159
"full employment budget" 28
Funding Act of 1790 35n5
Further Consolidated Appropriations Act of 2020 173

General Accounting Office 10
General Revenue Sharing program 187
Gingrich, Newt 65, 74
Gore, Al 71
government shutdown 168, 170–171
Graham, Lindsey 154
Gramm, Phil 48
Gramm-Rudman-Hollings II 48–51, 62, **63**
Grassley, Charles E. 124
Great Depression, The 13, 14–17
Great Recession, The 90, 105–107, 111, 114–117, 145, 176, 188, 193, 204
Great Society legislation, The 23–24
Greenspan, Alan 93
Gulf War 65, 66
"guns vs. butter" discipline 18, 20

Hamilton, Alexander 1, 3–4, 35n5, 194, 207
Harding, Warren 10
Harris, Kamala 179, 196
Hatch, Orrin 158
healthcare cost controls 30
healthcare entitlements 132, 141; cost increases in 30–31, 40; for the elderly 24; growth of 190–191, **190**; increased spending for 27; Medicare Catastrophic Care Act 187–188; new programs enacted by Congress 190; Obama budget 146; Reagan administration and 58; retrenchment of 53, 81; rollbacks in 135; Ryan and 135; steady growth of 188–190; Trump budget 156; *see also* Medicaid, Medicare, Social Security program
Health Care for All Americans Act of 1979 30
healthcare reform *see* Patient Protection and Affordable Care Act of 2010
Heroes Act 178
Hollings, Ernest 48
House Ways and Means Committee 4

income tax rates: Bush, George W. presidency 91; Carter budget 31–32; Democratic party's theory on 46–47; Kemp-Roth plan 41–42; Obama budget 132; party disputes on 140; raises in 9; Reagan administration 42; reductions in 19; Republican tax policy changes on 82; revenue losses from cuts to 106
individual income tax: Bush tax cuts and 191–193; as cornerstone of federal finances 18; EGTRRA 2001 impact on 91; ERTA 1981 **43**; establishment of 7; Kemp-Roth plan 41–42; Simpson-Bowles plan and 132; tax rates **163**; Trump tax cuts 157; during World War I 9; during World War II 17
individual retirement accounts (IRAs) 92
in-kind benefit programs 197
Internal Revenue Code 21
international tax system **164**
Iraq War 110

Jackson, Andrew 5
Jefferson, Thomas 1–6, 35n5

Jeffersonian Republicans 1–2, 5–6, 36n25
Jeffords, James M. 93
Jobs and Growth Tax Relief Reconciliation Act of 2003 (JGTRRA 2003) 96–98, **99**
Johnson, Lyndon 23–26
Johnson presidency: defense budgets 23–24; defense spending 24; tax preferences 24–25
Joint Select Committee on Deficit Reduction 137

Kemp, Jack 41
Kemp-Roth plan 41–42
Kennedy, Edward M. 30, 125
Kennedy presidency: budget program 23; defense spending 23
Kerry, John 99
Knutson, Harold 19
Korean War 20

Lewis, Jerry 121

Madison, James 1
Mahon, George H. 20
Manchin, Joseph, III 196
"marriage and family relief" bill 91, **95**
McCain, John 153–154
McConnell, Mitch: Affordable Care Act 'skinny' repeal negotiations 152–154; ANWR bill negotiations 161; Better Care Reconciliation Act compromise 152–154; as Big Six member 158; Bipartisan Budget Act of 2019 171–172; on border wall funding 170; coronavirus relief bill 177; healthcare reform cloture votes 125; negotiating debt limit increase 137; on party's goal with Obama administration 145; START II filibuster 131
Medicaid: Balanced Budget Act of 1997 impact on 81; Biden budget plan for 206; Reagan budget 58; Ryan proposal on 135; Trump targeting 155
Medicare: Balanced Budget Act of 1997 impact on 81; George W. Bush's modernization plan 103–104; prescription entitlement 114; Reagan budget 58; Ryan proposal on 135
Medicare Catastrophic Care Act of 1988 187–188
Medicare Hospital Insurance trust fund 194
Medicare Prescription Drug, Improvement, and Modernization Act of 2003 103–104, 190
Mellon, Andrew G. 10–11
Mexican-American War 5
Michel, Robert H. 65, 69
Military Construction and Veterans Affairs appropriations bill 145
military spending 12
Mills, Wilbur 25
minimum wage, federal 196
Mnuchin, Steven T. 158, 167–168, 171, 176–177
modern monetary theory (MMT) 205
Mondale, Walter 47
Murkowski, Lisa 153

national bank proposal 35n5
National Commission on Fiscal Responsibility and Reform 129, 132
National Governors Association 59
national health insurance 30
National Taxpayers Union (NTU) 32
New Deal's peacetime budgets 15
"New Look" strategy 22
Nixon, Richard 26–28
Nixon presidency: defense budgets 26; defense spending 26–27; welfare reform 27
nondefense spending: Balanced Budget Act of 1997 impact on 81; Bush, George H.W. presidency 68; Bush, George W. presidency 90, 98, 102; Clinton presidency 70; Obama presidency 130, 139, 145; Trump presidency 167–168, 171; *see also* defense spending
NSC-68 report 20

Obamacare *see* Patient Protection and Affordable Care Act of 2010
Obama presidency: Bipartisan Agreement of 2015 143–145; Bipartisan Budget Act of 2013 141–143; bipartisan deficit reduction working group 135; bipartisan outreach 131; Boehner's shutdown strategy 134–135; on Bush tax cuts 139; continuing Bush tax cuts 130–131; defense authorization bill 131; defense budgets 138–139; deficit reduction program 132–134; discretionary domestic spending 129, 132, 143, 146; economic stimulus

package 118–121, **120**; government shutdown 142; Great Recession challenges for 114; healthcare entitlements 146; healthcare policy victory 126; healthcare reform (*See* Patient Protection and Affordable Care Act of 2010); jobs bill 128; on nonbudgetary matters 131; nondefense spending 130, 139, 145; omnibus appropriations bill 142–143; public approval ratings 129; second term 140–145; signing second continuing resolution 167; spending cap adjustments 142; spending-GDP ratios 146; START II 131; State of the Union Address 131–132; Troubled Asset Relief Program (TARP) 118; Trump budget policy vs. **173–174**

Omnibus Budget Reconciliation Act of 1981 42–44, 45, **52**

Omnibus Budget Reconciliation Act of 1987 51–52

Omnibus Budget Reconciliation Act of 1990 65–67, **67**

Omnibus Budget Reconciliation Act of 1993 69, 72–74, **73**

O'Neill, Thomas P. 48

Organisation for Economic Co-operation and Development (OECD) 194

outlay-GDP 22, 174

Packwood, Robert W. 49, 50

pass-through businesses tax rates 160–162, **164**, 191, 206

Path to Prosperity budget plan 135–136, **136**

Patient Protection and Affordable Care Act of 2010: abortion services compromise 123–124; cloture vote 124; committee deliberations 123–124; committee markups 123; cost estimates 126–128, 190; deficit-neutral pledge 122; draft bill 123; health insurance exchanges 154; House vote 125–126; implementation restrictions 142; Obama's commitment to success of 154; Obama's reconciliation bill veto 144; primary goal 122; public approval of 155; repeal efforts 143, 150–152, 156; Senate vote 125; spending, revenue and deficit effects of **127**; tax changes affecting **163**; Trump's attacks against 154–155

Paul, Rand 160

Paulson, Henry M. 121

pay-as-you-go (PAYGO) 66, 98, 106–107, 128

Paycheck Protection Program (PPP) 177, 198

Pelosi, Nancy 118, 119, 170, 171, 176–177

Penn Wharton Budget research project 194

Pension Arrears Act of 1879 8

Perot, Ross 68

Planned Parenthood 144

"Pledge to America" 130

policy riders 75

post-Cold War 83, 101, 187 *see also* Cold War

postwar agenda 18

prescription drug coverage 103–104

presidential impoundments 28

presidents involved in legislative process 8–9

"Progressive Era" 9

protective tariff system 2, 11

public assistance entitlements 27, 58–59, 63, 103–104, 132, 138–141, 157, 188 *see also* healthcare entitlements, Medicaid, Medicare, Social Security program, social welfare programs

public debt: 1789–1860 **6**; 1860 5; 1893 8; 1920–1930 **12**; 1940–1946 **17**; 1997 82; 2019 204; fourfold increase in 191; increase in 8; during World War II **17**; *see also* debt-GDP ratios

public health funding in the ARPA 198

public works *see* federal public works projects

Randolph, Edmund 35n5

Reagan presidency: debt legacy 180; defense budgets 40, 46, 53–55, 62; defense buildup 54–56; defense spending 46, 48, 53–56; disregard for deficits 61, 100; domestic discretionary spending 55–56; economic recovery program 39–40; on entitlement programs 42, 56–57; healthcare entitlements and 58; income tax rates 42; national defense importance 40; retrenchment failure 102–103; revenue effects of legislation during **52**; on social safety net programs 42; Social Security trust fund reserves 56–57; spending-GDP

ratios 56, 58; tax increases during 44–45; tax policies 40–46, 180; tax preferences 42, 44, 49–52; Tax Reform Act of 1986 (TRA) 50; tax reform program 46–49; Treasury II proposal 48–49; welfare reform 58–60; welfare state, impact on 59–60
Rebuild America program 199–201
Reconstruction Finance Corporation (RFC) Act of 1932 13
Reid, Harry 124–125, 135
Report on a National Bank 1
Republican National Committee 41
restaurant stabilization program 198
retirement savings incentives 94, **95**
Revenue Act of 1932 13
Revenue Act of 1945 18
Revenue Act of 1964 23
Revenue Act of 1971 28
Revenue Act of 1978 31
Revenue and Expenditure Control Act of 1968 25
revenue-neutral tax reform 47–51, 61 *see also* tax reform
revenues, by category, 1980–2030 **193**
revenues, outlays, and surplus/deficit **33**
revenue sharing 55–56
Roosevelt, Franklin D. 13–14, 16, 18
Roosevelt, Theodore 9
Roosevelt presidency: defense budgets 18; defense spending 18; tax preferences, Congress's approval of 16
Roth, William V. 41
Rubin, Robert 74
Rudman, Warren 48
Ryan, Paul 135–136, 145, 151, 158
Ryan Budget Plan 135–136, **136**

Sanders, Bernie 196–197
Schumer, Charles E. 159, 170, 196
Shelby, Richard 171
Simpson, Alan K. 129
Simpson-Bowles Deficit Reduction Comprehensive Plan 132–134, **133**, 146
Sixteenth Amendment 9
Smoot-Hawley bill 13
Snowe, Olympia 119, 120, 124, 129
social insurance taxes 16, **166**, 193–194, **193**
Social Security Act of 1935 15
Social Security program: George W. Bush's reform plan 103; growth of **190**; as largest spending program 190; Nixon presidency 27; program reforms 187; tax increase 45; Truman's call to broaden 19
Social Security trust funds 31, 56–57, 134, 190, 194
social welfare programs: Bush, George H.W. presidency 102–103; Bush, George W. presidency 108–109; Carter administration 30; defense budget transfer as support for 22–23; Eisenhower administration 22; expansions of 2, 19–20; Ford administration 29; Johnson administration 23–24; Johnson's Great Society and 60; New Deal's 16, 19–20; Nixon administration 27; policy reform 29–30; Reagan administration 58–60; Reagan presidency 58–59; "workfare" proposal 59; *see also* healthcare entitlements, public assistance entitlements, Social Security program
Soviet military 29
Specter, Arlen 119, 120, 146n1
spending, 1789–1860 **6**
spending-GDP ratios: during the 1920s 12, **12**; Biden budget 206–207; George W. Bush budget 104, 108; Clinton budget 78; decrease in 187–188; defense 101, 110, 202; for domestic programs 55, 108, 111, 114; Ford budget 28; healthcare 191; increase in 112, 188; Medicaid 58; Medicare 58; Obama budget 146; pre-pandemic 188; public assistance entitlements and 27; Reagan budget 56, 58; for social security 190; during World War II **17**
state and local tax (SALT) deductions 159, 162, **163**, 178
State Children's Health Insurance Program (SCHIP) 81, 109 *see also* Children's Health Insurance Program (CHIP)
state debts 6
Story, Joseph 5
strategic arms reduction treaty (START I) 131
Stupak, Bart 124
supplemental security income program 27, 30–31, 77, 188
supply-side economics theory 41
surplus budgeting 82–83
surpluses/deficits, 1789–1860 **6**

surplus to deficit reversal, as percentage of GDP **112**

Taft, William Howard 9
tariff system 2, 5–11, 13, 179
taxable exemption levels 11
Tax Cuts and Jobs Act of 2017 (TCJA): Arctic National Wildlife Refuge (ANWR) 160; Big Six deliberations on 158–159; border adjustment tax (BAT) 159–160; budgetary impact of 165; budget resolution committee reviews 160–162; description of 157–158; economic effects of 165; major provisions of **163–164**; proposed changes 158–159; state and local tax (SALT) deductions 159, 162; tax law changes under 162–165; "Unified Framework for Fixing Our Broken Tax Code, The" 158–159
tax cut stimulus 23, 28, 31, 107
Tax Equity and Fiscal Responsibility Act of 1982 44–45
Tax Increase Prevention and Reconciliation Act of 2005 106
Taxpayer Protection Pledge 130
Taxpayer Relief Act of 1997 79, 80, **80**
Taxpayer Relief Act of 1999 82
tax preferences, Congress's approval of: Bush, George W. budget 99; Carter budget 31–32; Clinton budget 71, 77, 82; Ford budget 28; Johnson budget 24–25; proliferation of 32; Reagan budget 42, 44, 49–52; Roosevelt budget 16
tax reform 16, 31, 40–41, 46–47, 158, 166 *see also* revenue-neutral tax reform
Tax Reform Act of 1986 (TRA) 50–51, **51**, **52**, 157
tax system, goals of 194
Tea Party Republicans 134–135
Troubled Asset Relief Program (TARP) 118, 121
Truman, Harry 18–21
Trump presidency: American Health Care Act (AHCA) 151, **153**; attacks against Affordable Care Act 154–155; Better Care Reconciliation Act (BCRA) 152–154, **153**; Bipartisan Budget Act of 2015 167; Bipartisan Budget Act of 2018 168–169; Bipartisan Budget Act of 2019 171–172; border wall shutdown 170–171; budget policies 149–150; budget program 165–167; Consolidated Appropriations Act of 2017 167; Consolidated Appropriations Act of 2018 169; Consolidated Appropriations Act of 2019 170–171; Consolidated Appropriations Act of 2020 172–173; Coronavirus Aid, Relief, and Economic Security Act (CARES Act) 177–178; debt legacy 179–181; debt limit increases 167–168; defense budgets 165–166, 173; discretionary domestic spending 180, 199; domestic agenda 149; government shutdown 168; healthcare entitlements 156; Heroes Act 178; impeachment inquiry 149, 181n1; Medicaid 155; midterm elections 169; nondefense spending 167–168, 171; Obama budget baseline vs. **173–174**; Republic agenda during 150; tax cuts (*See* Tax Cuts and Jobs Act of 2017 (TCJA)); as tumultuous 149

"Unified Framework for Fixing Our Broken Tax Code, The" 158–159
U.S. Supreme Court 48–49, 88, 154, 155

veterans' pensions and benefits 8, 12
Vietnam War 24, 26

War of 1812 5
war operations—Overseas Contingency Operations 137, 144, 167, 171
wartime budget policies 17–22, 101
wartime debt 7
wartime taxation 5, 18, 21, 24, 97
water and power projects 15
Watergate scandal 28
Weinberger, Casper W. 53
welfare reform: Carter budget 29–31; Clinton budget 74, 77–78, 81; Nixon budget 27; Reagan budget 58–60
Wilson, Woodrow 9
Wolcott, Oliver 4
Working Families Tax Relief Act 99
World Health Organization 175
World War I 7, 9–10
World War II: budgetary impact of 17; defense spending 18; tax increases during 17; tax rates 17–18, **17**